BETWEEN WORLDS

BETWEEN WORLDS

WORLDS

Contemporary Asian-American Plays

Edited by MISHA BERSON

Theatre Communications Group
New York
1990

Acknowledgments

Many people generously gave their time and blessings to this project. For their willingness to participate and their illuminating interviews, I thank all of the playwrights. For his contacts, ideas, encouragement and friendship, I owe a special debt to Philip Kan Gotanda. Tisa Chang of Pan Asian Repertory, Eric Hayashi and Lane Nishikawa of the Asian American Theatre Company, Michele Garza of East West Players, Eugenie Chan of the Magic Theatre, Richard France and Christina Yao helped me lay my hands on many scripts, while Benjamin Tong, Frank Viviano and Janice Mirikitani shared their valuable insights with me. My dear friend Jim Leverett must also be thanked for getting me involved in this project; once I was, M. Elizabeth Osborn, my clearheaded and wonderfully supportive editor at Theatre Communications Group, kept me on the right track.

Finally, I want to acknowledge my good fortune in being able to witness the flowering of Asian-American theatre over the past dozen years. As a theatre critic in San Francisco, I've observed the early efforts of many talented Asian-American writers, actors and directors, and watched some of them develop into artists of vision and influence. They have entertained, enlightened and moved me, and for that I am most grateful.

—Misha Berson

Contents

Introduction
by Misha Berson

The six playwrights represented in this volume are strikingly diverse.

They are first-, second- and third-generation Americans with ancestral roots in China, Japan and the Philippines. They were reared as Baptists, Catholics and Buddhists, in bilingual households and in families where only English was spoken. Their plays vary greatly, ranging in style from naturalistic family drama to performance-art spectacle and mythic fable.

With such differing backgrounds and divergent theatrical sensibilities, what do these writers share in common? A vantage point. They are all Asian Americans, United States citizens of East Asian descent. And, in the scripts gathered here, they have all created characters who hover "between worlds," suspended between countries of origin and adopted homelands, between marriage and divorce, between life and death, between war and peace.

This anthology reflects the vitality of an expanding body of Asian-American stage literature. Today dramatists of Asian-American ancestry are distinguishing themselves in every branch of our national theatre: in the experimental sector, in regional companies, on Broadway, and, of course, in the lively national network of Asian-American theatre troupes.

But the prominent involvement of Asian Americans in mainstream theatre—as in popular literature, filmmaking, music and other mass media—has been hard-won and long overdue. Consider that people from the eastern part of Asia have been settling in the United States for well over one hundred years (roughly seven generations), and now constitute one of the fastest-growing and economically dynamic population groups in the country. They came at first from China and Japan, later from Korea and the Philippines, more recently from Laos, Cambodia and Vietnam. They came, and continue to come, for the same array of reasons most immigrants have landed on American soil: to escape war, tyranny, hunger and repression; to seek a better life in a prosperous new land. Why, then, were the visions of Asian Americans absent for so long from our theatrical mainstages?

Introduction

Cross-cultural differences surely played a part in this. Play-oriented Western theatre was an alien artistic genre for Asians more accustomed to epic, mythological music-drama forms. Additionally, many immigrant parents (Asian and non-Asian) actively discouraged their first-generation children from having anything to do with "show business," viewing it as a financially precarious, morally dubious career at best.

But even if gifted young Asian Americans won their parents over, they still faced intense racial discrimination from the society at large. Until well after World War II the majority of Asian Americans lived set apart in their own ethnic enclaves, in urban Chinatowns, Filipinotowns, Japantowns, and in certain rural regions of California and the West. Periodically subjected to restrictive legislation and brutal vigilante attacks, publicly scorned for their unfamiliar customs, languages and religions, Asian Americans were for many decades both praised and damned as a "silent" minority—clannish, intrinsically exotic, unalterably alien. Given the racial hostility they encountered (and, in some places, continue to encounter), keeping a low public profile made sense.

Certainly, Asian Americans found few open doors into mainstream theatre or film. Those who sought to preserve the rich Asian traditions of dance, drama and music created amateur performance groups and clubs in their own communities. The more populous Chinatowns in San Francisco, New York and other cities boasted spacious playhouses devoted to Chinese opera, venues that often featured visiting troupes from abroad. In another vein, some Asian-American variety artists found work on the lively "Chop Suey" vaudeville circuit, or in popular Chinatown nightclubs like San Francisco's Forbidden City. And a modest B-movie industry also developed, with Chinese-speaking actors performing in low-budget romance and action films.

But from the late 1800s to the 1950s, when "legit theatre" flourished throughout the U.S., no plays by or about Asian Americans appeared on Broadway or, presumably, in regional stock houses. Nor were any Asian-oriented shows produced in the 1930s by the government-sponsored Federal Theatre Project—a noteworthy omission, considering the agency's famed Negro unit and its productions in Spanish, German, Italian, French and Yiddish. (San Francisco's Federal Theatre unit did, however, produce a written history of Chinese theatre in California as part of an exhaustive theatre research project.)

For many years Asiatic people were in the ironic position of being rarely heard from but often seen. The dutiful houseboy and the inscrutable detective, the treacherous Dragon Lady and the submissive China Doll, the all-knowing mystic sage and the bloodthirsty "Chink" and "Jap" charging into battle—these ethnic stereotypes paraded through dozens of American plays, movies, cartoons and television series over the past century.

Conceived by non-Asian writers (and frequently played by non-Asian actors in exaggerated facial makeup), such caricatures had little to do with actual human behavior, and nothing at all to do with Asian self-definition. But the images were repeated often to instill distorted notions about Asian identity in the minds of an impressionable, ethnocentric general public.

One particularly absurd notion was that all Asiatic people—from Bangkok to Tokyo to San Francisco—looked, talked and behaved exactly alike. Another, that Asians were so exotic, so profoundly "different" from European Americans that they could live only at the margins of our society, never at its center.

The more hostile images of Asians tended to dovetail neatly with U.S. foreign-policy aims. According to Asian-American media scholar Benjamin Tong, the legion of enigmatic and treacherous "Oriental" villains helped stir up anti-Asian sentiments during the wars against Japan, Korea and Vietnam, helped rationalize the periodic government orders against Asian immigration, and helped justify the incarceration of one hundred thousand innocent Japanese Americans during World War II.

Movies and television conveyed these stereotypes most persuasively and in-sistently. But live theatre did its part too. There were Broadway musicals like *Chinese Honeymoon*, a 1902 hit imported from London, set in romanticized China locales with Caucasian chorus girls decked out in brocade pajamas and slant-eyed makeup. In some drawing-room comedies of the 1920s and '30s, it was chic for the idle rich to have comic Chinese servants at their beck and call. And just as white minstrels found fame impersonating blacks, some vaudeville performers prospered as "Chinese impersonators."

You could not even find sympathetic or sizable Asiatic *roles* in Broadway shows until after World War II. A shift began when U.S. soldiers returned from long stints in the Pacific, sometimes bringing Asian war brides home with them. As U.S. political influence spread eastward, intermarriages and social interactions between Asians and Caucasians increased. And as telecommunication systems grew more sophisticated, the global village became a reality.

In the 1950s Broadway reflected the public's new interest in the Far East with hit shows focusing on Asian characters. The wily Japanese peasant in *The Teahouse of the August Moon*, the Siamese monarch in *The King and I*, the Hong Kong bargirl in *The World of Suzy Wong*—these were sizable and sympathetic roles. But they were still *foreigners*, in *foreign* settings. And the larger the part, the more likely it would be played by a non-Asian actor.

Would there ever be plays about Asian Americans, with roles for Asian-American performers? Not until 1958, when the Richard Rodgers-Oscar Hammer-stein musical *Flower Drum Song* premiered on Broadway. Loosely adapted from a novel by Chinese-American author C.Y. Lee, *Flower Drum Song* was the first major show to be set in an Asian-American milieu—in this case, a postcard-picturesque version of San Francisco's Chinatown.

The plot concerned the intergenerational rift between a conservative Chinese father and an Americanized son who rebels against an arranged marriage. The premise had some validity, but *Flower Drum Song* rang false as an accurate picture of life in a big-city Chinatown. Its happy-go-lucky ghetto inhabitants seemed ex-empt from economic problems or racial bias, and utterly disconnected from the rest of American society. And the major characters—a wise Confucian patriarch, a China Doll vamp, a submissive, fresh-off-the-boat bride—acted like familiar Asian stereotypes dressed up in new clothes. (Ironically, the producers of the original pro-

Introduction

duction cast mostly Japanese-Americans in the major roles, insisting they could find no suitable Chinese-American actors.)

Clearly, the time had to arrive for Asian Americans to begin telling their own stories in their own authentic voices. The pent-up frustrations of this "silent" minority finally erupted in the 1960s and early 1970s, in the wake of the black movement for civil rights and ethnic pride. Young people of diverse Asian ancestry joined together to form a new political coalition. United under the "Asian-American" banner, they began to exert collective political clout, seek reparations for past injustices and challenge racial stereotyping.

From the beginning this movement had a very active cultural component, and spawned visual arts collectives, literary groups, independent film cooperatives and nonprofit theatre companies. According to the editors of *Aiiieeeee*, a landmark literary anthology published in 1974 by Howard University Press, Asian Americans had been kept "off the air, off the streets, and praised . . . for being Asiatically no-show." After decades of invisibility, they wrote, "it is clear we have a lot of elegant, angry, and bitter life to show."

The theatre became a logical place to express that elegance, anger and bitterness. In 1965 a group of Los Angeles actors of Japanese, Chinese and Korean descent formed the first Asian-American theatre group, East West Players. They began by dramatizing the work of Asian novelists like Yukio Mishima, and showcasing Asian-American actors in classic plays by Lorca, Goldoni and Gorky. Later, under the charismatic leadership of the actor-director Mako, they concentrated on plays by Asian Americans.

But Asian-American playwriting got its real jumpstart in 1973, when Frank Chin, Janis Chan, Jeffrey Chin and others founded the Asian American Theatre Workshop in San Francisco. Helped by donations of space and acting training from the American Conservatory Theatre, this exciting laboratory yielded the first major play by an Asian-American author: Frank Chin's *Chickencoop Chinaman*.

Incisive, irreverent and raunchy, *Chickencoop Chinaman* was for and about a restive young generation of Asian Americans. Audiences responded to its lampooning of both racist media stereotyping and self-stereotyping, and to characters shaped more by the gritty reality of multiracial America than by the distant culture of their ancestors.

Chin's play toured college campuses for over a year, bringing media attention and new recruits to the Asian American Theatre Workshop. National interest in Chin's work intensified after the American Place Theatre mounted his *The Year of the Dragon* in 1977, billing it as the first Asian-American drama ever produced in New York.

While Asian American Theatre and East West Players continued to develop, other companies sprang up. In New York actress Tisa Chang founded the Pan Asian Repertory. In Seattle the Asian Exclusion Act (later renamed the Northwest Asian American Theatre Company) opened, and, in Toronto, the Canadian Artists Group.

As soon as there were theatres to produce Asian-American scripts and actors eager to perform them, the ranks of Asian-American playwrights swelled. In addition to the writers anthologized here, many other noted dramatists and performance artists of Asian descent have emerged over the past decade. Some of the better known are Momoko Iko, James Yoshimura, R.A. Shiomi, Winston Tong, Milton Murayama, Rosanna Yamagiwa Alfaro, Genny Lim, Ernest Abuba, Daryl Chin, the late Warren Kubota, Edward Sakamoto, Mel Escueta, Velina Houston, Jon Shirota, Dom Magwili and Perry Miyake Jr.

At this writing, Asian-American theatres are still the primary artery for plays about Asian-American history and experience. But it must be emphasized that not all of the plays and playwrights in this anthology have been associated with the Asian-American theatre movement.

David Henry Hwang's first play was produced in his dorm at Stanford University. Many of his subsequent works have been premiered by the New York Shakespeare Festival, and his stunning M. Butterfly earned Hwang a Tony Award after it debuted on Broadway. Ping Chong and Jessica Hagedorn developed their unique multimedia formats in the experimental performance spheres of New York and San Francisco. Chong's background as a visual artist strongly informs his style, while Hagedorn's work as a poet and fiction writer have a powerful impact on hers. Laurence Yep wrote popular children's novels for ten years before joining a playwrights' laboratory and discovering his flair for drama. And though Philip Gotanda and Wakako Yamauchi remain closely allied with Asian-American troupes, they are now writing for regional theatres, film and television as well.

The plays contained in this volume were chosen, in part, to reflect the tremendous diversity of Asian Americans as artists and individuals—a diversity long denied by the "majority" culture. As Elaine Kim pointed out in her 1982 study, Asian American Literature, "Asian Americans who write are not necessarily 'typical' or 'representative' of their nationality or racial group. No one expects John Steinbeck or Herman Melville to present or typify all white Americans, or even all German Americans or Anglo Americans, but because Asian Americans have been unfamiliar to most American readers, their visions and expressions are sometimes erroneously generalized."

In the autobiographical remarks that precede each play, certain similarities of viewpoint do arise. Most of these writers claim a kind of dual identity as both observer and participant, outsider and insider, anthropologist and subject in their own homeland. They speak of wearing the tag of "otherness" our society still assigns members of racial-minority groups—including those who are U.S.-born and bred.

Ping Chong points out that this sense of "otherness" can prove useful to a writer. It can, he believes, result in a kind of double vision that allows one to work at the intersection of forms, at the crux of cultures, at the critical junctures where ethnic, aesthetic and social identities blur and blend.

As David Henry Hwang emphasizes, the United States remains the world's great experimental laboratory for cultural hybrids and convergences. As we move into the next century, new influxes of Asian and Hispanic immigrants are changing the demographics of many regions. Intermarriage is on the rise, more biracial children are being born, new waves of racial violence occur, and the battles over bilingual education and bilingual ballots rage on.

Only by rejecting the narrow, simplistic conceptions of race and ethnicity can a truly pluralistic American culture emerge—an inclusive culture that acknowledges our contradictions, honors our differences, celebrates our commonalities. This book, the first anthology of plays by Asian-American writers, was conceived in the spirit of that emergent culture, that ever-evolving mosaic of the American Dream.

Misha Berson is the theatre critic for the *San Francisco Bay Guardian* and is a senior contributor to *American Theatre* magazine. The first volume of her history of theatre in San Francisco, *The San Francisco Stage: From Gold Rush to Golden Spike, 1849–1869*, has just been published by the city's Performing Arts Library & Museum. She also teaches at San Francisco State University.

BETWEEN WORLDS

Nuit Blanche
A Select View of Earthlings

Ping Chong

in collaboration with Joel Beard, Tone Blevins, John Miglietta, Louise Smith, Pablo Vela, David Wolpe

Ping
Chong

I grew up first-generation Chinese-American in New York's Chinatown. My parents had the first Chinese coffee shop on Bayard Street.

I didn't realize how far away American culture at large was until I went to high school. Crossing Chinatown meant you were in Little Italy, so we were familiar with Italians. But then I went to high school, and for the first time I was part of a minority group.

Having grown up in a ghetto situation I really had a lot of adjusting to do. That's certainly profoundly influenced my work, because what happened was that I could never again take anything for granted. Nor was anything ever really familiar to me again. I started looking at America as if I was from another world, as an outsider.

Before I was born my family had been involved in Chinese opera. My grandfather and father were director-producers, my mother performed and had toured to Vietnam in the 1920s. The first theatre I saw was Chinese opera, but only in the reduced state of touring companies. I saw very little of it because by the time I was growing up my parents had more or less given it up. They did not encourage me to go into the arts, but they didn't try to stop me either.

From early on I was very attracted to visual art. I went to the High School of Art and Design, then to Pratt Institute, and after that I studied filmmaking. I had no desire to go into theatre; at that point I wanted to be a filmmaker.

As a young adult I felt like I was sitting on a fence staring at two cultures. I realized I could not return to my previous culture, because the community was too small. I could never have been an artist staying in Chinatown.

I think this feeling is classic, a uniquely first-generation situation for anyone who grows up in a ghetto. You go out into the bigger world, and start looking at it with the kind of objectivity an anthropologist has.

Theatre was really an accident for me. I knew Western painting well, but Western theatre was something I had no real connection to. I found it was totally ethnocentric, something that had nothing to do with my life. I wondered if, as an Asian, I would be totally misunderstood in this country because I don't carry the agreed-upon perceptual responses.

But I've always had the need to express myself in various ways. I remember someone telling me, "You're the kind of person who has to start from ground zero." He meant I'd have to develop something that was totally my own vocabulary.

I got interested in performance around the time I met Meredith Monk. It was the height of the 1960s, when all that performance ferment was going on in the New York art scene, and I got very involved in that. The sixties breakdown of traditional values and ideas about what art is and is not was a seminal influence on me. Actually, I'm a real potpourri of influences.

I made my first two performance pieces in 1972. One was a collaboration with Meredith Monk called *Paris*, and it turned out to be one of our most popular pieces together. We've since gone on to collaborate several more times; it's been a very fruitful relationship.

My second piece, which I did totally on my own, was called *Lazarus*. At that time I did not have a company, I did not have any overhead. I was totally penniless and did the whole production for about $100. The odd thing is that in my entire career this piece was my most uncompromising, and the most difficult for an audience to sit through. It was not about entertainment, it was not literary. It was very much visual theatre. I've never been that tough since!

There was no Asian pride movement going on in New York at the time, as far as I can remember. I had to resolve all those issues of being Asian-American myself. I wasn't particularly connected to the Asian community, because I didn't know anybody like myself in New York.

Early in my career my work was partially disguised autobiography. After I got through that phase I had this realization that the role of the outsider was more universal. I began dealing more with the problem of how whole cultures are unable to interact harmoniously.

Ping Chong

Many of my latter works are about this issue. I've found a positive way to use this sense of not totally belonging. I recognized that this relative objectivity I had was positive, it could help me show many people a view they themselves couldn't see. It's an outsider's perspective similar to that of certain writers I admire—V.S. Naipaul, Bruce Chatwin, Joseph Conrad.

I first did *Nuit Blanche* in 1981, at La Mama in New York. It's a favorite among the more than twenty pieces I've done, one of the shows I feel closest to.

I collect newspaper clippings of everything that happens to ring a bell. I was looking through them one day, and got the idea for a piece that would be a select view of earthlings. It was going to be a kind of global newspaper, though it didn't come out that way.

I wanted to do a piece that covered a lot of timelines in human history. *Nuit Blanche* is really about human history, about the way history evolves vis-à-vis the two characters in the plantation who wind up in their respective worlds later on. The Cambodian reference was a news item that I had collected. It was, for me, a mirror of human beings and our superstitions. By presenting humans as very primitive creatures I was saying how vulnerable we really are, how small our universe is.

Nuit Blanche was informed by the fact that I was reading books by Shiva Naipaul and V.S. Naipaul. It was the first show I did with the theme that has echoed over and over again in my later works: the vulnerability of human beings and the recurrence of destruction. I've always come back to that, to the cyclical nature of destruction.

The piece also represented a lot of stylistic experimentation for me. The sound and visual aspects were very elaborate. I did a lot of visual research, the most I've ever done for a piece; you can't really tell how visually rich the show was by just reading the script. I went to Washington and got the NASA tape of Neil Armstrong landing on the moon. I got projections of earth from a satellite. It all wound up in the performance.

It was also the first show where I really started to deal with actors as actors, where I actually directed them and included more conventional scenes. The works before were really visual theatre, distinctly art-centered.

Since I made *Nuit Blanche* my work has broken in two categories. There are the shows with conventional scenes, like *Kind Ness*. And there are the more choreographic works like *Angels of Swedenborg*, which is almost textless.

I think there's a kind of magic realism in my work, like that of the South American writers. It's that sense of reality being absolutely fantastical. Now I'm becoming more interested in spirituality in the twentieth century. My latest works deal with this great need, this sense of spiritual longing. They've gotten more like personal and spiritual journeys.

In spirit I'm close to my Chinese roots but in practice I'm very far from them. As another way of trying to feel positive about what I had lost when I left Chinatown, I began to think of the entire world as my culture. I've developed a commitment to the sense that we are all together on this one little planet. It's more and more important for us not to feel so foreign with one another.

It's an interesting transition that's happening in the twentieth century. The electronic age is tying us all in, and the inclination of human history is to conglomerate into larger and larger republics. If we don't ruin the planet first, it's likely we will someday belong to one enormous republic.

Biographical Information

A writer, director, choreographer and designer, Ping Chong has originated more than twenty interdisciplinary performance pieces and installations. His work has been presented at major venues in the United States and beyond, including the Brooklyn Academy of Music, the Walker Arts Center in Minneapolis, the Osaka World Festival in Japan and the Festival d'Automne in Paris. He has created several pieces with Meredith Monk, and often works in close collaboration with other performers and designers. Among his recent pieces are *Kind Ness* (1986), honored with a Playwrights USA Award from Theatre Communications Group and Home Box Office; *Plage Concrete* (1988), a triad of outdoor multimedia installations for the Three Rivers Festival in Pittsburgh; and *Noiresque: A State of Being* (1989), a joint production with Pan Asian Repertory Theatre.

Chong's extensive video work includes two television pieces codirected by Meredith Monk: *Paris* (1972) and *Turtle Dreams* (1982), winner of a grand prize at the Toronto Video Festival.

The recipient of an Obie award (for *Humboldt's Current* in 1977), Ping Chong has also collected two National Endowment for the Arts fellowships, a Guggenheim Fellowship and a National Institute for Music Theatre Award. The artistic director of Ping Chong and Company (formerly known as The Fiji Company), he resides in New York.

About the Play

The first performances of *Nuit Blanche* took place at La Mama in New York City in January of 1981. Four years later the piece was revived, again at La Mama. *Nuit Blanche* was the first volume issued in the VRI Theater Library's Contemporary Scripts series, appearing in 1986.

From the Program

PNOMPENH, Cambodia, Feb. 7 (AP) Premier Lon Nol says Cambodian soldiers who shot at a mythical monster that was believed to be devouring the moon during a recent eclipse wasted so much ammunition the army might have run short in case of attack . . . . The soldiers were trying to drive away Reahou, a legendary monster who is malevolent brother to the sun and the moon. According to tradition, only by making great noise could they prevent Reahou from gobbling up the moon during the eclipse, darkening their nights forever.

6

The Play

Nuit Blanche
A Select View of Earthlings

Dedicated to
Kenji Mizoguchi
& Manuel Alvarez Bravo

Bare stage backed by a large rear-projection screen, lit with soft blue light from above. As the audience enters, a recorded voice croons the ballad "Blue Skies" by Irving Berlin. At the conclusion of the song, the lights dim and a small, filmed image is projected onto the center of the screen. What the image depicts is not immediately recognizable; it seems to be a picture of clouds, or maybe water, a horse's head, or perhaps two figures on a country road. These separate images seem to emerge, disappear and reappear the longer one looks at the film. Accompanying the projection is a narrative sound progression: cold autumnal wind, a baby's squall, a horse and carriage approaching and then stopping, the tolling of bells and a preacher intoning the words of a burial service. Underneath the small image another projected image appears, a name: Abigail Smith—a name that does not recur at any time during the play. Below the name a birth date dissolves into place, followed by the death date, and, finally, the cause of death: Smallpox. These images, the tolling bells, and all the other overlapping sounds are erased by the lowering of a large black partition or wall that creates a shallow forestage area. A stagehand places a folding chair in the center.

Scene 1
A Congregation Hall

A respectable-looking gentleman enters, sits and addresses the audience directly in a measured fashion. He is formal, and it is clear that he is an old hand at

7

8

manipulating his audience. His exact profession, nationality and the events he speaks of are left deliberately ambiguous—crime, anarchy, terrorism, blackmail belong to all of us.

THE GENTLEMAN: Good evening everybody. And congratulations to those of you who arrived here tonight on your public transportation system and survived that experience once again. I understand you're having quite a problem with that system, but I think it's a good problem. It reminds you of the greater problems in the city, the country, the world. In our last meeting in the capital I felt somewhat nervous when I noticed some of our most fearless spokespeople casting me sympathetic glances when they heard I was coming here. I thought I must really be going on a dangerous mission, coming to "the heart of the beast" as this country has been called. But, you're not too bad; quite tame, quite human—and I hope as generous as you appear to be.

Events have reached a critical stage. Since the destruction of the supertanker *Sea Emperor* and the liquidation of Cardinal Morosco, the International Commissioner's tactics have changed. Massive, undisguised brutality has emerged from behind a facade of self-assured righteousness. In my own country, our dear leader has invoked emergency powers and once again uses every method to crush each dissident voice. You may have noticed certain disturbing political adjustments in your own country. Beware. I have personally lost many friends. At times the pressure seems unbearable but we are close now. We need food, clothing, media expertise, technical aid, money. You have the choice to participate now, or sit back in your chairs and see which way the wind will blow. You can analyze our motives, reread our manuals, digest our charters, talk to your spouse, your lawyer, your accountant, your cat—I will be here for two days. I have promised to return with three-and-a-half million dollars. There are many of you here. You have friends. You can do it. I know you can. You have a great opportunity to assist in making a more humane society, that will shine as a golden beacon in a sad world.

Blackout. Soundtrack: A series of electronic beeps and hisses sporadically piercing the silence of the blackout lead into the sound tapes of the first Apollo moon landing including: "One small step for man; one giant step for mankind." This soundtrack overlaps the first sequence of slides.

Scene 2
Murmurs of Earth: A Slide Sequence

This sequence and a later slide sequence in the piece were inspired by Carl Sagan's book Murmurs of Earth—*a chronicle of the sounds and images sent, as a record of life on earth, into outer space on the Voyager II spacecraft headed for Jupiter. The images selected for the sequence include natural and man-made structures,*

diverse animal and human groupings in color and in black-and-white. The selec-
tions were most often made to emphasize the peculiarities of earth life. They were
interspersed with black-and-white grid slides and images in both closeup and long
shot of the moon's surface and its topography. Toward the end of the sequence,
a stagehand brings on two ornate nineteenth-century chairs and a table. A
candelabra is lit and placed on the table. Then an elderly and stately-looking
patrician figure in a cape appears and sits a chair. At the end of the slide se-
quence, the camera recedes away from the moon until the view is from the earth
looking up at the moon. Soundtrack: The cry of a bird, and the huge flapping
of its wings, is heard. When this sound of a dark night recedes, a slide with the text:

Estancia La Mariposa
Midnight
1800s

appears, and we hear the quiet ticking of a grandfather clock in a sleeping
household.

Scene 3
Estancia La Mariposa

Once again the setting is unspecified, though it can geographically be located in
South America. The scene is played entirely in Spanish to distance the viewer
both historically and metaphysically. The action in the scene, however, is clear:
The man in the room is the ranch owner, who has returned from Buenos Aires
with presents for his daughter. The half-savage slave girl, Berenice, wakens the
rancher's daughter, Gloria, to meet her father, who presents her with gifts. He
is formal with the child. The absence of her mother is strongly felt. Berenice is
commanded to reveal each gift: first, a delicate miniature tea set; then a dangerous-
looking knife, which sends Berenice screaming from the room; and, finally, a magic
lantern which projects a black-and-white film in miniature scale in which a chim-
panzee is hunted and slaughtered by a tiger. As this grisly law-of-the-jungle event
comes to a close—to be repeated in human form later in the piece—Berenice returns
to escort the yawning child back to bed. With a bow to her father, she takes leave
of him; as this scene ends, the father and daughter can be heard reciting their
respective prayers in their respective rooms. On the rear-projection screen the follow-
ing slide text fades in:

Estancia La Mariposa
Afternoon
6 Years Later

Soundtrack: Cattle mooing, horses galloping, ranch hands shouting. Then quiet.

Scene 4
Estancia La Mariposa

Same setting. A sunny afternoon. A handsome young man expectantly waits, a gift in his hand. Berenice, the slave girl, is now a self-composed young woman. She enters very formally and with the slightest of bows signals the entrance of the blossoming Gloria, who is likewise formal in her shawl, a comb in her hair. With the simplest of gestures, she bows and points with her fan to the chair opposite her. The young man bows and composes himself. He is armed with a speech. Berenice discreetly sits off to the side, only her wild eyes and birdlike hands betraying the constrictions on her being. The young man rises.

THE YOUNG MAN: Señorita Santiago, I bring you a gift from my family's glorious magnolia orchard. May it blossom on the pampas as it has in North Carolina. May our friendship blossom as the flower. May the names of McQuade and Santiago be as close as two little baby lambs newly born on a cold winter's morning. This is for you, señorita— *(In an offhand manner)* I think you should have your girl take the wrappings off and let the light get at it.

GLORIA: You are too kind, señor. Berenice, pon las flores en un vaso.

Berenice goes for the vase.

I hope your journey was not too unpleasant.

THE YOUNG MAN: The unpleasantness of my journey was lightened by the prospect of its consummation.

GLORIA: You are too kind, señor.

Berenice returns with a single flower in a vase.

Oh, señor, the flower is beautiful. May I touch it?

THE YOUNG MAN: Of course.

Gloria for the first time breaks her composure and leans forward to stroke the petals.

GLORIA: The color is so pure . . . and the petals are so exquisitely formed . . . and the fragrance . . .

Berenice clears her throat to indicate the impropriety of Gloria's expressiveness.

(Regaining her composure and withdrawing her being) Señor, in all the years my father and I have cultivated our modest garden, we have never been blessed with such an exquisite horticultural specimen.

The young man, seeing it to be the right moment to bring up the subject of his visit, leans towards Gloria.

THE YOUNG MAN: Señorita, were you able to discuss—

Gloria, with a flick of her fan, interrupts the young man.

GLORIA: Perhaps the señor would care for some refreshment. Berenice, serve el té.

Gloria is showing signs of discomfort. Berenice leaves to fetch some tea. The young man, sensing something is wrong, careful of proprieties, sits back in his chair.

THE YOUNG MAN: Tea . . .? Of course . . . *(Again in an offhand manner)* She's Indian, isn't she?

GLORIA *(Absently fanning herself)*: Sí, señor.

THE YOUNG MAN: Señorita, were you able to discuss with your father, the matters we brought up at the end of our last conversation?

GLORIA *(Stops fanning herself)*: I am afraid, señor . . .

Already realizing what is coming, the young man lists the advantages of a union with a McQuade.

THE YOUNG MAN: You told him, didn't you, that I'd be willing to leave South Carolina . . . that I'd assume full responsibility for the management of this plantation . . .

GLORIA *(Distressed, but still composed)*: Sí, señor . . .

THE YOUNG MAN: . . . that I would maintain its present boundaries, that I would respect your country's imminent abolition of slavery . . .

GLORIA *(Trying to get a word in)*: I am afraid . . .

THE YOUNG MAN: . . . that I would include in the marriage contract the fact that you would owe primary responsibility to your father until the time of his death?

For the first time, Gloria looks at the young man.

GLORIA: I am afraid, señor, that my father has made a plan.

Silence.

THE YOUNG MAN: And the plan does not include me. It includes Señor Ortega.

GLORIA: Señor Ortega.

Berenice returns with the tea and carefully sets each thing down in the silence of the moment. Berenice's eyes dart about. The young man makes one last, desperate plea.

THE YOUNG MAN: You told him I'd be willing to convert to Catholicism?

GLORIA *(Hanging on for dear life to her composure)*: Señor . . . I have told him everything you wanted me to tell him.

She slowly pours the tea and offers it to him. Without a word, but with a hasty gesture of leavetaking, the young man departs. Berenice, sensing some disturbance, knits her brow.

Berenice?

BERENICE: Sí?

GLORIA: Yo quiero conserva estas flores.

BERENICE: Sí.

GLORIA: Envuelvelas en papel . . .

BERENICE: Sí.

GLORIA: Mét-elas en una caja de madera . . .

BERENICE: Sí.

GLORIA: Y después me las trae.

BERENICE: Sí.

GLORIA: Quiero verlas.

BERENICE *(Slowly)*: Sí . . . sí . . . sí . . . sí . . .

As this last conversation between lady and servant concludes, the stage lights are slowly dimming, leaving only a spotlight on the magnolia, and then this too fades away. A text slide appears on the rear-projection screen and gunshots, horses racing across a pampas and men shouting in exaltation are heard. Is it a revolution or a wedding?

Estancia La Mariposa
A Year Later

Scene 5
Estancia La Mariposa

Same setting. No one is on stage. Dappled sunlight shines and fades through the shades, then Berenice enters backwards in a black shawl and gown—her servant's uniform. She looks offstage in both directions to see if anyone is watching, then sits in her mistress's chair. She wildly mimics her mistress in conversation with a person in the opposite chair. Then she jumps up and plays the guest, grabbing a bonbon from a candy dish. Looking once again in both directions, she picks up her mistress's fan, seductively strolls downstage and tempts the audience in a wild, improbable gibberish. The lights fade to black as Berenice's voice fades away and the singing of nuns rises to the fore. A text slide appears:

1853   Slavery is abolished.
Berenice Huarpes makes her way
to North Carolina.

1854   Gloria Ortega dies in childbirth.

1863   La Mariposa is lost at
the gambling tables.

Scene 6
A Prehistoric Cave and Its Environs

This scene begins as a slide sequence of cave drawings in closeup, followed by a grouping of cave drawings on a wall, inside a cave with the opening at the right. Then a shadowplay begins, utilizing slides of the cave's environs as backdrop to a prehistoric manhunt. The effect is somewhat like a silent film since the backdrops have a bluish-white light. After a brisk chase through forests and mountains, two primal men confront each other on a high bluff, threatening each other with, respectively, a spear and a branch. This image freezes, fades and is replaced by a text slide:

Monday
October 4

Soundtrack: When the singing nuns fade out after the last Estancia La Mariposa sequence, the placid dripping of water into a cavern pool is heard in the darkness, followed by a pompous, condescending French tour guide and his retinue of foreign tourists, all chattering away in their own native tongues. This noise echoes throughout the cave. A bat flaps its wings overhead and then fades into the depths of the cave. An Italian and his lady are left behind gazing at the cave drawings. He muses out loud, wondering what manner of men could have made these drawings. Suddenly the sound of violent winds whips through the cave. Over this, the voices of wild dogs rise in a a cacophony. Then something can be heard moving about in the cave, and soon the silhouette of a man is seen. When he turns to reveal his profile, the scene has jumped back thousands of years in time. Throughout the manhunt that follows, the violent winds rise till the meeting on the bluff of hunter and prey. When the two men freeze into the unrecorded event that it was, the wind stops, and then we hear the sound of an airplane overhead, approaching, fading away.

Scene 7
A Laundry Room

The setting, suggested only by an ironing board, clothes basket and one of those metal stools with a pullout stepladder, is a private laundry business run by Miss B., a mulatto woman played by the same actress who appears as Berenice. Downstage is an oversized sheet, laid out flat on the ground as a white rectangle. The feeling is rural and southern, perhaps somewhere in the Carolinas. As the scene begins, Miss B. is harried by the heat and the work. For most of this scene, an insistent, repetitive zither score creates an atmosphere of lyricism and bustling activity in a rural home business. At the same time, behind Miss B. and her world, we see a black-and-white slide sequence of a handsome mulatto man walking through a poor part of town. There are some seventy slides; he moves along, smiling, putting his fingers through his hair, looking off, tilting his head and then finally moving out of frame, leaving only a desolate, burnt-out road and the hungry bark of a stray dog to close the scene.

THE CHILD'S VOICE *(Offstage)*: Miss B., Miss B.—what time is it?
MISS B. *(As she irons)*: It's not time yet, Hannah Pearl.
THE CHILD'S VOICE: Is it six o'clock?
MISS B.: It's not six o'clock yet. I'll tell you when it's six o'clock.
THE CHILD'S VOICE: But if I'm late for dinner . . .
MISS B.: I know. You're gonna get a whippin', I know.

Another voice offstage randomly announces bingo numbers as a kind of vocal counterpoint: N-31 . . . O-5 . . . T-36 . . ., etc.

THE CHILD'S VOICE: What's that?
LITTLE BOY'S VOICE: Cracker ball—you throw it. Watch.
THE CHILD'S VOICE: What are those things made of?

Meanwhile, on the rear-projection screen, the mulatto man is moving along the street; the zither music is buzzing and Miss B. is madly working along.

LITTLE BOY'S VOICE: I don't know. Here, you take one. You throw it. Not like that Like this.
THE CHILD'S VOICE: You gave me a dud.
LITTLE BOY'S VOICE: I didn't give you no dud. Watch. Now dance! Dance!
THE CHILD'S VOICE: Get away from me.
LITTLE BOY'S VOICE: Jump high, high!
THE CHILD'S VOICE: Ow! Quit it, quit it!
MISS B.: You kids quit it. . . . It's Tuesday.

Over the image of the mulatto man, a text slide appears:

Tuesday
October 5

FRANKLIN'S VOICE *(Offstage)*: Hi, B.
MISS B.: Morning, Franklin.
FRANKLIN'S VOICE: How ya doin' today?
MISS B.: I'm doin' fine. How're you?
FRANKLIN'S VOICE: I'm okay. Hey, B., I got two shirts for you.

Miss B. is now straightening the edges of the huge downstage sheet. Franklin throws his clothes on stage from the wings.

Uh-huh.
FRANKLIN'S VOICE: One of 'em's for my daddy, he says . . .
FRANKLIN'S VOICE AND MISS B.: No starch!

MISS B.: Yeah, I know, no starch.

FRANKLIN'S VOICE: How'd you know? Hey, B. I got one from me, too, it's blue, okay?

MISS B.: Okay.

FRANKLIN'S VOICE: You can do anything you want, just make it clean. Hey, B., I got something to show ya. It's my new knife.

MISS B. *(Friendly scolding)*: I ain't got time for knives today.

FRANKLIN'S VOICE: Aw, c'mon, B., just a minute?

MISS B.: On Thursday, I'll look at your knife. You come back for your shirts, I'll look at your knife.

FRANKLIN'S VOICE: Okay, you promise?

MISS B.: I promise, Franklin.

FRANKLIN: Till Thursday.

Meanwhile on the rear-projection screen, the mulatto man moves past a telephone pole. A text slide appears:

Wednesday
October 6

A rose-colored nun appears, her back to the audience. The audience will never see her face. She leaves walking out backwards. Miss B. has sat down with her bottle of Coca-Cola and her crossword puzzle. The rose-colored nun enters again, this time to address Miss B. The nun raises her arm in Christian salutation. Miss B. knows what the nun has come for.

THE NUN: Good morning, Mrs. Winfred.

Miss B. looks up and then back down at her puzzle, not too friendly. The nun does not notice.

MISS B.: Good morning, Sister.

THE NUN: How's business?

MISS B.: Oh, business is fine . . . how's God? I'm sorry, that was sacrilegious, I didn't really mean it.

THE NUN: Oh, he's fine. He appreciates your interest.

MISS B.: Oh, really? That's funny.

THE NUN: You know, we're having a raffle at the church this weekend.

MISS B.: Oh, Sister, wait a minute. Do you know . . . what is the Big Sky State? Big Sky . . . seven letters.

THE NUN: Dakota? No.

MISS B.: I'll put it in, but I don't think that's right.

THE NUN: Wyoming? You know, Mrs. Winfred—first prize is a color TV.

MISS B.: Yeah?

THE NUN: Remote control . . . only two dollars. *(She raises two fingers)*

MISS B.: Two dollars? Okay, I'll take . . . I'll take two chances, but I'll have to pay you later, because I don't have any money on me right now. No hard feelings . . .

THE NUN: No hard feelings. Mrs. Winfred, life is too short.

Meanwhile, on the rear-projection screen, the mulatto man appears to be smiling at whoever is looking at him, perhaps it is Miss B. As if the words "life is too short" signal some deep pain within her, Miss B. begins to sob uncontrollably.

THE CHILD'S VOICE (*Offstage*): Hey, Miss B.? You got one of them old bleach bottles . . . you know . . . like them old white ones with a handle, you know . . . you got one of them things?

The zither music stops as the child speaks. Miss B. picks up the ends of the over-sized sheet.

MISS B.: It's Thursday.

Miss B. flaps the sheet. It makes a loud sound and suggests an ocean wave, or a stormy cloud, or an avalanche on a snow-capped mountain. She quickly folds it up and the huge shape is now a crumpled ball in her arms. For a moment it appears to be a baby. She gets up abruptly and leaves the stage. Meanwhile, text appears over a slide of the mulatto man:

Thursday
October 7
Davenport Road
3:00 P.M.

Soundtrack: A plaintive piano and synthesizer score has quietly replaced the zither music. The child who was heard offstage earlier enters with her pull-toy; she calls the toy Freddie.

THE CHILD: C'mon . . . c'mon, Freddie . . . c'mon. Miss B.? Hey, Miss B.? Yoo-hoo? Hey, Miss B., we're makin' mud pies, I made me thirty already . . . . Hey, Miss B., can I get a drink of water? C'mon, Freddie, she don't mind . . . . I'm gettin' me a drink of water, Miss B. C'mon . . . c'mon . . .

As the child exits, Miss B. enters in her coat, a scarf over her head, carrying a suitcase. She puts the suitcase down, backs off from it, picks it up again, backs off and then puts it down by her side. The mulatto man has now left the screen, leaving only the empty, burnt-out street.

MISS B. (*To the audience*): At first I thought he'd gone to Nashville, to visit his uncle. Or Tuscaloosa, Mobile, or Orangeville, Louisiana, Fayetteville, or even down to New Orleans, I . . . sent him some letters down there and I found out that was not indeed the case, he hadn't gone down to Nashville to visit his uncle . . . . At first, I thought he'd gone on down to Galveston, y'know, to work on that oil rig down there—they make a lot of money. And I made a telephone call and I sent a telegram but he wasn't down there. There used to be quite a resemblance between . . . (*She points to her face*) I . . . I had a couple items I had to pick up, I had to go all the way downtown Jackson to get the ticket, 'cuz I'd always . . . wanted to travel.

Miss B. exits; she has left her world behind.

THE CHILD *(Reenters)*: C'mon, c'mon now. Thanks a lot, Miss B. Oh, hey, Miss B., could you save me one of them like you know, like one of them big old blue bottles like . . . like Wisk in 'em, you know? Could you save me one of them? I'm gonna make me a girl. C'mon, Freddie, you're gonna make me late.

Franklin enters as the child exits.

FRANKLIN: Hi, B. It's Franklin. It's Thursday. Thursday's here and so is Franklin. Hey, my shirts all set? Hey, c'mon down here. I got something I wanna show ya. I promised ya and I ain't gonna let you down. *(He pulls out a knife and brandishes it around macho style)* Huh!—you're pretty good, you're pretty, you . . . *(He is looking at himself in the mirror)* Huh—who is that masked man? Swashbuckler, that's who you are. Swashbuckler. Hey, B., c'mon down, you're missin' the show. B.? Hey. C'mon, B. . . . don't be rude to me . . . that's what I always say—don't be rude to me. 'Kay. Your last chance for romance, I'm gonna sell my house in town and give up the family jewels, isn't never gonna see me again. 'Kay, that's how you want it . . . bye-bye . . . bye . . . here goes Franklin . . . here goes . . . I'm gone.

The lights fade to black. Only the empty street remains, then that too fades out with the sound of the barking dog. Soundtrack: Nuns singing, then they fade before the next scene.

Scene 8
Murmurs of Earth II: The Second Slide Sequence

This slide sequence is similar to the first, but without the grid slides and the moon-landing shots. The tone of the second grouping, though varied, has a latent feeling of war, destruction and death. By the fifth slide, the stagehand starts to bring in the furniture for the next scene. A low black wall that spans the entire stage flies in; it divides the outer veranda, which is upstage, from the individual guest rooms in the foreground. Soundtrack: A wind blowing through.

Scene 9
The Haven of Peace

An American woman comes on stage and goes over to the telephone in her room. An American beachcomber-type also enters. The Haven of Peace is a resort hotel in a Third World country on the verge of a revolution. The atmosphere throughout the scene is languid, damp and quietly threatening. A sense of waiting pervades and the hotel itself seems eternally vague and indifferent. It is run by a European named Papa Willie who has long since forgotten Europe. His guests are European and American tourists—an enclave of foreigners. The slide sequence continues as the American woman enters and ends when she gets off the phone. The woman is dressed like a suburban housewife on tropical holiday in a country she doesn't like and doesn't try to understand. Yet there is no intentional bigotry, only a form of stupid innocence.

AMERICAN WOMAN: Hello, Mother? Mother? It's Judith. Yes, yes, Mother, it's me. What? No—no, no, Mom, we're not in the States yet. No, we're not home yet, Mother, we're still over here. What? No, the embassy's been closed for two weeks. No, no, Ed hasn't gone . . . Ed hasn't gone in for . . . what? No, no, we're not there anymore, either, we had to leave there, it was getting . . . . I can't hear you, Mother, can you hear me? Yes, yes, that is better . . . oh, oh, is that what that was? Well, we're in a hotel . . . oh, it's all right, you know, it's the same all over. How are you? Uh-huh . . . are your legs any better? . . . Yeah . . . huh . . . oh, really? What kind of medicine . . . oh, yeah, Digitalis . . .

The beachcomber is in his room cutting out news clippings and laughing occasionally to himself. His room is a shambles compared to that of the American woman.

BEACHCOMBER: Hey, I really like that song! Turn it up!

At this point, a tall man with dark glasses and a black attaché case enters. He has a South African accent. He is wearing some kind of African shirt, khaki pants and heavy boots. He seems coldly efficient, like a hired killer or a mercenary. He immediately settles into his room, opens the attaché case and gets to work. The audience cannot see what he is doing.

AMERICAN WOMAN: You only take those when you have a pain, Mother, don't take too many of those . . . yeah . . . they're not good . . . . Oh, he's fine, he's fine . . .

At this point, a native waiter crosses the veranda, practicing out loud the new nationalist slogans. He repeats like a parrot.

WAITER: The wave of the future is Nationalism.

AMERICAN WOMAN: Oh, wait, just a minute, Mom! *(She leans out over the wall)* Oh, boy . . . hello. *(Back to telephone)* Oh, no, it was nothing, Mother. Well, he's not here right now. He went into town to rent a car. Oh, Mother, it's all right, there's plenty of other Americans here. I'm fine. Look, he'll be back any minute . . . in fact, Mom, you know what, I better get off . . . yeah, well, he might be trying to call me and I really should cut it short and if anything should . . . uh-huh . . . uh-huh . . . well, I just didn't want you to worry so . . . yeah . . . well, I know . . . yeah, Ma, I love you, too . . . I'll see you soon, okay? All right? Okay, bye-bye, Mom . . . bye, Mother . . . bye-bye . . .

*Soundtrack: Ice-cold chimes suddenly rattle in the air, we hear the pounding of
the surf. The beachcomber leaves his room with his snorkeling equipment. A text
slide appears:*

The Haven of Peace

*The American woman also leaves her room. The native waiter crosses the veranda
once again.*

WAITER: The loiterer is the exploiter of the State!
MAN IN DARK GLASSES: Hey, boy! *(He does not go to the window)*
WAITER: Yessir?
MAN IN DARK GLASSES: Where's my drink?
WAITER: What you got?
MAN IN DARK GLASSES: I told you, gin and tonic.
WAITER: Gin and tonic. You want ice?
MAN IN DARK GLASSES: Of course, I want ice.
WAITER: No ice. You want lemon?

*A time slide comes on. For the rest of the scene, time slides will appear, even
over the shadowplay:*

11:15

MAN IN DARK GLASSES: Lime.

*The waiter exits and returns with drink. He stands outside, peering in, over the
wall, watching what the man is making in his attaché case. An airplane flies
by overhead. The man notices the waiter watching and stares him down.*

WAITER: Gin and tonic.

He waits for a tip. Which is not forthcoming.

MAN IN DARK GLASSES: Yeah, well, uh . . . cheers.

The waiter realizes he won't get a tip. Flips his serving tray in the air.

WAITER: Okay. Sure thing.

*The beachcomber appears outside the man in dark glasses' door. The American
woman is now on the veranda, looking at postcards.*

BEACHCOMBER: Hey! Anybody in there?

Waiter crosses, whistling.

AMERICAN WOMAN: Oh, boy!
WAITER *(Stops reluctantly)*: Yes, missy?
AMERICAN WOMAN: Could you bring me another coffee?
WAITER: Café?

AMERICAN WOMAN: Café, yes.

WAITER: Okay, sure thing. Oh, missy, pas de lait.

AMERICAN WOMAN: Excuse me?

WAITER *(Impatient)*: Oh, no milk in the hotel, we haven't had any milk for about a week now . . .

AMERICAN WOMAN: Yes, yes, that's right. Black is fine.

BEACHCOMBER: Hello!

Soundtrack: When the waiter leaves the American woman on the veranda, she picks up a postcard and her voice is heard on tape.

AMERICAN WOMAN'S VOICE: "Dear Bunny, Funny-looking fella, isn't he? *(Referring to the chimpanzee on the card)* Ed and I are finally on our way home. It's been one long haul here in the wilds. Hope to see you on Thursday. Miss ya! Love, Judith."

When "Love, Judith" comes on the tape, it echoes and repeats itself several times until it fades away. On the rear-projection screen, a time slide:

11:45

Then the sound of the pounding surf and the gulls. There is a slight lapse before the waiter returns with the coffee. Time is passing languidly by at the Haven of Peace.

WAITER: Café, missy.

AMERICAN WOMAN: Oh, um, do I pay you for these? *(She means the postcards)*

WAITER: Okay, sure thing.

AMERICAN WOMAN: How much?

WAITER: How many?

AMERICAN WOMAN: Three.

WAITER: Two.

AMERICAN WOMAN *(Trying to identify the foreign coins)*: Two. What's that?

BEACHCOMBER *(Offstage)*: I'm your neighbor from down the hall. Have you got a second?

The man in dark glasses does not pay any attention.

WAITER: One.

AMERICAN WOMAN: There's another.

WAITER: Two . . . one more . . .

He's trying to cheat her, but she knows. He backs off.

Okay, sure thing!

AMERICAN WOMAN: Oh, boy!

WAITER: Yes, missy?

AMERICAN WOMAN: I've noticed . . . why are they taking away all that furniture?

WAITER (*Standing himself up straight*): What the big man give, the big man can take away.

The answer is obviously unsatisfactory to the American woman and she exits. The beachcomber enters and walks into the man with dark glasses' room. Another time slide comes on.

12:32

BEACHCOMBER: Oh, hi! Just thought I'd drop in and see who my new neighbor was. There's a . . . a lot of commotion going on around here . . . d'ya know what's going on? Hey! That's a nice radio you got there . . . yeah . . . . So, uh . . . you been down to the beach yet . . . huh?

During this scene, the man in dark glasses gets up and threateningly walks toward the beachcomber, trying to intimidate him out the door.

MAN IN DARK GLASSES: No, you?

BEACHCOMBER: Oh, yeah, yeah . . . I been practically living down there . . . . Um . . . you got a cigarette . . . well . . . anything you need, you just let me know . . . I'm just two doors down the hall . . . just gimme a knock . . .

MAN IN DARK GLASSES: Get out.

Time slides appear:

12:32

then

13:58

Everyone has left the stage. The Haven of Peace is alone with the sunlight through the latticework and the smell . . . . The ocean splashes on the rocks nearby. It is afternoon. Soundtrack. The ice-cold tinkle of chimes again breaks the silence. Once, twice and three times. A formal-looking Oriental gentleman appears alone on the veranda in a white summer suit, a cup of coffee in his hand. He never speaks. It is apparent that he is the only one at the Haven of Peace who is not in any danger. It is possible that he is the cause of the danger. As he strolls along the veranda, enjoying the sea air, the rose-colored nun enters begging for funds. He gives generously.

ROSE-COLORED NUN: Excusez moi . . . pour les enfants? Merci, monsieur! Merci!

Shortly after, the sound of fishermen can be heard, with the slapping of their nets. Papa Willie enters, a man in his early fifties, dressed in loose-fitting native garb and sunglasses. There is an odd quality about him. He gives the impression of living in another time and place. He stands with his back to the audience, looking upstage toward the rear-projection screen, which is an aqua color. The Oriental gentleman does likewise. Papa Willie breaks the silence.

PAPA WILLIE: Yes . . . yes . . . my collection, my collection . . . oh, well, you are very kind . . . very kind . . . oh, I know, all the books quote me now. If you see a book on shells that doesn't quote me, it's not worth reading. Oh, no . . . . After you . . . Ruis! *(Ruis is the native waiter)* Follow me! No, no, after you.

Papa Willie and the Oriental exit.

RUIS'S VOICE *(Offstage)*: Right away, Papa Willie! Tips and gratuities undermine the welfare of the Working Class.

Time slide:

18:00

The beachcomber crosses the veranda with a soft drink and a crumpled paper bag. He throws the bag up in the air and bats it with his fist, then listlessly moves off. The rear-projection screen lights up from behind to reveal a shadowplay. Papa Willie and the Oriental enter and sit down on two deck chairs. A beach table, on which is a cocktail shaker and glasses, is between them. Downstage of them, just above the wall partition, the American woman enters, trying to get the attention of the man in dark glasses, who has returned to his room after Papa Willie and the Oriental's exit.

AMERICAN WOMAN: Hello . . . hello . . . are you in there? Hello . . .

PAPA WILLIE *(In shadowplay)*: Would you care for a cigarette? *(The Oriental makes a gesture)* You don't smoke. Well, I know smoking is not very popular these days . . . . They are English, you know. I get them at the airport. A most kind friend, a steward, brings them in to me weekly from Belgium. *(He points up in the air)* Sabena.

RUIS'S VOICE *(Offstage)*: Papa Willie, Papa Willie, look what I found!

AMERICAN WOMAN *(Still trying to get in)*: Hi . . . . It's your neighbor, Judith Elsen, from next door . . . uh . . . I was wondering if you've seen Mr. Willie.

Time slide:

18:15

MAN IN DARK GLASSES *(With cigar in mouth)*: Haven't seen him.

AMERICAN WOMAN: Could you open your door for a moment? Please?

MAN IN DARK GLASSES *(Doesn't want to let her in)*: Well, he was in the lobby when I checked in.

AMERICAN WOMAN: Well, I just checked the lobby, he's not there.

MAN IN DARK GLASSES: Just a minute . . . *(He curses under his breath, comes to the wall to speak with her)*

AMERICAN WOMAN: Excuse me? Hi . . . I'm sorry to bother you.

MAN IN DARK GLASSES: That's quite all right. *(It isn't)* Listen, have you checked on the . . . uh . . . the roof?

AMERICAN WOMAN (*Not noticing that he is being snide*): Yes, I checked the . . . well, I checked the veranda, and I checked out in the lobby. I checked the dining room and the guy next door's room. I . . .

MAN IN DARK GLASSES: Yeah, well, look . . . he's not in here unless he got in without my seeing . . .

AMERICAN WOMAN (*Out of nowhere*): Are you English?

MAN IN DARK GLASSES (*Curtly*): No.

AMERICAN WOMAN: Oh, I'm sorry . . .

MAN IN DARK GLASSES: Do I sound English?

AMERICAN WOMAN: No.

MAN IN DARK GLASSES: Actually, I'm South African . . . you been there?

AMERICAN WOMAN: No . . . no, I haven't.

MAN IN DARK GLASSES: Most beautiful beaches in the world.

Time slide:

18:16

AMERICAN WOMAN: Oh.

MAN IN DARK GLASSES: Look, sorry I can't help you . . .

AMERICAN WOMAN: Maybe you've heard some news on the radio then . . .

MAN IN DARK GLASSES: Yeah, but . . . uh . . . I don't have a radio.

Soundtrack: The radio music abruptly stops. Ticking like a time bomb begins.
Time slide:

18:17

AMERICAN WOMAN: Oh . . . I . . . uh . . . gee, I thought I heard one . . . must be someone else, I guess . . .

MAN IN DARK GLASSES: Yeah . . . must be.

Time slide:

18:19

AMERICAN WOMAN: Oh, well, I'm . . . uh . . . I'm in a little bit of a bind here . . . you see, I'm trying to find out about the traffic from town, and I . . . trying to talk to the boy, it just doesn't seem to register . . . do you know the language? How would you ask him about the traffic situation?

MAN IN DARK GLASSES: Mbala dgai dophay.

AMERICAN WOMAN: Oh. Could you do me a favor? Could you just write that down? I don't think I'm going to be able to remember it . . .

MAN IN DARK GLASSES: No. You see, I'd like to write it down for you, but I can't. You see, because there's a certain musicality to the language—

AMERICAN WOMAN: Just use arrows or something . . .

MAN IN DARK GLASSES: You can't use arrows, madam—

AMERICAN WOMAN: Please, please! I really appreciate—
MAN IN DARK GLASSES: Madam—
AMERICAN WOMAN: Just write it down for me . . . please . . .

Time slide:

18:20

MAN IN DARK GLASSES: Right.

Papa Willie, in shadowplay, laughs and gestures. The American woman enters the room and snoops around. The man in dark glasses sits and starts to write.

AMERICAN WOMAN: Oh. I see you're a whiskey drinker . . . that's . . . uh . . . that's an interesting item you have there. What is that?
MAN IN DARK GLASSES: That, that's nothing. *(Closes attaché case)* Look, I've written it out for you, so . . . *(Notices the American woman looking at his whiskey)* Care for a drink?

Soundtrack: Ticking, ticking, ticking like a bomb.

AMERICAN WOMAN: Oh, uh . . . sure . . .

The beachcomber, who has been asleep in his room, is stabbed to death by a person in black, with a black stocking over his head.

Is . . . um . . . is that a hunting knife?
MAN IN DARK GLASSES: Yeah. *(He has a knife strapped to his leg. He pulls down his pant leg)*
AMERICAN WOMAN: You know what . . . this is a terrible place.

She is beginning to feel uneasy with him. He knows it and plays it out.

MAN IN DARK GLASSES: South Africa's fantastic . . . fantastic . . .

She is nervously reaching for the sheet of paper with the translation on it. He holds it out just slightly so that she has to reach for it.

Yeah, well uh look . . . there it is, all written out for you. *(He relaxes his grip and lets her go, psychologically speaking)*
AMERICAN WOMAN: Oh. That's wonderful . . . mbala piria dogai dophayyoay . . .
MAN IN DARK GLASSES: That'll get you anything you like . . . the sun, the moon and the stars.
AMERICAN WOMAN: Oh. Thank you. *(As she turns to leave)* How are you getting out?
MAN IN DARK GLASSES: Well, I'm not getting out, I'm arriving. I'm staying.
AMERICAN WOMAN: Oh, is it your job?
MAN IN DARK GLASSES: Yeah, yeah, it's my job. Well, that's how it is, you know, some of us gotta go, some of us gotta stay.

AMERICAN WOMAN: Oh, that's a shame. Well, gee . . . I wish you the best of luck . . . and . . . . Oh, if you see Mr. Willie, would you tell him I'm looking for him? My name's Judith Elsen, Number 6.

Time slide:

18:30

MAN IN DARK GLASSES: Judith Elsen. Number 6.

The American woman is out on the veranda.

AMERICAN WOMAN: Oh . . . and uh . . . if you do hear any news on the radio or something . . .

Time slide:

18:40

Suddenly the lights in the veranda black out. The ice-cold chimes tinkle again and again. The American woman is grabbed from behind by a figure in black and dragged offstage.

PAPA WILLIE (*In shadowplay*): But, you were asking about Karen. (*The Oriental nods*) Oh, yes, she used to come here quite often. That was years ago. Long before she became so famous. Oh, she was so young, so elegant—painted fingers. I propose a toast—to Karen, may she rest in peace.

They toast. Meanwhile, downstage, the beeping of the man in dark glasses' quartz watch signals him for his departure. He leaves. Then several figures in black enter silently to plunder what's left of the Haven of Peace. One of them is obviously the leader. They remove everything on stage, including the corpse of the beachcomber.

Oh, do you like it? I'm so glad. It's called Tang, T-A-N-G, Tang—it's from America.

The Oriental picks up a large shell that was resting on the table and walks along the shore with it as Papa Willie continues. Papa Willie points to the shell.

I offered them to the museum at Daba. After my death, of course. Oh, no, for myself, I don't care, but I don't want my life's work to be broken up and scattered. You understand. Do you know—they refused them. They did not understand what I was offering them, they were not interested, thank you very much. Shells, shells, shells, we have nothing but shells in this country. Why is he making such a fuss?

The Oriental is looking offstage, not really listening. Papa Willie offers more Tang.

Encore? (*The Oriental gestures*) No. I know, I know. It has been my pleasure.

The Oriental bows. Papa Willie waves him off without rising from his chair. He is alone.

Well, I look on it as a blessing in disguise. They would have been broken, scattered, dispersed—like the scarabs in Cairo.

Ruis the waiter enters with a shell.

RUIS: Look what I found for you, Papa Willie.
PAPA WILLIE: Oh, very nice, very nice. Yes.

Ruis then looks out to sea with Papa Willie. A quiet, elegiac moment.

RUIS: Papa Willie—you think some day I have a hotel of my own?

Papa Willie shrugs and the sound of gunshots rises. Blackout. Soundtrack: Gunshots crossfade into airplane engines revving up.

Scene 10
Airport

When the lights fade up, the wall is still separating the foreground from the background. The tails of airplanes cross the stage from right to left, suggesting a runway. On the rear-projection screen, the black-and-white grid slides fade in. Then the plane engines subside and the plaintive music heard earlier in Scene 7 with Miss B. fades up as she and others cross the stage with their luggage. Papa Willie is sitting downstage in front of the wall in a waiting area. The last grid slide fades out to be replaced by Landsart Satellite slides of various parts of the earth seen from space. Miss B. settles downstage, next to Papa Willie. Flight announcements in various languages—some humorous—punctuate the scene, but the plaintive music dominates. A flight board which shows an accumulation of arrivals and departures appears toward the end of the scene, after the Landsart slides. Behind the wall, various passengers wait with their belongings.

MISS B.: Mind if I sit here?
PAPA WILLIE: Of course, of course.
MISS B. *(After settling and furtively eyeing the old man)*: Do you know the Spanish word for custard?
PAPA WILLIE: Custard. How many letters?
MISS B.: Four.
PAPA WILLIE: Flan. F-L-Ah-N . . . flan.
MISS B.: F-L-Ah? . . .
PAPA WILLIE: A.
MISS B.: A. Flan. It fits. Thank you very much.

*Flight announcements are called out. The Landsart slides change. The music con-
tinues. Then, for no apparent reason, Miss B. hands her ticket to Papa Willie,
who has been reading* Paris Match.

PAPA WILLIE: Berenice Winfred. Is this you?

MISS B.: It's me.

PAPA WILLIE: It's a very beautiful name.

MISS B.: Thank you.

PAPA WILLIE: It's a name from my co . . . from what used to be my country. Where
my family comes from.

*It should be noted at this point that the actor who plays Papa Willie also plays
the father of Gloria Ortega, and remembered that Miss B. is played by the same
actress who played Berenice Huarpes.*

MISS B.: It's not a real common name, Berenice.

PAPA WILLIE: I know. You have a long journey ahead of you. (*He is looking at her
ticket*) A stopover in Shannon.

MISS B. (*Childlike*): Ireland.

PAPA WILLIE: Ireland. I have never been there.

MISS B.: You've never been there?

PAPA WILLIE: You must drink some Irish coffee for me.

MISS B. (*Pause*): I don't drink coffee, I drink tea.

Announcement.

MISS B.: Care for a Lifesaver? These are butterscotch . . . I like butterscotch because
it's not too sweet . . . because you have a little sweetness, you know . . . it's a
lot . . . (*Hands Papa Willie a towelette*) If you wanna save that one, I have one
you can use now. I have plenty. You know, they give them to you in the
bathroom. You know, that little girl . . . it's not where you help yourself. I think
they must put some kind of perfume on them, some kind of smell.

Papa Willie doesn't know quite what to do with the towelette.

PAPA WILLIE: They are very hygienic.

Announcement: It is Miss B.'s flight to Greensboro.

MISS B.: That's my flight.

PAPA WILLIE (*He rises, and in his old-world manner*): Madam, I wish you a bon voyage.

MISS B. (*Shyly*): Bon voyage.

*Soundtrack: The music rises and fades out as Papa Willie leaves, and the parti-
tion wall rises out of sight. Blackout. Soundtrack: Once again gunshots are heard,
but, repeatedly, there is an eerie moan, as if some kind of indefinable animal
were dying. It is a loud cosmic moan that wavers and rises, over and over again.*

*Snippets of the Apollo moon landing, the zither music from Scene 7, "Blue Skies"
and strange singing in a foreign tongue are heard.*

Scene 11
A Tropical Sacrificial Place

*Blood-red lights fade up. A huge beast lies heaving on its side, dying. Two pup-
peteers manipulate the beast's neck, as well as its belly, to rise and fall. Its eyes,
lit from within, glow like embers. The entire cast comes forward, and lays out
candles, fruit, incense and paper money. Also laid on the beast are strands of
blinking Christmas lights. The last figure to arrive, the Oriental, takes out a wad
of money and throws it in the air. The money flutters about, to land on the dying
beast. The noises dissolve into a collage of night sounds: crickets, wind, water.
A film of the moon, seen through branches of a tree, is projected onto the screen.
This calm is broken by the members of the cast lining up downstage. They bow.
The film continues, as do the night sounds, and the dead Reahou lies still.*

END OF PLAY

The Wash

Philip Kan Gotanda

Philip Kan
Gotanda

I am a Sansei, a third-generation Japanese American, and I was raised in Stockton, California. My father emigrated from Hawaii to the mainland to go to medical school, married my mother, and settled in Stockton, which has a large Japanese-American community.

As I define myself as an Asian-American writer, I find two themes keep coming up: one is the Camps, the other is racism in general. Both my mother and father were sent to internment camps during World War II. They went to Rohrer, Arkansas, with most other Japanese Americans from Stockton. It's a strange irony, because my father went to medical school at the University of Arkansas, moved to Stockton to practice medicine, and what happened? They sent him back to Arkansas.

As I was growing up little mention was made of the Camps, just these references now and then. But even though I wasn't born in Camp and we didn't talk about it much, it's still a very big part of my life. Whether you speak about the Camps or don't speak about them, the experience is passed on generationally.

It's a psychic scar, almost like an abused-child syndrome. My parents were American-born, part of America's family, and suddenly they were punished and incarcerated. People in that situation start to take on a great deal of guilt. You start thinking, "I must have done something wrong to be treated this way by my country. I have to be really good or something else will befall me."

In my own Japanese-American community there was a tacit distrust of the whole white world. When we moved into an all-white neighborhood my mother said to me, "Philip, you're going to play with your white friends, and that's fine. But if things ever go wrong or turn bad, you can't trust them."

That's the explicit message I was given, but there was an implicit one too: "It's wiser and better to stay within your own community. Don't be too high-profile." I believe that all comes from the Camps.

But I always wanted to express myself creatively. I grew up in the era of Bob Dylan and the Beatles. You gravitate to those expressions that you're exposed to, so I gravitated to rock 'n' roll. As soon as I picked up a guitar I started to write songs and get together a band. I kept playing through my college years at the University of California, Santa Cruz.

Our band was kind of unique in that we always played original music. Right from the beginning I was exploring in songs what it was to be Asian-American. I just felt I had to write about who and what I was, especially during the emergence of the Asian-American movement in the latter part of the 1960s and into the early 1970s.

I sang at a lot of political functions, but outside the community few people were interested. I went to Los Angeles to pitch my songs to record companies and couldn't get through the door. They wouldn't even listen to my tapes. I was singing at little clubs in Los Angeles, Santa Barbara and San Francisco, but getting nowhere.

I went to Japan for a year to study ceramics, and when I returned I decided to enter a profession like my parents wanted me to do. I chose law because my lawyer friends were doing good work with class-action suits and impact litigation. But once in law school I realized I didn't belong there, I still wanted to do creative things.

While I was in the lecture hall, or clerking at North Beach-Chinatown Legal Aid, I would work on writing this rock musical based on a Japanese folk tale. I called it *The Avocado Kid*, and sent it down to Mako at the East West Players in Los Angeles. As soon as I graduated he told me, "Come on down to L.A., we want to do this." I did and that was it for being a lawyer.

Working with East West Players was my first real exposure to the Asian-American theatre scene, and then I came back to San Francisco to work with the Asian American Theatre Company. Suddenly I had a context. I found I could do all the things I wanted to do, say the things I had wanted to say in music—but in theatre there was more support for it.

Philip Kan Gotanda

I began to experience this tremendous sense of freedom. All the people involved in the theatre were Asian Americans. For the first time we were in charge, and we set the rules. We didn't have to explain things to each other—whatever we wanted to do, we just did it. At times it was rough, at times it was raw, but at least it was ours.

All of this grew out of a much larger Asian-American movement happening in California. From its early days it was a cultural movement—people were involved in printmaking, street poetry, publications, music, filmmaking. As the blacks and Hispanic Americans emerged, so did we.

Around this time I was also in a rock band with David Hwang and Ric Shiomi, a Canadian playwright. We played a lot of music together, and spent a lot of time talking about what we wanted to do as writers, what it meant to the Asian-American community, what it meant to the larger theatrical community, the international picture.

We always believed we were part of an emerging story that needed to be told, one of many American stories. It turned out to be much more complex than we realized, what with the economic ascendancy of Japan, the influx of Southeast Asian refugees, the changing situation in Hong Kong. But it was always important to us to think about our role in the international scene.

I spent most of my time from 1979 to around 1985 writing plays for Asian-American theatres: AATC, East West Players, Pan Asian Repertory in New York. The other, more mainstream theatre companies were not interested in what I was doing.

That changed gradually for me. My first breaks occurred when *Song for a Nisei Fisherman* and *The Wash* were done in Los Angeles at the Mark Taper Forum's "New Theatre For Now" series, and when *The Dream of Kitamura* was produced at Theater of the Open Eye in New York. Doing *Yankee Dawg You Die*, a play about two Asian-American actors of different generations, at Berkeley Repertory Theatre was another breakthrough.

In my writing I have looked back in time, at my parents and at my grandparents, who lived in Japan. I figured that if I told their stories I could move on to my own generation, and then on to speculating about what life might be like for the next generation of Japanese Americans.

The Wash, which I began writing in 1984, focuses on a Nisei couple about my parents' age. It was inspired by several things. I had a conversation with a friend whose mother had left her father, which was very unusual for an older Nisei couple. I was also doing research on elderly Japanese-American widows and widowers, and had collected a lot of information about that. And I recall another friend telling me that even though she was divorced, her ex-husband still came over to mow her lawn.

All of this came together. The lawn became the laundry, and the other stories went into the plot of *The Wash*. The play was developed at the Mark Taper Forum, and after many drafts it premiered in 1986 at the Eureka Theatre in San Francisco.

When I later translated it into a screenplay I had to ask myself, "Whose story is this?" My answer was that it's both the husband's and the wife's story. Ultimately, the central character of both the play and the screenplay is the marriage itself.

Even though I wrote from the dual perspective of Nobu and Masi, I was really trying to explore a Nisei woman's life. I come from a male-dominated background; I'm one of three sons. I had written about a Nisei man, modeled on my father, in *Song for a Nisei Fisherman*, but didn't feel I had a handle on the female psyche. The only way to deal with that was interview a lot of Nisei women, hear their stories and get their opinions on many issues. Those interviews helped me create the character of Masi.

Another conscious decision I made in *The Wash* was to juxtapose quiet scenes with very explosive moments. There is a lot of indirection in the conversation of Japanese Americans. They talk around issues in everyday dialogue; what's *not* said is often as important as what *is* said.

I also wanted to show the sexuality of the older characters. Japanese Americans are sometimes perceived as almost asexual in this culture, and showing sexual intimacy between older people has always been sort of taboo. So I dealt with that very consciously too.

The conflict between the daughter Judy, who is married to an African American and has a child, and her father Nobu, who won't accept his biracial grandchild, was another important theme for me. Every minority group—Hispanics, African Americans, Asian Americans—has inherent racial biases, and I think it's imperative that we confront that. There's a lot of tension in America right now, and unless these issues are addressed and people are educated there could be some serious racial violence on the horizon.

I think a writer can, at times, help steward a change in a particular direction. The Japanese-American community now has an intermarriage rate of over 50 percent. In *The Wash* I've tried to promote the idea of being inclusive, of accepting and including biracial children as part of the next generation of Asian Americans, and simply as Americans.

You can make a good argument that theatre has been a very strong force in bringing the Asian-American stories and perspective to the larger media. Now writers like David Hwang and me are beginning to go out into the television and film world too, just as we hoped we would.

I'm happy to be working more in the mainstream regional theatres and in the entertainment industry, but I still believe there is an Asian-American theatre and an Asian-American literature. "Asian America" is, in itself, a political term. It hearkens back to the time when people from many different cultures and backgrounds—Chinese, Japanese, Filipino, Korean, Vietnamese—found they had something in common. There was a political reason why we should work together, given racism and the context of America. We found that under this banner of Asian American we could move forward.

34 *Biographical Information*

Philip Kan Gotanda began his arts career as a musician and songwriter. His first play, the rock musical *The Avocado Kid*, debuted in 1979 at East West Players, followed by *A Song for a Nisei Fisherman*, *The Dream of Kitamura*, *Bullet Headed Birds*, (all first presented at the Asian American Theatre Company) and *The Wash*. His latest completed work, *Yankee Dawg You Die*, has been produced by the Berkeley Repertory Company, the Los Angeles Theatre Center, Pan Asian Repertory, Playwrights Horizons and Wisdom Bridge.

A member of New Dramatists, Gotanda is the recipient of a National Endowment for the Arts fellowship, three Rockefeller Playwriting Awards, a McKnight Fellowship and the 1989 Will Glickman Playwriting Award for *Yankee Dawg You Die*. Recently Gotanda was invited to Tokyo, for the Japanese-language debut of *A Song for a Nisei Fisherman* at the Bunka-za Gekijo.

Gotanda is currently at work on theatre, television and film projects, and he continues to serve as co-dramaturge (with David Henry Hwang) for the Asian American Theatre Company. He resides in San Francisco with his wife, actress Diane Takei.

About the Play

Originally sponsored by a Henry and Chiyo Kuwahara Arts Grant of the Japanese American Citizens League, *The Wash* was first produced in workshop form at the Mark Taper Forum's 1985 New Theatre For Now Festival. The play's world premiere occurred in 1987 at the Eureka Theatre Company in San Francisco, in a production directed by Richard Seyd. *The Wash* was published in *West Coast Plays* that same year.

A film version of *The Wash*, with a screenplay by Gotanda, was released in 1988. Produced by American Playhouse-Lumiere Productions and directed by Michael Uno, it will air on public television in 1990.

Characters

NOBU MATSUMOTO, Nisei (second-generation Japanese American), 68 years old, retired produce man. Separated from wife, Masi. Lives alone in the family house.

MASI MATSUMOTO, Nisei, 67 years old. Left Nobu. Does housework for a living. Lives in a small apartment by herself.

KIYOKO HASEGAWA, 55-ish, originally from Japan. Previously married to an American soldier. Widow. Seeing Nobu. Owns and runs a small Japanese restaurant.

SADAO NAKASATO, Nisei, 65 years old, widower. Seeing Masi. Retired pharmacist.

MARSHA MATSUMOTO, Sansei (third-generation Japanese American), 33 years old, single. Older daughter of Nobu and Masi. Works as a dental hygienist in nearby big city.

JUDY ADAMS, Sansei, 29 years old, married to James with a baby. Younger daughter, fifth-grade teacher. Presently not working.

CHIYO FROELICH, originally from Japan, but has lived most of her adult life in the U.S. Late 40s, divorced, friend of Kiyoko. Owns and runs a small beauty salon next door to Kiyoko's restaurant.

BLACKIE, Hawaiian Nisei, 55-ish. Speaks with a thick pidgin accent. Works as the cook at Kiyoko's restaurant.

Setting

Stage center is Nobu's place, the "old family home." Stage right is Kiyoko's restaurant. Stage left is Masi's small bedroom apartment. A clothesline runs across the upstage area. The downstage area is used to play several scenes that take place elsewhere.

The set should be realistic but *elemental*, allowing for an underlying abstract feeling. Nobu's place is the most complete, with Masi's and Kiyoko's places more minimal, and Marsha's and Judy's places being represented by only a table and chairs.

The set as a whole must be constructed so that entrances, exits and crossovers may be easily viewed by the audience. This is because actors' movements from one area to another, both as focus action and as half-light action, are an integral part of the storytelling.

The play takes place in the present over a period of six months—July to January.

The Play

The Wash

ACT ONE

Scene 1

Nobu's place, the old family home. The kitchen is upstage. A sink, refrigerator, stove. There is a kitchen table with a pile of dirty clothes on it. On the stove, a pot of water is boiling. In the washrack there is a teapot, some dishes, chopsticks, etc. Stage left is a door that leads to the outside, the proverbial side-door entrance into the kitchen that everyone uses. Upstage right is a door leading to the hallway and bedrooms.

    Down right, a TV. A long couch is angled facing it. On a long coffee table in front of the couch sits the yet undeveloped skeleton of a large kite Nobu is building. During the play, the kite becomes more and more pronounced in its construction.

    The pile of dirty clothes is in a shaft of light. Lights come up to half revealing Nobu asleep lengthwise on the couch, facing the TV, a newspaper sprawled over his chest. Mouth open, snoring loudly. TV lights come up. Nobu can be seen in the flickering light of the television screen. Lights come up full. Nobu awakens with a start, newspaper falling to the floor. He pulls himself upright and just sits and stares into space for a moment, trying to awaken. Then he picks up the newspaper, tosses it in a heap on the couch. He checks to examine the *progress he's making on the kite. He carefully sets the kite back on the table and shuffles over to the stove to shut the boiling water off. He gets a plate and a pair of chopsticks from the washrack, takes the two hot dogs that were cooking out of the pot and puts them on the plate. Then he gets some tea out and puts it into the teapot which he has taken from the rack. He moves to throw out the hot-dog water to boil some new water, then stops. Thinks. Proceeds to pour the hot-dog water into the teapot and use it to make tea. Nobu reaches into the refrigerator and pulls out a bowl of cold rice covered over in cellophane and a small bottle of French's mustard. He uncovers the rice, scoops some of it into a rice bowl using his chopsticks, pours hot tea over it. It starts to spill; he quickly bends down and slurps up the excess. He opens the mustard and, using his chopsticks again, shovels a healthy portion of mustard onto his hot dogs. He licks the mustard off his chopsticks. Then he carefully makes his way back to the couch with the plate of hot dogs and a bowl of rice. He sets the food down on the coffee table and begins to eat while working on the kite and watching television.*

Masi enters through the side door with two large brown paper bags. She's struggling to open and close the door with both hands full. Nobu turns around and notices her but gives no greeting and makes no effort to help her. She is not upset by his actions. She appears to have no expectation for him to assist her. Masi sets both bags on the kitchen table and catches her breath.

MASI *(Putting tomatoes and Japanese eggplant from one of the bags into refrigerator)*: If you have any more dirty clothes I can take them now. Nobu? Is this everything?

NOBU *(Not turning, eating)*: Want some hot dog?

MASI: No, I ate before. Got these from Mr. Rossi. The tomatoes are soft so eat them right away. *(She gets up, folds paper bag and puts it into drawer. She knows this place well. Walks over and checks his shirt collar from behind)* No more clothes?

NOBU *(Brushing her hand away)*: No, already.

Masi goes over to the other bag and begins unpacking the freshly washed clothes in neat piles on the kitchen table.

MASI: I just finished cleaning Dr. Harrison's place. You should see the bathrooms. If you see the family walk down the street, they look so clean and neat. But the toilets, *kitanai* [dirty].

Finished unpacking, Masi takes a cup out of the rack and pours herself a cup of tea. She walks over to the couch and sits down next to Nobu and watches TV. She takes a sip of tea and makes a face.

NOBU: Hot-dog water.

Masi decides not to drink it. She looks at the unfinished kite frame.

MASI: You gonna fly this one? *(Picks up the kite)* Nobu, why don't you at least try a different design this—

NOBU *(Taking kite)*: My old man did it this way.

Masi gets up and starts to pick up the old clothes on the floor, fold them and put them in the second bag.

MASI: Have you talked to the kids? *(No response)* Marsha said she stopped by. *(Beat)* You know if you don't see Judy's baby soon he's going to be all grown up. Nobu?
NOBU: No.

Masi gives up trying to talk to him at all. Finishes putting old clothes into the bag.

MASI: No more dirty clothes, Nobu? *(Nobu shakes his head without turning away from the TV)* All right, then I'm going.

Masi leaves with the bag of old clothes. Nobu continues to watch TV for a few moments, then turns and stares at the door. Dim to half, with the TV light illuminating Nobu. Marsha appears in a pool of light looking towards Nobu.

MARSHA: Dad?

Nobu turns to look at Marsha momentarily, then back to the television. Judy appears in a pool of light, holding Timothy. Marsha fades out.

JUDY: Mom?

Masi, moving away, turns to look at Judy momentarily, then exits. Judy fades out. Lights fade on Nobu and Masi. We hear Japanese restaurant Muzak.

Scene 2

Kiyoko's restaurant, afternoon, next day, upstage right. On upstage side wall there is a service window. Left of it is a swinging door that leads into kitchen. There is a small counter space with three or four small stools. Downstage there are one or two small tables with chairs.

    Lights come up. Blackie can be seen in the service window. He is taking a big swig of Budweiser. Kiyoko appears and gives him a dirty look. Blackie's been caught in the act.

KIYOKO: Blackie.
BLACKIE: It make my cooking get mo' better. *(Kiyoko stares, no response)* It make *me* get mo' better. *(Kiyoko continues to stare)* I'm thirsty. I wanted a beer.
KIYOKO *(Taking bottle away)*: You're always thirsty, you're always hungry. You're the cook. You're supposed to cook the food, not eat it all up. Now go wipe the tables.

She hands him a towel and scoots him out the swinging door.

BLACKIE: It makes my cooking get mo' better. If *I* feel better, my cooking get mo' better. No bull lie, yo.
KIYOKO: Your face gets red like a tomato and everything tastes like *shoyu* [soy sauce].

Blackie stops and scratches his butt. Kiyoko knocks his hand away.

Don't scratch your *oshiri*. You're the cook, 'member?

Nobu enters.

NOBU: *Kiyoko, dō desu ka* [how are you]?
KIYOKO (*Grabbing towel away from Blackie*): Give me that. (*Walks past Nobu, ignoring him*)
BLACKIE: Hey, brudda, you in the doghouse!
NOBU: What?

Kiyoko finishes taking a few swipes at a tabletop.

Kiyoko, tempura special, *onegai* [please] . . .

Kiyoko ignores him again, moving behind the counter, wiping.

BLACKIE (*To Nobu*): You in the doghouse. But it going pass. (*He exits into kitchen area*)
NOBU (*Moving to counter and seating himself*): What? What?

Kiyoko tosses a small plate of tsukemono *[pickles] in front of him and continues to wipe around him. Nobu looks at the plate.*

You know I don't like this kind of pickle.

KIYOKO (*Looks at him hard, tossing towel on the counter*): I'll get your tea. (*She exits into kitchen*)
BLACKIE (*Pokes head out of service window holding Nobu's plate in one hand*): We drop food on the floor, we pick it up. If we like you . . . (*Mimes throwing the food away*) But, if you in the doghouse . . . (*Mimes dropping food back on plate, then barks at it*)

Blackie withdraws as Kiyoko enters with Nobu's tea.

NOBU (*To Kiyoko*): I like eggplant. You know that. You always give me eggplant pickle.
KIYOKO (*Pouring tea*): Out of season.
NOBU: Masi brought some by yesterday with the wash.
KIYOKO: Nobu-chan, I *said* I'd do the wash for you. You gotta washing machine at your place. I can just come over and—
NOBU: No, no, too much trouble. I can do it myself. I don't like cucumber pickle.
KIYOKO: Nobu, how could you forget?
NOBU: I didn't. You did.
KIYOKO: I kept dropping hints . . .
NOBU: I like *eggplant*. You know that.
KIYOKO: All last week.
NOBU: Eggplant! Eggplant!
KIYOKO (*Pause, glaring at him*): WE RAN OUT!

Kiyoko stomps into the kitchen. Nobu sits there stunned and very puzzled. Blackie enters carrying a plate of food and sets it down in front of Nobu.

BLACKIE: Tempura special.

Blackie watches while sipping on a beer. Nobu is about to put a fork-load into his mouth, then stops. Looks at food, then at Blackie. Blackie makes a barking sound and grins. Suddenly something dawns on Nobu.

NOBU: Her birthday, I forgot her birthday . . .

Cross-fade to Masi's apartment.

Scene 3

Masi's place, three weeks later. Small apartment, with bedroom downstage from main room. Sadao, seated on sofa, in a pool of light. Masi is in half-light at counter fixing two cups of Sanka.

SADAO: We were all sitting around in somebody's living room, when someone said, "How come you still wear your wedding ring?" They weren't being mean. That's why we were there. To ask those kinds of things. I didn't know what to say. Speechless. Then someone else said, "Sadao, you always complain about not meeting people, not being able to start a new life—how come you still wear your ring?" I began to cry. Like a little boy. I remember thinking, "How strange. I am crying in front of all these people that I don't know. And yet I feel no shame." The room was so still. All you could hear was my crying. Then I heard a tapping sound. I looked up and noticed a woman sitting across from me, slapping the sandals she was wearing against the bottom of her feet. Tap, tap, tap . . . . I said I didn't know why. It just never crossed my mind to take it off. "Why should I take the ring off?" Then one of the widows, the one who formed the group, said, "Because you're not married anymore."

Lights come up on the rest of the apartment area. Masi wasn't quite prepared for Sadao's sharing such personal details and is a bit unsure how to respond. Sadao in turn fears he may have gotten a bit carried away.

MASI (*Bringing coffee over*): Cream? It's nondairy creamer. (*Sadao shakes head*) If you want tea?
SADAO: No, this is fine. I ran on a bit, didn't I?
MASI: No, no, it's all right. (*Pause*) It's just Sanka.
SADAO: Good. Otherwise the caffeine keeps me up all night. Have you tried decaffeinated coffee?

Masi motions to the Sanka, unsure of what he means.

No, the bean. The actually make a decaffeinated bean.
MASI: No, we never did anything like that. Just instant. Yuban makes a good in-

stant coffee. That's what I usually drink. But I don't have any since I moved over here.

SADAO: No, I've never tried it.

MASI: I'll have to get some next time I go shopping.

SADAO: They have this process they use. On the bean. I mean they don't grow a decaffeinated bean. I don't know what's worse. The caffeine in it or the chemicals they use to get the caffeine out. *(Laughs at his own joke, gathering momentum)* I have a little grinder. A Braun? You know a Braun?

Masi doesn't know what it is. Awkward pause.

MASI: We never did anything like that. We just drink instant.

SADAO: I like Sanka. I have to drink it all the time. Doctor's orders. *(Imitating)* "If you drink coffee, Sadao, drink Sanka!" *(He laughs valiantly at his attempt at humor. Masi stares at her cup. He notices and offers a feeble explanation)* Blood pressure . . .

They both drink in silence. Suddenly Sadao remembers something.

Oh. Excuse me. I'll be right back. I left something in the car . . .

Sadao's voice trails off as he exits. Masi sits there uncomfortably. This isn't working out. Sadao returns with a fishing pole and reel wrapped up like presents. Nobu appears in half-light at his place watching TV, his face illuminated by the flickering screen's glow.

MASI *(Surprised)*: Sadao, what's this?

Sadao holds out pole.

I can't.

SADAO: No, no, it's for you.

MASI: But Sadao . . .

SADAO: No, no, it's for *you.*

MASI *(One hand on it)*: Sadao, you shouldn't have.

SADAO: Go 'head. Open it up.

MASI *(Takes it and begins unwrapping it)*: No, I can't accept this. I don't have anything for you.

Masi unwraps pole, which is broken down into pieces. Sadao sets reel on table and takes pole from Masi.

SADAO: Here, let me show you. *(Puts it together)* There. *(Hands it back. Remembers reel, hands it to her)* Oh, and here's this.

Masi now has a reel and pole in her hands. Sadao realizes she can't unwrap the reel with both hands full and takes pole away. She unwraps the reel. Sadao promptly takes it away from her and puts the pole and reel together.

See, it goes like this. And then you're all set to catch fish. *(Hands it back to Masi)* I told you I was going to take you. Now you can't refuse.

MASI: Yeah, but . . .

SADAO: Thought I was kidding, huh?

MASI: But this is so expensive. I know how much these things cost, 'cause of Nobu. I don't know anything about fishing. He's the fisherman. I just pack the lunch and off he goes.

SADAO: Well, this time you're going and it's lots of fun. Economical, too. You get to eat what you catch.

MASI: But you have to do all that walking.

SADAO: No, who said that? We sit on the bank and fish from there. We'll pack a good lunch—I'll make it—you bring the cards so we can play blackjack. We have to practice.

MASI: I don't play.

SADAO: That's why we have to practice so we can go to Tahoe. If there's a good game on we'll have to watch it. I'll bring my portable TV. I love the Giants.

MASI: What about fishing?

SADAO: Only if we have time. See, this is how you cast out. *(Demonstrating)* You hook your index finger around the line here. Turn the bail and . . . *(He casts)*

Nobu, still in half-light, gets up to phone Masi. Phone rings. Masi goes over and answers it. It's Nobu. Slowly lights dim on Sadao and rest of apartment so that just Masi and Nobu are lit.

MASI: Hello.

NOBU: You coming to pick up the clothes?

MASI: Nobu? I was just there. You mean next week? Don't worry, I'll be there. I do it every week, don't I? Nobu?

NOBU: I'm not worried. You all right?

MASI: Yes, I'm all right. Did you want something? *(No response)* I got more vegetables. Do you need some more?

NOBU: No. *(Pause)* Can you bring more eggplant?

MASI: I don't have any more.

NOBU: All right, then.

MASI: I'll ask Mr. Rossi. He can always get lots more. *(Pause)* Was there something else? Did you want something?

NOBU: No.

Pause.

MASI: Nobu, I have to go now.

NOBU: I went fishing so I got a lot of dirty clothes.

MASI: All right. Don't worry, I'll be by.

NOBU: I'm not worried.

MASI: Bye.

NOBU: Bye.

Dim to darkness.

Scene 4

Kiyoko's restaurant, three weeks later, night. Kiyoko, Chiyo, Blackie are playing five-card stud. When the scene starts they each have one card down and two up. Chiyo is in the process of dealing the next card, Kiyoko to her left, Blackie to her right. Chiyo wears a poker visor. Five empty beer bottles sit in front of Blackie, who is working on a sixth. He is not drunk, though. Hawaiian music is playing on his large portable tape player.

CHIYO *(Examining her hand)*: He's got a wife. You said so yourself.

KIYOKO: They're separated.

CHIYO: He wants to get back together. I know his kind. She left him. They can't get over that. He only wants you for one thing—your "tempura." Yeah. He's over your restaurant everyday, *desho* [isn't that so]? You feeding him. He's eating up all your profits.

Chiyo and Kiyoko notice Blackie chugging down the rest of his beer, making strange gurgling sounds. They stare.

BLACKIE: You gotta drink beer when you're playing poker or you aren't playing poker. You're just playing cards. I don't like cards, hate cards. *(Holds up another beer)* I *love* poker.

KIYOKO: Nobu is a good man.

CHIYO: You like to mother him, you like that kind of thing. But you don't know about men.

KIYOKO: And you do, heh?

CHIYO: You don't get out of this restaurant of yours. I tell you, "Go out, go out." "No, I gotta work, work . . ." *(Noticing something)* Wait, wait, someone didn't ante. We only bet once, a nickel, right? *(Counting)* See. Someone didn't ante.

KIYOKO: I did.

CHIYO: So did I.

They turn to Blackie, who's guzzling a beer.

BLACKIE: Huh? Oh, yeah. *(Innocently tosses money in)*

CHIYO *(Begins to deal; to Kiyoko)*: Two sixes—a pair of saxophones. *(To Blackie)* A three of diamonds gives you . . . nothing. *(To self)* Eight of puppy toes to the dealer, working on a possible club flush. *(To Kiyoko)* Pair of saxes high. I just can't see myself going out with him.

KIYOKO: Nobu is an honest man. Not like that guy you've been seeing. Check.

CHIYO: Ray, his name is Ray. Blackie.

BLACKIE *(Carefully examining his cards)*: Yeah, I know.

KIYOKO: That time Blackie gave Nobu too much change. Remember? He walked all the way back from his house to return it—twenty-five cents.

CHIYO: Good investment. He gets a $4.50 combo plate free now. *(To Blackie)* Your bet.

BLACKIE: Don't rush me, don't rush me.

CHIYO *(To Blackie)*: You're queen high, working on a possible nothing. *(Motioning to her own cards)* Possible club flush here and . . . *(Pointing to Kiyoko's hand)* A pair of saxes there, possible three-of-a-kind. *(To Kiyoko)* I just think you can do better, that's all I'm saying. Besides, he's so old.

KIYOKO: I don't want to talk about it.

Blackie finally decides to bet but Chiyo ignores him and goes right ahead.

CHIYO: Dealer bets a nickel.

KIYOKO: He's not old.

CHIYO: Is he good in bed?

KIYOKO: He's sixty-eight years old, Chiyo. I raise you a dime.

CHIYO: So he really is old. See you and I bump you a quarter.

BLACKIE: I love it when the wahines talk dirt. *(They stare at him)* Jeez, just joking. Don't lose your coconut.

As Blackie begins putting in the bets he missed Kiyoko and Chiyo continue on.

KIYOKO *(Tossing quarter in)*: I call.

CHIYO *(Starting to deal; to Kiyoko)*: Nine of spades. No help there. *(To Blackie)* A trois. Oh, a pair of threes. *(To self)* And for the dealer . . . another club. Read 'em and weep. Four puppy toes looking mighty pretty. Flush, very possible. *(To Kiyoko)* Pair of saxes still high.

KIYOKO: Chiyo, you don't know him like I do. Check.

She notices Blackie sucking on his beer.

He checks, too.

CHIYO: I'm just saying you could find someone else. Someone younger, more fun.

KIYOKO *(Irritated)*: You watch too many soap operas, Chiyo. Life's not like that. Men don't fall into your lap.

CHIYO *(Upset at being lectured to)*: Fifty cents.

BLACKIE *(Impressed)*: Fifty cents . . .

KIYOKO: I *like Nobu.* One dollar.

BLACKIE *(In disbelief)*: One dollar . . .

CHIYO: All right, all right, white hair doesn't bother me. It's no hair I can't stand. *(Tosses in dollar)* Call you. You got the three-of-kind?

KIYOKO: Pair of sixes, that's all. You got the flush?

CHIYO: Pair of eights! Hah!

Kiyoko's disgusted. Chiyo's about to grab the pot when Blackie puts down his cards. Kiyoko and Chiyo stare in disbelief.

BLACKIE *(Puffing up like a rooster)*: Excusez-moi's, but I got three trois's.

CHIYO: Blackie . . .

Blackie shovels the pot in. Kiyoko pushes the cards to Chiyo, who examines them skeptically.

KIYOKO *(To Chiyo)*: Your wash. *(To Blackie)* Blackie, cut.

Blackie cuts the shuffled deck and Kiyoko begins to deal.

BLACKIE *(Holding up beer)*: Hate cards. *Love* poker. *(He starts to guzzle)*

KIYOKO *(Dealing)*: Today is the fifteenth, *neh* [isn't it]? *(Stops, reflecting)* Harry would have been fifty-nine this week.

Chiyo and Blackie exchange glances. Cross-fade to Nobu's place.

Scene 5

Nobu's place, same day as previous scene. Nobu's seated and Marsha's working in the kitchen.

NOBU: What do you mean, "Be nice to Mama"?

MARSHA: All I'm saying is, just try to be nice to her when she gets here. Say something nice about the way she looks or about her—

NOBU: I'm always nice to Mama. I'm always good to her. *(Pause)* Why the hell she has to live over there? Huh? How come Mama's got to live way over there?

Masi enters carring a small paper bag.

MARSHA: Hi Mom, come on in. *(Taking bag)* Here let me help you. Dad's already here.

MASI *(To Nobu)*: Just some leftover fruit that was in the icebox. Starting to rot so eat it right away.

Masi and Nobu acknowledge each other awkwardly.

MARSHA: Judy and the baby couldn't make it.

MASI: She called me.

Nobu's expression reveals he didn't know they were coming.

MARSHA *(Offering explanation to Nobu)*: Jimmy wasn't going to come. *(Pause)* Sit down, sit down. Dinner's almost ready in a minute. Roast beef. Dad, coffee? Tea for you, Mom?

Marsha goes to kitchen. Silence.

NOBU: I told her we can eat at her place. *(Beat)* She wanted to cook dinner here.

Pause.

MASI: Her place is cozy, *neh*?

NOBU: Marsha's? Looks like the rooms back in Camp.

MASI: Nobu, the Camps were over forty years ago. At least she's clean. Not like the younger one.

Pause.

NOBU: How you been?

MASI: All right.

NOBU: *Isogashi no* [Busy]?

MASI: No. The usual.

NOBU: I called the other night, no one answered. *(Masi doesn't offer an explanation)* How you been?

MARSHA *(Interrupts, carrying in an ashtray)*: Dad, Mom's taking a ceramics class. Judy got her to go. *(Hands him the ashtray)* She made this. *(Nobu stares at it)*

MASI: It's an ashtray.

NOBU: You don't smoke.

MASI: I'll get Daddy's coffee. *(She exits with cup)*

MARSHA: Dad, just say you like it. That's all you have to say. Just say it's nice.

NOBU: Yeah, but she doesn't smoke. Why make an ashtray if you don't smoke?

Masi returns with a cup of coffee for Nobu and tea for herself. Marsha gives Nobu an encouraging nudge and exits into kitchen.

(Holding ashtray) It's a nice ashtray. Is this where you go all the time? I call in the evening. I guess that's where you must be. *(Pause)* Remember those dances they used to have in the Camps? You were a good dancer. You were. Best in the Camps.

MASI: You couldn't dance at all. You were awful.

NOBU: Remember that fellow Chester Yoshikawa? That friend of yours?

MASI: He could dance so good.

NOBU: Remember that dance you were supposed to meet me out front of the canteen? We were all going to meet there and then go to the dance together. Shig, Chester, and a couple others. Everybody else, they went on ahead. I waited and waited . . .

MASI: Nobu, that was forty years ago.

NOBU: Yeah, I know, but remember you were supposed to meet—

MASI: That's over forty years ago. How can I remember something like that?

NOBU: You didn't show up. Chester didn't show up either.

Masi puts cream and sugar into Nobu's coffee.

MASI: Nobu, didn't we talk about this? I'm sure we did. Probably something came up and I had to help Mama and Papa.

NOBU: Where were you, huh?

MASI: How am I supposed to remember that far back? Chester died in Italy with the rest of the 442 boys.

NOBU: Where the hell were you?

MASI: How in the hell am I supposed to remember that far back!

NOBU *(Noticing his coffee)*: You put the cream and sugar in. That's not mine. *(Pushes coffee away)*

MASI: That's right. You like to put the cream and sugar in yourself.

NOBU: I like to put it in myself.

MASI (*Pushing the cup towards him*): It's the way you like it, the same thing.

NOBU (*Pushes it back*): No, it's not the same thing.

MASI: All right, all right, I'll drink it myself. Here, you can drink mine. (*She shoves her tea to Nobu and grabs the coffee cup*)

NOBU: What are you doing—wait, wait.

MASI: I don't mind.

Masi starts to raise cup, but Nobu reaches for it.

NOBU: It's no good for you, Mama. Your blood pressure. Remember what Doc Takei—

MASI (*Clinging to cup*): Who gives a damn. You make such a fuss about it. *Monku, monku, monku* [Kvetch, kvetch, kvetch]. *I'll* drink it.

NOBU (*Struggling with Masi*): It's no good for you, Mama.

Coffee spills onto table. Marsha appears with a towel.

NOBU (*To Masi*): Clean it up.

MASI: I'm not going to clean it up.

MARSHA: I'll clean it up.

While Marsha starts to wipe the table, Masi grabs Nobu's coffee cup and exits into the kitchen.

MASI: I'll get him more coffee.

MARSHA: Dad.

Masi returns with Nobu's coffee and sets it down in front of him, turns and quickly exits.

(*Chasing after Masi*) Mom . . .

Nobu is left alone with his cup of coffee. He slowly puts in the cream and sugar himself. Raises the cup to his lips but cannot drink. Sets it back down and stares at it. Marsha returns and sadly watches her father. Dim to darkness.

Scene 6

Masi's place, three weeks later, afternoon. Masi's at the clothesline. Judy's visiting with Timothy.

JUDY: I don't see how you had two of us, Mom. I need sleep. Large doses of it. Jimmy's so lazy sometimes. I even kick him "accidentally" when Timothy starts crying. Think he gets up to feed the baby?

MASI: Daddy used to.

JUDY: Used to what?

MASI: Get up at night and feed you kids.

JUDY: Dad? You're kidding.

MASI: He used to sing to you. No wonder you kids would cry.

They laugh.

JUDY: I saw your new phone-answering machine.
MASI *(Proud)*: Yeah. For messages.
JUDY *(Kidding)*: What? You got a new boyfriend?
MASI: Judy.
JUDY: Well, why not Mom? You moved out. It's about time you start meeting new people. Once you get a divorce you're going to have to do that any—
MASI: I'm not getting a divorce.
JUDY: What are you going to do? You live here, Dad's over there . . . *(No response)* You can't do that forever.
MASI: I just do his wash. That's all I do. Just his wash. *(Pause; she hangs clothes)* I think you should call Dad.
JUDY: Mom, what can I say to him? I can't talk about my husband, I can't talk about my baby. All he can talk about is how he can't show his face at Tak's barber shop because I married a *kurochan* [black].
MASI: Judy, he's not going to call you.
JUDY: That's because he might get Jimmy. *(Beat)* Can you imagine Dad trying to talk to Jimmy.

They laugh; settle down.

MASI: Judy. He needs you.
JUDY: Why can't he accept it. Why can't he just say, "It's okay, it's okay, Judy"? I just need him to say that much.
MASI: He can't.

Dim to darkness.

Scene 7

Kiyoko's restaurant, that same evening. We hear the rhythmic pounding of fists on flesh. A pool of light comes up on Nobu and Kiyoko. Kiyoko is standing in back of Nobu pounding his back with her fists. She is massaging Nobu. This is a supreme joy for him. Kiyoko likes doing it for him.

KIYOKO *(Not stopping)*: Enough?
NOBU *(Voice vibrating from the steady blows)*: Nooo . . .

They continue in silence, both enjoying the activity.

KIYOKO: Enough?
NOBU: Noo . . .
KIYOKO *(Her arms are just too tired; stopping)*: Ahh . . .
NOBU *(Stretching)*: Oisho [Ahh]! Masi used to do it. Sometimes Marsha does it now.

KIYOKO (*Pouring tea*): You're lucky you have children, Nobu. Especially daughters. Harry and I wanted children. They're good, *neh*.

Nobu wants to give her something but can't bring himself to do it. Makes small talk instead.

NOBU: How come you take the bus? (*Kiyoko doesn't understand his comment*) You have that Honda. At your place, *desho*?

KIYOKO: Ahh. Datsun. Just to work. Just to work I take the bus. Got into the habit after Harry died.

Awkward silence. Nobu abruptly pulls out a small gift-wrapped box and holds it out to Kiyoko.

NOBU: Here.

Kiyoko is too surprised to take it.

Anata no tanjobi no puresento. Hayo akenesai. [Your birthday present. Hurry, open it.]

KIYOKO (*Taking it*): Ara! Nobu . . . (*Opens it and holds up the earrings*) Nobu-chan.

NOBU: Earrings. *Inamasu Jewelry Store no neki o tōtara me ni tsuitanda ne.* [I was walking by Inamasu's store when I spotted them.]

KIYOKO: *Mah, kirei, Nobu-chan. Tsukete miru.* [They're pretty, Nobu. Let me try them on.]

Kiyoko exits. Nobu in pool of light. Memory sequence: Masi appears in pool of light.

MASI: Why don't you want me anymore? (*No response*) We don't sleep . . . . You know what I mean and don't give me that kind of look. Is it me? The way my body . . . I've seen those magazines you keep in the back closet with your fishing gear. I mean, it's all right. I'm just trying to know about us. What happened?

NOBU: Nothing. Nothing happened. What's gotten into you?

MASI: Then why don't you . . . sleep with me?

NOBU: By the time I get home from work I'm tired. I work all day long, I'm standing the whole time. I told you never to touch my fishing equipment.

MASI: What about those magazines?

NOBU: I'll throw 'em out, okay? First thing tomorrow I'll throw 'em in the trash and burn 'em. That make you feel better? (*Masi is hurt by his angry response*) Masi? (*No response*) Masi. You're pretty. You are.

MASI: Don't lie to me. I hate it when you lie to me.

NOBU: I'm not lying. (*Masi refuses to believe him*) What the hell do you expect? We got old. Not just you. Me. Me. Look. Look at me. You call this a catch? You still want this?

MASI (*Quietly*): Yes. (*Nobu doesn't know what to say*) Why don't you want me?

Memory ends. Masi withdraws into shadows. Kiyoko returns to Nobu with the earrings on. Lights come up.

KIYOKO *(Posing)*: Nobu-chan?
NOBU: *Suteki da-nah* [Looks beautiful].

Kiyoko attempts to embrace Nobu. It's too uncomfortable for Nobu and he gently pushes her away. Kiyoko is quite embarrassed.

KIYOKO: How come you do that to me? *(No response)* Don't you like it?
NOBU: I like it. But I don't like it, too.

Dim to darkness.

Scene 8

Masi's apartment, three weeks later. Couch has a rumpled blanket on it. Morning. Sadao is standing holding the door open for a surprised Marsha. Sadao is dressed only in pants and an undershirt. Marsha is holding a box of manju [Japanese pastry]. They have never met.

SADAO: Good morning.
MARSHA: Is my mother . . . . Is Mrs. Matsumoto here?
MASI *(Off)*: Who is it?
SADAO: Come on in, please come in.

Masi enters in a bathrobe with her hair tied up in a towel, as if just washed.

MASI *(Momentarily caught off guard)*: Oh, hi, Marsha. Come in.
MARSHA *(Entering hesitantly)*: Hello, Mom.
MASI: This is Sadao Nakasato. *(To Sadao)* My eldest one, Marsha.
SADAO: Hello Marsha.
MARSHA: Hello.

Awkward pause. Marsha remembers her package.

Oh. I just thought I'd bring some *manju* by. *(Hands it to Masi)* I didn't think it was that early. Next time I guess I'll call first.

Masi gives the package to Sadao, who sets it on the counter.

SADAO: Hmm, love *manju*. One of my favorites. Especially the ones with the *kinako* on top. The brown powdery stuff?
MARSHA: I meant to drop it off last night but I called and no one was here.
MASI: Oh, we got in late from fishing.
SADAO: We caught the limit.
MASI *(Looking at phone-answering machine)*: I have to remember to turn this machine on.

SADAO: In fact, Masi caught more than me.

MASI: Teamwork. I catch them and Sadao takes them off the hook. Sit down and have breakfast with us. Sit, sit.

MARSHA: That's okay, Mom.

MASI: It was so late last night, I told Sadao to sleep on the couch. So he did. He said he would cook breakfast for me in the morning. Right over there on the couch.

Masi and Sadao are nodding to each other in agreement. Marsha doesn't move.

SADAO: Waffles.

MASI: You sure you know how?

SADAO: I can make them, good ones. From scratch. And they're low cholesterol.

MASI: Sit down, sit down.

MARSHA: No, no, Mom. I really should be going. I'm going to stop over at the house. To see Dad, too.

MASI: Wait, wait . . . *(Wrapping up two packages of fish in newspaper)*

MARSHA: Mom, I don't want any fish.

MASI *(Handing her a package)*: Then give some to Brad. Here.

MARSHA: Mom, remember? I'm not seeing him anymore.

MASI: Then give them to Dad.

MARSHA: What do I tell him?

MASI *(Momentary pause)*: Just give it to him. No use wasting it. He can eat fish morning, noon, and night.

Masi hustles Marsha towards the door.

SADAO: No waffles? They're low cholesterol.

MARSHA: Uh, no thanks. Nice to meet you, Mr. Nakasato.

Marsha pauses at the door. She and Masi exchange glances.

Bye, Mom. *(She exits)*

MASI *(Calling after)*: Tell Daddy I'll bring his clothes, that I've been busy. And tell him to put his old clothes in a pile where I can see it. Last time I couldn't find one of his underwear and he got mad at me. *(Closes door)* It was under the icebox.

As Sadao rambles on, Masi seems lost in her thoughts.

SADAO *(Caught up in his cooking)*: Everything's low cholesterol. Except for the Cool Whip. But that doesn't count because that's optional. Where's the MSG? That's my secret. My daughter gets so mad at me, "Dad, you're a pharmacist, you should know better than to use MSG." She's a health-food nut . . .

Sadao is bending down to look in a lower cabinet for the MSG. As he disappears, Masi moves into a pool of light. Memory sequence: Nobu appears in a pool of light.

NOBU: No, Masi, I said size eight, size eight hooks.

MASI: You told me to buy size six, not size eight. That's not what you told me.

NOBU: I get home from the store I expect you to . . . Jesus Christ . . . (*Starting to pace*) Shig, all day long ordering me around, "Do this, do that." I even gotta get up five o'clock this morning to pick up the produce 'cause his own damn son-in-law's a lazy son-of-a-bitch. And he yells at *me* if it don't look good in the cases. (*Mimicking*) "No, that's wrong Nobu, that's all wrong—do it this way."

MASI: Nobu. Nobu, you didn't tell me to get size eight hooks. You told me size—

NOBU: I said size eight. I said size eight hooks. (*Pause*) This is my house. Masi? After I come home from that damn store—here . . . . This is *my* house.

Silence.

MASI (*Quietly*): I'm sorry. I'm wrong. You said size eight hooks.

Nobu withdraws. Lights up. Sadao gets up with the MSG.

SADAO: You don't mind, do you? Masi? The *ajinomoto* [MSG]. Is it okay with you?

MASI: Yes, yes, it's fine.

SADAO (*Aware of Masi's pensiveness*): Sometimes I add prune juice but then you have to go easy on the MSG. The flavor doesn't mix. It's mostly for medicinal reasons, though. The prune juice. But it really does add a nice hint of flavor to the waffles, but you really can't overdo it. Everything in moderation. I think these people got a little carried away with this MSG thing. Of course, I'm not running a Chinese restaurant, either, I'm just talking about a tiny pinch of the stuff . . .

During this speech, Nobu is seen lit in half-light looking at his unfinished kite frame. As lights go to half on Sadao and Masi, Nobu is fully lit in a pool of light. He lifts the kite above his head and begins to move it as if it were flying. For a moment Nobu appears like a child making believe his kite is soaring high above in the clouds. As Nobu goes to half-light, Judy is lit carrying Timothy in front of her with a papoose carrier.

Scene 9

Kiyoko and Chiyo approach Judy as she passes by carrying Timothy.

KIYOKO: You are Judy, *neh.*

JUDY (*Cautious*): Yes?

KIYOKO: I am a friend of your father. My name is Kiyoko Hasegawa.

CHIYO: Chiyo Froelich.

KIYOKO: I run this restaurant. Hasegawa's.

CHIYO: Chiyo's Hair Salon, right next door.

JUDY (*Still unsure*): Hi.

KIYOKO: We are having a small get-together at my place for your father.

CHIYO: A birthday party.

They notice the baby.

KIYOKO: Oh, hello, Timothy.
CHIYO: Nobu should see him.

Awkward pause.

JUDY (*Starting to leave*): It's nice meeting you. Excuse me . . .
CHIYO (*To Kiyoko*): Show Judy your earrings. Kiyoko, show her.
KIYOKO: Chiyo.
CHIYO: He gave them to her. Your father. For her birthday.
KIYOKO: For my birthday. He comes to my restaurant almost every day. He likes my cooking. That's how come I know him so good.
CHIYO (*Kidding*): He's so *mendokusai* [troublesome]. I don't like cucumber pickle, I like eggplant. *Monku, monku* all the time.

Lights start to fade.

KIYOKO: Oh, it is no trouble at all. I like to do things like that. I like to cook for Nobu . . .

Dim to darkness. Cross-fade to Nobu with kite. Masi in half-light moves away from Sadao with the fishing pole. She begins to practice her cast.

Scene 10

Nobu puts down the kite frame. Thinks. Picks up the phone and dials Masi. In half-light at Masi's place, Sadao is at the counter making waffles. He hears the phone machine click on but does not answer it. Masi is off to the side, in a pool of light, engrossed in her casting.

NOBU: Masi? You got any . . . (*From his surprised expression we know that he has gotten Masi's answering machine. He doesn't know how to deal with it*) Masi? (*Listening to the message which finally ends*) I am Nobu Matsumoto. My telephone number is 751-8263. (*Not sure if he said his name*) I am Nobu Matsumoto.

He hangs up. Picks up his kite and stares at it. Masi is working on perfecting her casting technique, putting together all the little things that Sadao has taught her. She goes through one complete cycle without a hitch. Very smooth. Having done the whole thing without a mistake gives her tremendous satisfaction. She smiles to herself. It feels good. She begins again. Lights fade.

END OF ACT ONE

Scene 11

Kiyoko's restaurant, four weeks later. Surprise birthday party for Nobu. Judy stands by herself out front, picking at the food. Blackie and Marsha are in the kitchen and Kiyoko and Chiyo scurry about with last-minute preparations. Over the restaurant speakers we hear the forties tune "String of Pearls."

KIYOKO *(Calling)*: Blackie! Hurry up with the chicken teri! *(Checking the food items)* Ara! I forgot the dip. Chiyo, go talk, go talk.

Kiyoko pushes Chiyo towards Judy, then hurries back into the kitchen as Blackie and Marsha enter, carrying more food. Marsha is holding her nose.

CHIYO *(To Judy in passing)*: Nobu's favorite song. *(Stops momentarily, touching Judy's hair)* You come see me, I know what to do with it.

Chiyo heads back to the kitchen as Marsha and Blackie are setting their dishes down.

BLACKIE: If you think that stink, wait till you try my famous *hom-yu.*

MARSHA *(Attempting to be polite)*: No, really, it wasn't that bad.

BLACKIE: All Orientals gotta have stink food. It's part of our culture. Chinese, Japanese, Koreans, Filipinos—we all got one dish that is so stink. Chinese got this thing they call *ham-ha*, shrimp paste. My mudda used to cook with it. Whew! Stink like something went die.

Chiyo enters.

Filipinos got fish-gut paste, *bagaoong*; Koreans, *kimchee*. Whew!

CHIYO *(Admonishing)*: Blackie.

BLACKIE *(Ignoring Chiyo)*: And us Buddhaheads eat *takuan*, the pickled horseradish. When you open up the bottle, the neighbors call to see if your toilet went explode!

CHIYO *(Poking her head into the kitchen)*: Kiyoko! He's at it again!

BLACKIE: Next time you come I make you my *hom-yu.*

MARSHA: *Hom-yu? (To Judy)* You know *hom-yu?*

BLACKIE: Whatsa matter? You kids live on Mars? You never heard of *hom-yu? Hom-yu*. Steamed pork hash. It's my specialty. Gotta have the stinky fish on top. That's the secret. Lottsa *Pake* [Chinese] places don't use that fish anymore. Know why? Too stink! Chase all the *haole* [white] customers away. Take pork butt, chop it into small pieces. Four water chestnuts, chopped. Teaspoon of corn-starch—

Kiyoko enters with dip, Chiyo trailing.

Philip Kan Gotanda

56 KIYOKO: Blackie! Blackie! Go do the cake!

MARSHA *(To Blackie)*: I'll help you.

CHIYO: Kiyoko, when is he coming?

KIYOKO *(To Marsha)*: No, no . . . *(To Chiyo)* He should be on his way . . . *(To Marsha)* You shouldn't help anymore. Eat, eat. Talk to Chiyo.

MARSHA *(Overlapping)*: We met already . . .

KIYOKO *(To Blackie)*: Go, go, put the candles on the cake. No beer, either.

BLACKIE *(Exiting, calling back to Marsha while scratching his butt)*: Stinky fish. Don't forget the stinky fish . . .

KIYOKO *(Following him out)*: Don't scratch your . . . *(She remembers her guests)*

Chiyo approaches Judy and Marsha.

CHIYO: I've never seen her like this. She's acting like a kid back there. *(Catching her breath and looking the two daughters over)* You're Judy, *neh*, the fifth-grade teacher? And you're the dental . . .

MARSHA *(Overlapping)*: . . . hygienist, I told you earlier . . .

CHIYO: . . . hygienist—yeah, yeah you told me before. *(Quietly laughs about her mistake; calms down)* So. What do you think of the two of them? Nobu and Kiyoko?

Awkward pause.

MARSHA: I think it's . . . good. I think it's good.

Chiyo looks to Judy, who is silent.

CHIYO *(Touching Judy's hair gently)*: You come see me. I know what to do with it. *(She turns and walks back towards the kitchen)*

MARSHA: Judy.

JUDY: This is stupid. What am I doing here?

MARSHA: We're doing this for Dad.

JUDY: You really think he's going to want us here? Do you?

Kiyoko enters tentatively, followed by Chiyo.

KIYOKO: Blackie called—Nobu's not home, so he's coming. *(To Marsha, feigning enthusiasm)* I'm so glad you could make it. Judy said you weren't sure whether you could all come or not.

MARSHA: Oh no, no. We wouldn't have missed it.

KIYOKO: Nobu-chan will be so happy you are here.

MARSHA: It was very kind of you to invite us.

KIYOKO: Oh no, no, no. I wanted all of you here. *(To Judy)* Where is the baby?

JUDY: Jimmy's home babysitting him.

CHIYO: Next time you bring him. We got plenty of room here.

KIYOKO: Yes, please, please. Next time you bring the baby and Jimmy, too. I want to get to know all of Nobu-chan's family.

BLACKIE (*Rushing in with his ukulele*): HAYO [Hurry]! HAYO! THE BUGGA'S COM-
    ING! THE BUGGA'S COMING!
KIYOKO: I'll get the cake. Hide! Hide!
BLACKIE: I got the lights.
CHIYO (*To Marsha and Judy*): Over here, over here . . .

*Darkness. Nobu enters cautiously. The lights come up abruptly, then begin a
slow fade through the rest of the scene.*

ALL: SURPRISE!

*Nobu sees Judy and Marsha. He is in shock. Chiyo and Blackie lead everyone
in a rousing version of "Happy Birthday" as Kiyoko enters with a birthday cake
decorated with burning candles. He is attempting to appear happy, but he is becoming more and more upset that his daughters are there. Lights continue their slow
fade through the song, which is beginning to fall apart. Kiyoko is now standing
next to Nobu holding the cake out in front of him. She senses something is wrong.
The song ends with Blackie and Kiyoko mumbling the last few lyrics. Silence.
Nobu's face is illuminated by the glowing candles. Nobu makes no move to blow
out the candles. The moment is now uncomfortable. Kiyoko is very upset.*

KIYOKO: Nobu-chan, please.

Pause.

JUDY (*Irritated*): Dad.

*Nobu still refuses to blow out the candles. The moment is now extremely awkward.
No one knows what to do.*

MARSHA (*Gently*): Daddy.

*Slowly Nobu leans forward and with a forceful breath extinguishes the candles.
Blackout.*

Scene 12

*Masi's place, same night. Sadao and Masi in bed. Both are propped up, Sadao
intently watching TV and Masi peering at the TV over the magazine she holds
in front of her. Sadao keeps switching the channels with his remote control. Each
time Masi starts to settle into a program, Sadao switches the channel, causing
her to jerk her head from the shock.*

MASI: Sadao? (*He's busy switching channels*) Sadao?
SADAO: Hmm?
MASI: Could you please keep it on one?
SADAO (*Realizing what he's been doing*): Oh. I'm sorry. (*Starts switching channels again*)
    Which one? This one? How's this?

MASI: Fine, fine. That's fine. *(They settle into watching TV)* Sadao?

SADAO: Hmm?

MASI: I don't feel good. *(Pause)* I think something's wrong with me.

SADAO: What, what? Want me to call Doc Takei?

MASI: No, no . . .

SADAO: You have a fever? Headache? What's wrong?

MASI: No, no, nothing like that. *(Pause; thinking)* I'm too happy.

SADAO: What?

MASI: I feel . . . too happy. *(Sadao stares at her uncomprehending)* I used to feel like this as a kid, I think. But it was . . . different.

SADAO: You feel too happy?

MASI: When you're a kid you get ice cream and 'member how you used to feel? Happy, right? But then you eat it all up and it's gone, or, you eat too much of it and you throw up. But this just goes on and on.

SADAO: You mean us? *(Masi nods)* Yeah, but this is a little different than ice cream, don't you—

MASI: Of course, of course, Sadao.

SADAO: What about with Nobu? Didn't you go through this with him? *(Masi shakes her head)* I mean in the beginning when you first met? When you got married?

MASI: No, it wasn't like that. *(Pause)* I think something's wrong with me. You know how they say there's no such thing as an accident? That you really wanted it to happen and so it did? I don't think I ever really cared for Nobu. Not the way he cared for me. There was someone else who liked me in Camp. I liked him, too. I married Nobu. Something's wrong with me, huh? Now you make me feel too happy. I don't like it. It makes me . . . unhappy.

They both laugh. Sadao reaches out and places his hand on top of hers. They exchange warm smiles.

Was she in a lot of pain? *(Sadao doesn't follow her comment)* Your wife. Towards the end. In the hospital.

SADAO: She just slept all the time. No, not too much. After about two weeks she went into a coma and that was it. You can't tell. Cancer's like that. Mary was pretty lucky, I guess. *(Pause; thinking)* There's nothing wrong with you. Really, there isn't. *(Pause; trying to decide whether to say something or not)* You scare me. You know that? Sometimes you scare me half to death. I don't want to go through that again. I told myself, "Never, ever again." Dead is better than feeling that kind of pain. But this . . . this is . . . I don't know . . . . To get a second chance . . . *(Pause)* There's nothing good about growing old. You spend most of your time taking medicine and going to the doctor so you won't die. The rest of the time you spend going to the funerals of your friends who did die, and they were taking the same medicine and seeing the same doctors so what's the use, anyway? Huh? *(Sarcastically)* The golden years . . . . Look at us. Here we are. At our age. In bed together. Not even married. Can you imagine what the kids are thinking?

MASI: We're not doing anything wrong.

SADAO: Of course, I know, I know.

MASI: We're not doing anything wrong, Sadao. We're not.

SADAO: I know. But when I really think about what we're doing . . . it embarrasses the hell out of me!

They look at each other, then suddenly burst out laughing. They gradually calm down.

MASI: I scare you half to death. And you . . . you make me feel so good I feel awful.

They look at each other for a moment, then slowly reach out and embrace. Dim to darkness.

Scene 13

Kiyoko's restaurant, one week later. Nobu is sitting at the counter sipping sake and eating eggplant pickles. Blackie is watching him from the service window. He comes out sipping on a beer.

BLACKIE *(Takes a big gulp)*: Know why I like to drink beer? Know why? *(As Nobu looks up, he answers his own question with a loud satisfying burp)* Ahh. I like to let things out. Makes me feel good. Don't like to keep things bottled up inside. Not good for you. Give you an ulcer. Cancer. Maybe you just blow up and disappear altogether, huh. *(Laughs at his own joke. Notices Nobu isn't laughing)* That's the problem with you *katonks*. You buggas from the mainland all the time too serious. *(Nobu glances back towards the door)* No worry, no worry. Kiyoko going be back soon. Chiyo's place—yak, yak, yak. Hey, you had lots of girlfriends when you was small-kid time? *(Nobu shrugs)* Strong silent type, huh. Me? Lottsa wahines. All the time like to play with Blackie. *(Mimicking the girls)* "Blackie, darling, you're so cute . . . you're so funny." . . . But I not all the time cute. I not all the time funny. How come you all the time come around here and you still got one wife?

NOBU: We're separated.

BLACKIE: So when you gonna get the divorce?

NOBU: No. *(Blackie doesn't understand)* No.

BLACKIE: What about Kiyoko? *(No response. Nobu keeps drinking)* I don't like you. I like you. I don't like you 'cause you make Kiyoko feel lousy. I like you 'cause you make her happy. Hey, she's my boss—who you think catch hell if she not feeling good? Hey, I don't like catching hell for what you do—

NOBU: It's none of your business—Kiyoko and me.

BLACKIE: None of my business? Hey, brudda, Kiyoko may be feeding your face but I'm the guy who's cooking your meals. *(Nobu stares down at his pickles)* Nobu?

NOBU: What?

BLACKIE: You like Kiyoko? *(No response)* Well, do you?

NOBU *(Under his breath)*: Yeah, I guess so.

BLACKIE: "Yeah, I guess so" what?

NOBU *(Mumbling)*: I like Kiyoko.

BLACKIE: Jesus. Talking to you *katonks* is like pulling teeth.

NOBU: I LIKE KIYOKO! I like Kiyoko.

Blackie sips on beer while Nobu glares at him. Blackie leans forward towards Nobu and burps loudly.

BLACKIE: Feels good, huh?

Dim to darkness.

Scene 14

Nobu's place, one week later. Evening. Masi enters carrying the wash in a brown paper bag. She unpiles the clothes and stacks them neatly on the kitchen table. She picks up the old clothes off the floor, folds them, and puts them in the bag. As she looks up, one gets the sense that she is trying to decide whether to say hello to Nobu or just leave. She looks for a moment towards the hallway, then decides otherwise. Just as she turns and starts to make her way towards the door with the bag, Nobu enters from the hallway.

NOBU: Masi, is that you?

Nobu realizes that she's leaving without bothering to say hello. Masi senses this and feels guilty.

MASI: I was going. I'm a little late. I was just going to leave the clothes and go. *(As she speaks, she notices the dirty dishes on the coffee table. She puts down the bag and proceeds to clean up the mess as she continues to talk)* I didn't know you were in the back . . . *(She takes the dishes to the sink. Nobu just watches)* Nobu, why don't you wash the dishes once in a while? Clean up.

NOBU: Place is a dump anyway. *(Masi stops and looks at him. He presses point)* Place is a dump, Mama. Neighborhood's no good. Full of colored people, Mexicans . . .

MASI *(Putting dishes in sink)*: Well, move then. Move to the north side like me. I kept saying that all along. For the kids—better schools, better neighborhood . . . . Think you listen to me? *(Mimicking Nobu)* "I don't like *Hakujin*—white people make me nervous." So you don't like white people, you don't like black people, you don't like Mexicans . . . . So who do you like? Huh? *Monku, monku, monku* . . .

NOBU *(Muttering)*: I don't mind Mexicans. *(Pause)* I told Shig, "You can't keep stocking all that Japanese things when the *Nihonjins* [Japanese] are moving out of the neighborhood. You gotta sell to the Mexicans and not all that cheap crap, too, 'cause they can tell." Think Shig listens to me? He's the big store owner.

The big man. If I was running the store it woulda been different. *(Pause)* And your old man said he'd get me that store.

MASI: It wasn't his fault. He didn't plan on the war, Nobu.

NOBU: He promised he could set me . . .

MASI *(Overlapping)*: It wasn't his fault.

NOBU: . . . up in business or anything else I wanted to do.

MASI: IT WASN'T HIS FAULT!

Silence.

Who wanted to be in the relocation camps? Did you? Do you think he wanted to be in there? It broke Papa's heart. He spent his entire life building up that farm. Papa was a proud man. A very proud man. It broke his heart when he lost it.

NOBU: I'm just saying I'd run the business different. Shig is a *baka* [fool]. That's all I'm saying.

MASI: You're retired. Shig passed away eight years ago. The store's not even . . .

NOBU *(Overlapping)*: If all the Japanese move out you can't keep selling all that Japanese things, you can't. That's all I'm saying.

MASI: . . . there anymore. It's a cleaners.

Silence. Masi picks up the paper bag of old clothes and starts to move towards the door. She's had enough.

NOBU: Masi?

MASI *(Stops)*: What?

NOBU: Mr. Rossi give you any more fish?

MASI *(Uncomfortable, lying)*: No. Not lately.

Pause.

NOBU: Mama?

MASI: Is your back bothering you, Nobu? *(No response)* Want me to *momo* [massage] it for you?

Nobu nods. As Masi moves to put the bag down, Nobu removes his undershirt. He seats himself. Masi begins to massage his shoulders from behind. They continue in silence. Nobu is enjoying the moment. He begins to laugh quietly to himself.

What?

NOBU: When I started work at your papa's farm, he wanted to put me in the packing shed. I said, "No, I want to work in the fields." It was so hot, 110 degrees out there. He thought I was nuts. But I knew every day at eight in the morning and twelve noon, you and your sister would bring the water out to us.

MASI *(Laughing as she recalls)*: Nobu.

NOBU: I wanted to watch you.

MASI: You would just stand there with your cup, staring at me.

NOBU: Hell, I didn't know what to say.

MASI: You drank so much water, Lila and I thought maybe you had rabies. We used to call you "Nobu, the Mad Dog."

They laugh.

Papa liked you.

NOBU: Boy, he was a tough son-of-a-bitch.

MASI: I didn't think anyone could keep up with Papa. But you could work like a horse. You and Papa. Proud. Stubborn.

Masi massages Nobu in silence.

NOBU: Mama? Why don't you cook me breakfast?

MASI: What?

NOBU: Cook me breakfast. I miss my hot rice and raw egg in the morning.

MASI: It's late Nobu. You have your wash. I'm not going to come all the way back over here just to cook you—

NOBU: Just breakfast. Then in the morning when we get up you can go back to your place.

Masi stops, realizing he is asking her to spend the night. Silence. Masi does not move. Nobu stares ahead. More silence. Then, tentatively, she moves her hands forward and begins to massage him. A faint smile appears on Nobu's face. Dim to darkness.

Scene 15

Kiyoko's restaurant, one week later. Blackie, after hours, is seated in semidarkness, feet up on table, accompanying himself on the ukulele and singing a sad Hawaiian folk song, "Manuela Boy."

BLACKIE *(Singing):*
Manuela Boy, my dear boy,
You no mo' hila, hila.
No mo' five cent, no mo' house
You go Aala Paka hia moe.

Mama work at the big hotel,
Brudda go to school.
Sister go with the haole boy,
Papa make his living shooting pool.

The tourist like filet mignon
And caviar it's true,

But they never lived till they went taste
Papa's Friday ole Hawaiian stew . . .

As Blackie sings, lights up on Masi's place. Sadao stands before the door Masi has just opened. In Sadao's right hand he holds a suitcase and in his left, several fishing poles. On his head sits a fishing hat. Sadao has come to move in with Masi. For a moment they look at each other in silence. Then Masi invites him in. Sadao enters. Dim to darkness.

Scene 16

Nobu's place, three days later, late afternoon. Judy has stopped by with Timothy. Judy sets the baby down on the kitchen table upstage of Nobu. Nobu turns to look at Judy, then returns to working on the kite and watching TV. This is the first time Judy has visited Nobu since their breakup over her marriage. He has never seen Timothy.

JUDY (*Moving down towards Nobu*): I was just driving by and I thought I'd stop in. (*No response*) You doing okay, Dad? (*Silence*) You know, Mom? I just wanted to say—
NOBU: Did he come?
JUDY (*Exasperated*): No, he did not.
NOBU: He can come to the house now.
JUDY: "He can come to the house now"? Jesus Christ. Dad, he isn't one of your children. He doesn't need your permission. He's . . .
NOBU (*Overlapping*): This is my house. He needs my permission.
JUDY: . . . a grown man. I don't want to fight. I didn't come here to fight with you, Dad.
NOBU: I *said* he can come—
JUDY: He won't come, he doesn't like you!

Silence.

NOBU: Damn *kurochan* . . .
JUDY: He's black, not *kurochan*—it's black. (*Pause*) Everybody marries out, okay? *Sanseis* don't like *Sanseis*.
NOBU: Tak's son married a *Nihonjin*, Shig's daughter did, your cousin Patsy . . .
JUDY (*Overlapping*): Okay, okay, I didn't, I didn't, all right?
NOBU: . . . did, Marsha's going to.

Pause. Nobu looks back to Timothy.

JUDY: But *happa* [multiracial] kids are the next generation, too.

NOBU: *No.* Japanese marry other Japanese, their kids are *Yonsei* [fourth-generation Japanese American]—not these damn *ainoko* [multiracial]!

Silence.

JUDY: You're gonna die out, you know that. You're gonna be extinct and nobody's gonna give a goddamn.

Timothy has begun to cry softly. Judy goes over and picks the baby up, trying to soothe him. Composing herself, Judy decides to try one last time to say what she came to tell her father. She walks back to Nobu, this time carrying Timothy with her.

Dad? *(No response)* Dad, you know, Mom's moving out of the house? I didn't put her up to it. Honest. *(Silence. Nobu stares straight ahead. She begins to cry)* If I did . . . I'm sorry.

More silence from Nobu. Judy gives up trying to talk to this man. As she turns to leave, she notices Nobu. He is looking towards her, at Timothy. Something in his expression makes Judy bring the baby over to Nobu. She holds the baby out to him.

Timothy. Your grandson.

For a moment there is hesitation. We are not sure whether Nobu is going to take the baby. Then, Nobu reaches out and takes Timothy. Judy watches as Nobu awkwardly holds his grandson for the first time. As Judy begins to withdraw from the scene upstage into a pool of light, Marsha also appears upstage in her own separate light. Nobu remains lit holding Timothy. He begins to hum the traditional Japanese lullaby "Donguri." Marsha and Judy watch Nobu and Timothy as they speak.

MARSHA: You didn't tell Dad, did you?
JUDY: No. I just brought the baby by.
MARSHA: It's going to kill him when he finds out.
JUDY: He's got that other woman.
MARSHA: Judy. *(Pause)* Maybe he already knows about Mom and Mr. Nakasato.
JUDY: I don't think so. I really don't think so.

They continue to watch as Nobu begins to sing the "Donguri" song to Timothy.

NOBU *(Singing)*:
Donguri koro koro, koro gatte
O-ike ni hamatte, saa taihen
Dojo o ga dette kite, kon-nichiwa
Botchan/Timothy isshoni, asobimasho . . .

Marsha and Judy fade out first. Nobu is left alone in pool of light singing to Timothy. As he fades out we hear the whir of a coffee grinder.

Scene 17

*Masi's place, two days later. Masi has asked Judy and Marsha over for a talk.
She has just told them that she is going over to see Nobu. She is going to tell
him that she wants a divorce and to marry again. The two daughters sit uneasily
while Masi is at the counter preparing coffee. Masi is trying to get the Braun
grinder to work. She's getting the feel of it by pushing the button. We hear the
whir of the spinning rotor blade. She's ready. Takes the plastic top off and pours
the beans in, then presses the start button. Just as the grinder picks up top speed
Masi accidentally pulls the plastic top off. Beans go flying every which way: pelting
her face, bouncing off the cabinets. Quiet. Masi peeks from behind her hands.
A couple of beans embedded in her hair fall to the counter. Masi is upset. The
daughters are embarrassed. Normally, this would be a funny situation for them.*

MARSHA (*Getting up*): I'll clean it up.

*Marsha starts to pick up the beans scattered on the floor. Judy starts to giggle—
it's all too ridiculous.*

JUDY (*Trying to suppress her laughter*): I'm sorry, I'm sorry . . . (*Masi begins to laugh*)
God, what a mess.

MASI (*To Marsha*): Let it go, don't bother. I'll take care of it later.

JUDY (*Finds a man's sock; teasing*): What's this? This belong to Mr. Nakasato?

MASI (*Grabbing it*): Judy.

MARSHA: Why didn't you just leave sooner? You didn't have to stick around for us.

MASI: I didn't. (*Pause*) I was . . . I was scared.

MARSHA: Of Dad?

MASI: I don't know. Everything.

JUDY: Was it 'cause I kept harping on you to move out on him all those years? Is
that why you left?

MARSHA: What's the difference?

JUDY: Marsha.

Pause.

MASI: Dad was always trying to beat me down, every little thing. "How come you
can't do this, how come you can't do that"—nothing was ever right. Every time
I opened my mouth I was always wrong—he was always right. He always had
to be right. (*Pause*) There are things you kids don't know. I didn't want to talk
about them to you, but . . . Daddy and I, we didn't sleep . . .

JUDY (*Overlapping*): That's okay, Mom. Really, it's okay . . .

MASI: . . . together. Every time I wanted to, he would push me away. Ten, fifteen
years he didn't want me. (*Pause*) We were having one of our arguments, just
like always. And he was going on and on about how it was my fault this and
my fault that. And I was trying to explain my side of it, when he turned on
me, "Shut up, Mama. You don't know anything. You're *stupid*." Stupid. After

forty-two years of letting him be right he called me that. And I understood. He didn't even need me to make him be right anymore. He just needed me to be stupid. I was tired. I couldn't fight him anymore. He won. He finally made me feel like shit. (*Judy and Marsha are shocked by her strong language*) That was the night I left him and came over to your place. (*Nodding towards Judy*) I like Sadao. I like Sadao very much.

Dim to darkness.

Scene 18

Nobu's place, same day. "String of Pearls" can be heard playing faintly in the background. He's fixing himself in front of a small wall mirror. He adjusts the collar of his shirt and tugs at his sweater until it looks right. Nobu checks his watch. As he begins to pick up some of the scattered clothes on the floor, Masi enters. Music ends. Nobu quickly moves to the sofa. Masi goes over to the kitchen area and takes clothes out of the bag, setting them neatly on the table. She picks up the dirty clothes off the floor, folds them, and puts them into the bag. As she's doing this, Nobu gets up, shuffles over to the stove, and turns on the flame to heat some water. He stands there and watches the water heat up.

MASI (*Sits down on sofa*): I want to talk, Nobu.

No response. Nobu gets tea out and pours some into pot.

I have something to tell you.

NOBU (*Moving back to couch*): Want some tea?

As Nobu sits, Masi gets up and moves towards the sink area. She gets a sponge and wipes off the tea leaves he has spilled on the counter. Nobu turns the TV on and stares at it.

MASI: You know Dorothy and Henry's son, George?

NOBU: The pharmacist or something?

MASI: No, the lawyer one. He's the lawyer one. I went to see him. (*Turns off the stove flame*) I went to see about a divorce. About getting one. (*No response*) I want to get married again. So I went to George to see about a divorce. I wanted to tell you first so you'd know. I didn't want you to hear from someone else. I know how you hate that kind of thing. Thinking something's going on behind your back.

NOBU: Wait, wait, wait a second . . . . You want a divorce? You want to get . . . . What? What's all this?

MASI: It's the best thing, Nobu. We've been separated how long now? How long have we been living different places?

NOBU: I don't know. I never thought about it. Not too long.

MASI: Thirteen months.

NOBU: Thirteen months, who cares? I never thought about it. I don't understand, Masi.

MASI: It's the same thing as being divorced isn't it?

NOBU: It doesn't seem that long. You moved out of this house. It wasn't my idea. It was your idea. I never liked it.

MASI: It doesn't matter whose idea it was. It's been over a year since we—

NOBU: You want to get married? Yeah, I know it's been over a year, but I always thought . . . you know, that we'd—

MASI: It's been over a year, Nobu.

NOBU: I know! I said I know.

MASI: I've been seeing someone. It wasn't planned or anything. It just happened.

NOBU: What do you mean, "seeing someone"? What do you mean?

MASI: He's very nice. A widower. He takes me fishing. He has a nice vegetable garden that he—

NOBU: Who is he? Do I know him? Is it someone I know?

MASI: His name is Sadao Nakasato. His wife died about two years ago. He's related to Dorothy and Henry. Nobu, it's the best thing for both of us.

NOBU: You keep saying it's the best thing, the best thing. (Pause) Masi, why did you sleep with me that night?

Silence.

MASI: Aren't you seeing somebody?

NOBU: No. Not like that.

MASI: But the kids said she's very nice. That she invited—

NOBU: It's totally different! I'm not seeing anyone! (Pause) How long have you been seeing this guy? How long?

MASI: Please, Nobu. You always get what *you* want. I always let you have your way. For once just let—

NOBU: HOW LONG!?

MASI: About five months.

NOBU: FIVE MONTHS! How come you never told me? Do the girls know too? The girls know! Everybody knows? Five months. FIVE GODDAMN MONTHS AND I DON'T KNOW!! (He breaks the kite)

MASI: I asked them not to tell you.

NOBU: Why? Why the hell not? Don't I have a right to know??

MASI: Because I knew you'd react this way. Just like this. Yelling and screaming just like you always do.

NOBU: Everybody in this whole goddamn town knows except me! How could you do this to me! Masi! HOW COULD YOU DO THIS TO ME?? (He has her by the shoulders and is shaking her violently)

MASI (Quietly): Are you going to hit me?

Pause. Nobu slowly composes himself and lets her go.

Because I want to be happy, Nobu. I have the right to be happy.

Masi exits. Nobu is left standing alone. Dim to darkness.

Scene 19

Kiyoko's restaurant, same day, evening. Chiyo and Kiyoko seated at table in pool of light.

KIYOKO: Nine years. That is how long it has been. Nine years since Harry passed away. He never treated me like this. I call, I go over there. Harry never treated me like this.

CHIYO: Kiyoko. Maybe you have to stop thinking about Nobu. Hmm? Maybe . . . maybe you should give him up. *(Silence)* Kiyoko. Lots more fish in the ocean. Lots more. Go out with us. Come on.

KIYOKO: I don't do those kinds of things.

CHIYO: I'll introduce you to some new guys. Remember Ray—you met him? I've been telling him about—

KIYOKO: I don't do those kinds of things. *(Pause)* It's not easy for me, Chiyo. *(Silence)* When Harry died, right after? I started taking the bus to work. I had a car, I could drive. It was easier to drive. I took the bus. For twenty-five years you go to sleep with him, wake up next to him. He shaves while you shower, comes in from the yard all sweaty. Then he's gone. No more Harry in bed. No more the smell of aftershave in the towel you're drying off with. No more sweaty Harry coming up and hugging me. I had a car. I took the bus. I missed men's smells. I missed the smell of men. Every morning I would get up and walk to the corner to take the bus. It would be full of all these men going to work. And it would be full of all these men coming home from work. I would sit there pretending to read my magazine . . . *(Inhales, discovering the different smells)* Soap . . . just-washed skin . . . aftershave lotion . . . sweat . . .

Lights come up to half in the restaurant. Blackie bursts through the kitchen doors holding a plate of his famous hom-yu. Brings it over and sets it down on the table, which is now in a full pool of light.

BLACKIE: Hom-yu! Hom-yu!

CHIYO: *Kusai yo* [Stinky]!

KIYOKO: Blackie!

BLACKIE: I know stink. But stink goooood!

It stinks to holy hell. Chiyo can't stand it. Kiyoko is quite moved by Blackie's gesture, though she too is having a difficult time with its odor. Blackie grins proudly. Dim to darkness.

Nobu's place, two days later. Knock at the door and Marsha enters carrying a brown paper bag. Nobu watching TV.

MARSHA: Mom asked me to drop these by and to pick up the dirty clothes. *(No response. She unpacks the newly washed clothes)* Kiyoko's been calling me. She's worried about you. She says you won't see anybody. Why don't you just talk to her, Dad?

NOBU: How come you didn't tell me? All the time you come here and you never mention it once. You. I feel so goddamned ashamed. How can I even show my face? All the time right under my nose. Everyone laughing at me behind my—

MARSHA: Dad, Dad, it's not like that at all. I just didn't think it was all that important to tell—

NOBU: Oh, come on! Mom told you not to tell me so she could go sneaking 'round with that son-of-a-bitch!

MARSHA: All right, all right, but it's not like that at all. No one's trying to hide anything from you and no one's laughing at you.

NOBU *(Moving her towards the couch and pushing her down)*: Sit down, sit down over here. Tell me about it. Who is he? What does he do? Tell me 'bout him! Tell me!

MARSHA *(Seated)*: What do you want me to say? Huh, Dad? They're happy. He's a nice man.

NOBU: "He's a nice man." What the hell's that supposed to mean?

MARSHA: He treats her like a very special person.

NOBU: Well, everyone does that in the beginning. In the beginning it's so easy to be—

MARSHA: She laughs. All the time she's laughing. They're like two little kids. They hold hands. Did you ever do that? I'm embarrassed to be around them. He takes her fishing. He has a little camper and they drive up to . . .

NOBU: All right, all right . . .

MARSHA: . . . Lake Berryessa and camp overnight. He teaches her how to bait the hook, cast it out, and even to tie the hook. I mean you never even took her fishing . . .

NOBU: She doesn't like fishing. I tried to take her lots of times, she wouldn't go.

MARSHA: They even dig up worms in his garden at his house. I saw them. Side by side . . .

NOBU: All right, I said.

MARSHA: . . . sitting on the ground digging up worms and putting them in a coffee can!

NOBU *(Overlapping)*: ALL RIGHT! ALL RIGHT!

MARSHA: . . . I MEAN DID YOU EVER DO THAT FOR MOM!! *(Pause)* Did you? *(Getting worked up again)* You're so . . . so stupid. You are. You're stupid. All you had to say was, "Come back. Please come back." You didn't even have to say, "I'm sorry."

NOBU (*Overlapping*): I'm your father . . .

MARSHA: Mom would've come back. She would've. That's all you had to say. Three lousy words: "Please come back."

NOBU (*Overlapping*): I'm your father . . .

MARSHA: You ruined everything. It's too late! YOU WRECKED EVERYTHING!! (*Pause. Composing herself*) I'm so mixed up. When I look at Mom I'm happy for her. When I think about you . . . I don't know. You have Kiyoko.

NOBU: That's not the same. I'm talking about your mama.

MARSHA: Dad, Kiyoko cares a great deal about you. She's been calling Judy and me day and night.

NOBU: She knocks on the door but I don't let her in. She's not Mama.

MARSHA: Dad. What do you want me to say? That's the way it is. I used to keep thinking you two would get back together. I couldn't imagine life any other way. But slowly I just got used to it. Mom over there and you here. Then all this happened. I mean, sometimes I can't recognize Mom anymore . . . . What do you want me to say? You'll get used to it.

Nobu pauses, upset.

NOBU (*Stubbornly*): No.

MARSHA (*Looks at her father sadly*): You'll get used to it.

Dim to darkness.

Scene 21

Judy's place, two days later. Masi is at the clothesline hanging clothes. Judy, holding Timothy, is with Masi. Nobu suddenly rushes in. Masi and Judy are surprised. Nobu appears very upset.

MASI: Nobu . . .

JUDY: Hello, Dad . . .

NOBU (*To Masi, ignoring Judy*): It's no good, Mama. It's no good at all. You come home. You come home now, Mama. You come home. It's no good . . .

JUDY (*Overlapping, trying to calm Nobu down*): Dad? Dad, take it easy . . . take it easy . . . (*Trying to get him seated*) Sit down, sit down . . .

NOBU (*Yanking arm away from Judy*): I DON'T WANT TO SIT! I WANT MAMA TO COME HOME!

Shocked silence.

JUDY (*Upset, quietly*): I'll get some coffee for you, Dad.

Judy does not exit. Masi doesn't know what to do. She's never seen Nobu like this.

NOBU: You come home, Mama. Just like always. You don't need to live over here. You come home. Just like always. That's the way it is . . .

MASI *(Overlapping)*: Nobu, Nobu . . . . You don't understand, Nobu. I can't come home. I can't come home anymore—

NOBU: I DON'T CARE! I DON'T CARE ABOUT ANY OF THAT STUFF, MAMA! *(Pause. Breaking down, he begins to plead)* I won't yell at you, anymore. I won't yell, I promise, Mama. I won't *monku* about the store or about your papa . . . I'm sorry . . . I'm sorry. Masi, it's no good. Please come home. Please come home . . . . Please . . .

Neither Masi nor Judy knows how to cope with this situation. Nobu continues to plead. Dim to darkness.

Scene 22

Lights up on Kiyoko's restaurant, one day later. Chiyo is dialing Nobu's number. A concerned Blackie stands guard next to her. Kiyoko has told them not to bother with him anymore. Kiyoko appears and watches them from the service window. She makes no attempt to stop them. In half-light, Nobu composes himself and leaves Judy's place. We follow him as he begins to make his way back home. However, he stops in front of Masi's place and stares at it. Chiyo lets the phone ring and ring. Finally she and Blackie exchange disappointed looks. At that point Kiyoko bursts in on them.

KIYOKO: How come you keep doing that? Huh? Don't phone him anymore. I told you, didn't I?

Blackie and Chiyo look sheepishly at Kiyoko. Kiyoko's feigned anger is very transparent to all three parties and only adds to the discomfort of the situation. As the scene darkens, Nobu arrives at his house. Nobu appears in a pool of light. He stands there for a moment in silence, still carrying some of the emotional turmoil from his previous scene with Masi. He reaches behind the sofa and pulls up a long, narrow object wrapped in cloth. As he unwraps it, we see what it is: a shotgun. Nobu sits down in the chair with the gun across his lap, staring into the darkness. As the lights do a slow fade on Nobu, the mournful wail of a shakuhachi [bamboo flute] is heard.

Scene 23

Masi's place, one week later. Nobu stands inside with the shotgun. In half-light, Sadao is asleep in the bedroom.

NOBU: Where is he? *(Masi stares at the gun)*

MASI: He went to buy the newspaper.

NOBU *(Notices Masi watching him cautiously)*: It's not loaded. *(Pause)* At first I said, "No, no, no, I can't believe it. I can't believe it." I got so pissed off. I got my gun and drove over here. I drove around the block twenty or thirty times thinking "I'm gonna shoot this son-of-a-bitch, I'm gonna shoot him." I drove right up, rang the doorbell. No one answered. I kept ringing, ringing . . . . I went back to the car and waited. You cheated on me. How could you do that to me? I'm a good husband! I'm a good husband, Masi . . . . I kept seeing you two. The two of you together. I kept seeing that. It made me sick. I kept thinking, "I'm gonna shoot that son-of-a-bitch. I'm gonna shoot him. I waited in the car. It was three o'clock in the morning when I woke up. It was so cold in the car. You weren't back. I got worried I might catch a cold, and my back—you know how my back gets. I drove home, took a hot bath, and went to sleep. I've been sick in bed all week. I just wanted to show you. Both of you. That's why I brought it. Don't worry. It's not loaded. (*He cracks the shotgun and shows her that it is not loaded*) I just wanted to show both of you how it was, how I was feeling. But it's all right. You two. It's all right now.

Nobu sets the gun against the wall. Masi watches him, trying to decide if it is indeed safe.

MASI: Nobu.

NOBU: Yeah?

MASI: He's taking a nap. In the bedroom. He likes to do that after dinner.

NOBU: What is he? An old man or something?

MASI: He just likes to take naps. You do too.

NOBU: In front of the TV. But I don't go into the bedroom and lie down. Well, where is he? Bring him out. Don't I get to meet him?

MASI: You sure? (*She looks at him for a long while. She believes him. She turns to go wake Sadao up, then stops*) Chester Yoshikawa? That night in the Camps when I didn't show up for the dance? Chester Yoshikawa? We just talked. That's all.

Masi leaves for the bedroom. Nobu looks slowly around the apartment. It's Masi and yet it isn't. Nobu suddenly has no desire to meet Sadao. He doesn't want to see them together in this apartment. Nobu exits abruptly. Masi appears cautiously leading out a yawning Sadao. They look around. No Nobu. All they see is his shotgun leaning against the wall.

Scene 24

Same day. Marsha and Judy appear in a pool of light far upstage. Marsha is holding a small kite and slowly moves it above Timothy, who is held by Judy. They sit in silence for a time.

JUDY: I can't believe he gave the kite to Timothy. He gets so mad if you even touch them. And he never flies them.

Pause.

MARSHA (*Moving the kite*): No. He never flies them.

The lights dim to half. They turn to watch the action taking place center stage.

Scene 25

Two days later, darkness. The TV light comes on, lighting Nobu's face. A pool of light comes up on Nobu, seated on sofa, watching TV. No kite on the coffee table. Masi appears in another pool of light. She stands, staring pensively downstage into space. In her arms she is holding the brown paper bag of newly washed clothes. She turns and moves towards Nobu's place. As she enters the lights come up full on the house.

Masi goes over to the kitchen table and takes out the newly washed clothes, stacking them in neat piles on the table. She then proceeds to pick up the old clothes scattered on the floor and puts them in the bag. She picks up the bag and moves towards the door, then stops. She makes up her mind about something she has been struggling with for a while. Masi returns to the kitchen and leaves the bag of old clothes on the table. As she opens the door to go, Masi looks back at Nobu and watches him for a brief moment. During this whole time, Nobu has never turned around to look at Masi, though he is very aware of what is going on. Masi sadly turns and exits.

Lights dim with Nobu silently watching TV. Briefly, Nobu's face is lit by the dancing light of the television screen. At this same instant, the brown paper bag of wash on the table is illuminated by a shaft of light. Nobu's phone begins to ring. He turns to look at it. Blackout on Nobu. The wash fades into darkness. The phone continues to ring for a few moments. Then, silence.

END OF PLAY

Tenement Lover
no palm trees/
in new york city

Jessica Hagedorn

Jessica
Hagedorn

I was born and raised in Manila, the Philippines. My family came to this country in the 1960s during my adolescence, and I did the rest of my growing up in San Francisco.

I've been writing pretty much all my life. My grandfather was a writer, and when I was six or seven years old I was writing what I used to call my "little novels." They were four pages long, and I would illustrate them.

I always wanted to work in theatre—as a performer, a writer, a director. So rather than going to college I entered the American Conservatory Theatre's training program. I got a lot out of it: it opened up a lot of things for me as a performer, and also taught me what I *didn't* want to do. The training combined disciplines like t'ai chi and martial arts with acting, mime and fencing, all that Western physicality. I think it was quite a full education in theatre arts, and we also got to work at night in ACT productions.

I continued to write, mostly poetry. My first published book of poems came out in 1972, when I was in my early twenties. It was a collection called *Four Young Women*, edited by Kenneth Rexroth. Around that same time I got involved with a collective of women writers and artists of color. We published an anthology, *Third World Women in the Early 1970s*, which is how I met and worked with Ntozake Shange and Thulani Davis. Both women have been important to my development as a writer-performer. All three of us were interested in doing poetry in collaboration

76

with artists working in other media—dance, music, film. My primary interest at the time was music. I always wanted to have a band.

Back then rock music meant more to me than just music. It was theatrical and, in its own crude way, conceptual. The road into it wasn't academic—if you wanted to perform you didn't have to go to endless acting classes, because rock 'n' roll was a way to hone those skills. And rock audiences were very open.

I put together a band called the West Coast Gangster Choir, and we worked all over Northern California—in Oakland, in San Jose, in Stockton, at colleges and universities. I would write these bits, these little theatrical moments between the songs. That was the sort of theatre I wanted to do, and there was no name for it then.

I knew I didn't want to write mainstream plays. I wanted to write for performance and eventually for film, so I just started doing it, and the band became another direction. I never thought I'd drop theatre for music, one medium for another. I simply thought I was adding to the form. The form might involve writing, staging, acting, music, but it always meant creating a spectacle that expressed my vision—whether it was on a stage or in a nightclub.

I got very involved in the cultural stew of San Francisco, which included a lot of other Asian-American artists. It was great growing up there as an artist in that era because there was a strong artistic community, especially among artists of color. No one thought anything was too strange or weird to try. We supported each other; it was a climate in which you felt nurtured. There was a real sense of generosity among peers.

By 1978 the scene was winding down, and I moved to New York. I think the move toughened up my work a lot because living in New York is so tough. I welcomed the change, because I wanted more muscle and less sentimentality in what I wrote. I don't mean it has to all be hard and brutal, but I think that sometimes the toughness is what can make you weep.

I first wrote *Tenement Lover* as a song. It became a kind of anthem for my band, which by then was known as The Gangster Choir. The song expressed my reactions to living conditions in New York and my adjustment to the change. In 1981 The Kitchen invited me to do a show, so I decided to incorporate the song and the band into one piece and have it be about otherness on many levels.

Doing *Tenement Lover* helped me grapple with a new life in New York, and with what it meant to be a Filipino there. I found it completely bizarre at first. San

Francisco was a very Filipino town, with a large Filipino population. New York had a much smaller Filipino community—it's sizeable now, but wasn't when I arrived. I felt strange; people would assume I was Puerto Rican, which is a totally different thing.

My director, Thulani Davis, suggested that I work Bongbong, a character I'd written about before, into *Tenement Lover.* She said, "You have this thing about Bongbong, he's always placed in an alien environment and he has to react to it. Why don't you use him in this?"

I tried it, and it turned out that Bongbong was a great thread to tie together the piece. I see him as the quintessential immigrant. He's a version of me, but more naive and more spiritual.

Doing *Tenement Lover* was the first time I had enough of a budget to realize the visual elements of my work. I had tableaus running through the piece of the bathing beauty character and the guerrilla, the mysterious man scooping up seashells. I also had slides of the Philippines projected, mostly landscapes. The photographer who took them had gone up into the mountains and shot rice fields, sometimes using red filters so that they looked like brilliant-colored abstractions, like landscapes on Mars.

I wanted to communicate to the audience in several ways. There was a visual story with no dialogue spoken, there were Bongbong's letters, there were songs performed live by the band. All these fragments may have seemed disjointed to some people, but by the end you could see the connections.

Tenement Lover turned out to be a very important piece for me. In it I began to explore, with a style that I'm still using, themes that continue to obsess me— otherness, the idea of revolution on many levels, terrorism, dominant culture vs. so-called minority culture. And the idea of home, what homesickness and home mean.

I also wanted to address the political situation in the Philippines. It was important to me at the time, because I hated the Marcos regime. I'm political, and find I'm overtly more political the older I get. I used to dance around that commitment and say, "Let my work speak for myself. It's there, if you want to find it." Now I'll just say yes, I want to include those reflections in my work. I don't pretend to have the answers, but the thing about grappling with politics in art is that the *questions* can be so interesting.

Does my work belong to an Asian-American aesthetic? I think there's a multicultural aesthetic, in the sense that you can draw from many different cultures that have similar experiences. For example, black music really influenced the way I write poetry. Certain rhythms go along with certain forms of jazz and R&B I listen to. But it gets kind of sticky when you try to define these things. I don't want limitations imposed on me.

I do know I've been influenced by other Asian-American performance artists. Ping Chong's *Nuit Blanche* had a lot of impact on me. It was so visually pristine, so clean, and yet Ping was playing with so many ideas. That taught me a lot. I also loved some of the early work of Winston Tong.

I'm still working in various media—theatre, poetry and fiction. The last theatre piece I did, with the group Thought Music, was a meditation on racism called *Teenytown*. We tried to get racism out of its American context and take a view that included a much bigger picture. We were using images from popular U.S. culture— music and films and jokes—but we wanted to reflect the world.

In all my writing there are always these characters who have a sense of displacement, a sense of being in self-exile, belonging nowhere—or anywhere. I think these themes are the human story. When it comes down to it, it's all about finding shelter, finding your identity. I don't care whether you're an immigrant or native-born, you're discovering who and what and where you are all the time.

When I think of home now I mean three places. The San Francisco Bay area really colored my work. New York is where I live. But Manila will always have a hold on me. What is the threshold of my dreams? I really don't think of myself as a citizen of one country, but as a citizen of the world.

Biographical Information

Born in the Philippines, raised in Manila and San Francisco, Jessica Hagedorn is an eclectic artist conversant in several media.

Hagedorn has authored two collections of poems and short fiction, *Dangerous Music* and *Pet Food & Tropical Apparitions* (both Momo's Press). Her writing can also be found in many literary magazines and in anthologies such as *Early Ripening: American Women's Poetry Now* (Pandora Press) and *Stealing the Language* (Beacon Press).

As a performance artist, Hagedorn performed original work in experimental venues throughout the country, including Dance Theatre Workshop, the Walker Art Center, Intersection, and the Public Theater. As musician, she was founder-director of the influential art-rock band The Gangster Choir.

A Nun's Story, Hagedorn's dance-theatre collaboration with Blondell Cummings, was broadcast on public television's *Alive From Off Center* in 1988. WYNC's *The Radio Stage* produced her radio drama *Holy Food* in 1989, airing it nationally.

Hagedorn currently resides in New York City with her daughter, and performs with the group Thought Music (Laurie Carlos, Robbie McCauley, John Woo). *Dogeaters*, her novel about the Philippines, will be published in 1990 by Pantheon Books.

About the Play

"Tenement Lover" began as a song, composed by Jessica Hagedorn and recorded by her band, The Gangster Choir, on John Giorno's anthology record, *A Diamond Hidden in the Mouth of a Corpse* (Giorno Poetry Systems label, 1986).

In 1981, with support from The Kitchen and The Basement Workshop, Hagedorn expanded the song into a full-length performance piece titled *Tenement Lover: no palm trees/ in new york city*. It premiered in New York that same year, directed by Thulani Davis, with music composed and performed by Jessica Hagedorn & The Gangster Choir, and by Lawrence "Butch" Morris. The version of the play published here is a 1989 revision.

The poem "Ming the Merciless" appears in Hagedorn's *Pet Food & Tropical Apparitions* (Momo's Press).

The Play

Tenement Lover
no palm trees/
in new york city

Slides of the Philippines are projected in silence; these are closeup shots of the actual terrain, shot through red filters. Voice of the Narrator comes on somewhere in the middle of the slide sequence; this can be performed live or on tape.

NARRATOR'S VOICE: What is the definition of *anting-anting?* Talisman, charm, or amulet . . . . Crocodile-tooth, twin-tailed lizard, whale spine, snake fang, two-headed snake, shark's fin, rooster's spur . . . *(Pause)* There are three known ways of obtaining *anting-anting:* (1) by finding a flowering *tanglad*, generally a nonflowering plant, and dipping its flower in a bottle of oil . . . (2) by obtaining the fallen tooth of a *carabao*, in the belief that the strength of the *carabao* transfers to the possessor . . . (3) by finding a live octopus inside a coconut and eating it.

On tape, the ominous "Alchemy" by Butch Morris begins. The sound of waves crashing against the shore, eerie and mysterious. The Beachcomber makes his entrance in the dim light. He is carrying a child's beach pail, and wears a loose floral-print shirt, torn pants, no shoes. From the pail, he takes pebbles and shells and scatters them on the stage, thus creating our unnamed tropical "beach." Depending on the site and the situation, this beach could be confined to one specific area—downstage, for example—while the Narrator and her band of musician/performers could be set in another area opposite. The Beachcomber could also transform the entire stage into one big beach, making it as elaborate or as minimal

81

as the director decides. After the Beachcomber literally sets the stage, he exits.

Two chairs are preset, one behind the other, to simulate the front and back seats of a limousine. The Beachcomber now makes an entrance dressed as the Chauffeur, with dark sunglasses hiding his eyes. He opens the imaginary door to the imaginary limo for the Sunbather/Tourist, who is preferably blonde and can be dressed in beach/tourist attire—e.g., shorts and tank top, bathing suit and short robe. She carries a large beachbag filled with books, magazines, lotions, and a roll of barbed wire.

As she steps out of the limo, the Sunbather barely acknowledges the Chauffeur's presence, except for a perfunctory nod. She is also wearing dark sunglasses.

The Sunbather waits until the Chauffeur has set up her mat, lounge chair, and umbrella; when he is done, she dismisses him with a wave of her hand. When he exits, she pulls out the barbed wire. Slowly, the Sunbather stretches the wire across the stage, splitting the playing area into two distinct worlds: the "real" world where the Narrator and the band emerge from the shadows, and the Sunbather's exclusive and private domain.

More slides of jungle terrain are projected. The Narrator/Lead Singer steps up to the microphone. As she speaks, the "Alchemy" soundtrack slowly fades out.

NARRATOR: Antonio Gargazulio-Duarte, also known as Bongbong to family and friends, has been in North America for less than two years and is slowly going mad. He doesn't know it, of course—having left his birthplace, the Philippines, because his sanity was at stake . . . (*Pause*) As he often told his friend, the painter Frisquito: "I can no longer tolerate contradiction. This country is full of contradiction. If I stay, I shall go crazy." (*Pause*) Frisquito told Bongbong: "There's nothing wrong with being crazy. Being crazy is good for art. The thing to do is to get comfortable with it." Unfortunately for Bongbong, he isn't sure he is an artist unlike his friend Frisquito. To save himself, Bongbong buys a one-way plane ticket to North America via Guam and Honolulu. It is approximately a 27-hour flight, according to the cheerful travel agent, who also happens to be Bongbong's mother. Bongbong leaves Manila on the morning of his twenty-ninth birthday.

Slides are projected: images of tribal members in mountain villages, images of a woman swimming in a pool. On tape, the voice of a newscaster is heard. (Note: Other news items can be substituted, as these newscasts were related to a specific time in the Marcos regime.)

NEWSCASTER: Within eight hours of his rousing arrival at Manila International Airport, Pope John Paul was feted at a formal reception in Malacanang Palace, the glittering presidential mansion. With the Marcoses seated stiffly at his side, the Pope scolded the President in some of the sternest language that diplomacy admits . . . . Discarding a prepared reply, Marcos seemed chastened in his first response: "Forgive us, Holy Father. Now that you are here, we resolve that we shall wipe out all conflicts and set up a society that is harmonious, to attain the ends of God."

The Narrator or different band members take turns reading the letters that follow out loud. Simultaneously, on the other side of the barbed wire, the Sunbather is turning her body from side to side, lying on her stomach, oiling herself, thumbing idly through magazines, etc.

LETTER FROM BONGBONG #1:

Dear Frisquito:

Everyone is a liar. My sister is the biggest one of them all. I am a liar. I lie to myself every second of the day. I look in the mirror and I don't know what's there. My sister hates me. I hate her. She is inhuman. But then, she doesn't know how to be human. She thinks I'm inhuman. I am surrounded by androids. Do you know what that is? I'm glad I never took acid.

I wish I was a movie star.

Love,
Bongbong.

Lights come up on a woman, possibly the Narrator, watching television. She does not move, totally transfixed by the images. Occasionally, she munches on banana chips, which she takes from a bag in her lap. During the course of this tableau, different characters can walk in and out of her tenement apartment. They might take some chips from her, light a cigarette, slam doors. She is oblivious to them, her attention totally focused on the monitor.

THE IMMIGRANT SECTION: LUDIVINDA'S STORY *(Either spoken live by the woman watching television, or on tape):* I like New York okay. I like my apartment okay. It's no house, but it's a nice place, *di ba?* We had a house when I was growing up in the Philippines . . . it was made of bamboo with a thatched roof, really I'm not kidding, and we had to walk a long way to take a bath. You should have seen the first place Tito and I had here in New York. Terrible *talaga.* Rats and cockroaches all over, even though I kept cleaning and cleaning, I went to sleep with a mop and broom right next to me, it was terrible but nothing helped. No one ever fixed anything that broke. The walls were falling, the ceiling was cracked. Am I in America? I kept asking my husband. *(Pause)* I like New York okay. I like my new apartment okay. It's not a house, but it's a nice place. We had a house when I was growing up back home, but it was made of bamboo with a thatched roof, and we had to walk a long way to take a bath . . . . I'm so happy with my new apartment now I don't care if we're broke—I just stay home and watch TV, is okay, I don't care if I never go out. *I watch all the programs! (Pause)* We didn't have a television in the Philippines. *(Pause)* And my family was afraid when I left them to marry Tito. *What are you afraid of?* I asked them. *I'm going to America! (Pause)* Tito was a marine . . . stationed at the base near where we lived. *(Pause)* We didn't know what a Puerto Rican was—it was funny when my family met him. *Ano ba iyan?* MENUDO? But Tito's American, I told them—something close to being Spanish, not dark at all. *I'm dark.* But Tito doesn't mind, he calls me beautiful. *(Pause)* Tito liked being in the marrines. He says it's too hard in the outside world. But now with two kids, he can't go back in the marines—they keep telling him he's got too many dependents . . . *(Pause)* I'm twenty-four years old, and I'm glad we're off welfare. You should have seen our first apartment. Rats, roaches, the walls falling in. Are we in America? I asked my husband. *(Pause)* Once I worked as a clerk to help out with the family income. It made Tito so crazy! The only job he can get is as a security guard. We don't have a bank account because it isn't worth it—we keep taking out as soon as we put in. *(Pause)* Tito hated me working, especially when he hadn't started his guard job and he had to stay home with the kids. "It's not right," he kept saying, "I don't feel like a man." I lost my job anyway, so it all worked out. I guess. *(Pause)* Tito's a good man—he doesn't drink or get high. He doesn't look at other women. One time I got angry with him. Only once. *(Pause)* We went to visit his friends in Brooklyn and I was feeling homesick. His friend's wife spoke Tagalog and asked me how come we never go dancing like they did. I got angry and asked Tito when we got home how come we never did that, dancing I mean—I love dancing, don't you? All Tito had to say was we better not see those people anymore because I was getting too jealous. *(Pause)* They were his only friends. *(Pause)* It's nice to have friends, but if they give you trouble I'd just as soon stay home . . . *(Pause)* We have two television sets, one in color. Tito watches sports games, but I like talk shows. Actually, I'll watch anything. So do the kids—we watch TV all day and all night, sometimes. *(Pause)* One of my real worries is that I'll never see my family back home again . . . and my parents will die and all this time will pass and I'll never have the money to go back . . . and this wavy black line, this black line that's been appearing on the bottom half of the screen of our color set . . . I can't call the repairman, we don't have any money, I just pretend the black line isn't there. Every day the black line gets worse, sometimes the pictures on the screen turn orange or pink, I think I'm going blind but no one else seems to notice . . . . Look, I tell my husband, it's going *bad.* It's on the *blink* . . . . What are we going to do? *(Pause)* Is okay, Tito tells me. Go watch the little set. I can't—I hate black-and-white TV—I keep telling Tito he should know this about me, I've told him many times, the same thing over and over again . . . *(Pause)* "Black-and-white's more realistic," he tells me, "you'll get used to it."

She keeps watching television. The Sunbather keeps sunbathing.

VOICE OF NEWSCASTER: President Marcos' announcement that martial law had ended was received with mixed emotion. The president's wife, however, looked grim. The former beauty queen lingered in the shadows as the president made his speech. Still very much the international jet-setter, the glamorous First Lady nevertheless allowed herself to be photographed on the verge of tears . . .

BONGBONG WRITES ANOTHER LETTER TO FRISQUITO:

Dear Frisquito:

I can't seem to find a job. I have no skills, and no college degree. My sister thinks I should apply at a business college and go into computer programming. The idea makes me sick. I am twenty-nine years old and no good at anything.

Yesterday I considered getting a job as a busboy at a restaurant, but my sister was horrified. She was certain everyone in Manila would hear about it (which they will) and she swears she'll kill herself out of shame. Not a bad idea, but I am not a murderer.

If I went back to Manila, I could be a movie star.

Love,

Bongbong.

In the beach area, the Beachcomber/Chauffeur makes another entrance, this time dressed as a Waiter. His face is covered by a mask of a smiling man. He carries a fancy drink in a coconut shell on a tray, the kind of elaborate drink served with paper parasols. He hands the drink to the Sunbather, bows, then exits. The Sunbather sips her drink, gazing at the audience from behind her dark sunglasses.

THE BAND SINGS A SONG:

Sleazy Desire / New York Reggae

Urban existence
Livin' hand to mouth
Stress is the factor
That cranks this town
Barbed-wire kisses
I can't get down
Rumors of war
Are goin' down . . .

Sleazy desire
All night and day
Got to get mine
Before it gets away

I can't get
Enough to eat
I'm livin' the lowlife
On the street

I want it fast
I want it slow
My bags are packed
I got no place to go
(2x)

Inflame me
Don't tame me
Sleazy desire
All night and day
Got to get mine
Before it gets away
Barbed-wire kisses
I can't get down
Rumors of war
Are goin' round . . .

BONGBONG'S LETTER #3:

Dear Frisquito:

I enrolled in business college today so my sister would shut up. I plan on leaving the house every morning and pretending I'm going to school. That way no one will bother me.

I don't understand anything. Everyone is an artist, but I don't see them doing anything. Which is what I don't understand. I think I may come back to Manila soon, but somehow I feel I'm being trapped into staying here . . .

Love,

B.

A man dressed in camouflage, his face partially covered by a red bandanna, guerrilla-style, creeps onto the beach. The Sunbather does not notice him at first, but when she does, she's not sure of what she sees. She slowly gets up from where she has been lounging and backs away from him as he stalks her. The scene should have a tense but dreamy quality. The Guerrilla comes closer and closer. They both exit.

NEWSCASTER INTERVIEWS BROOKE SHIELDS *(On tape)*:
NEWSCASTER: What did you think, Brooke?
BROOKE: Those were real diamonds in Mrs. Marcos' dress. I think that's neat!

Repeat question and answer 3x.

HER DEEPEST FEARS: THE NARRATOR'S MONOLOGUE: When I go home, back to the islands and my father's house, the same movie keeps unfolding in my head. They come and kill everyone in the house, and I'll just happen to be there. By chance, I tell myself. Except I know it's all part of my destiny. *(Pause)* There are three bedrooms in my father's house. My grandmother, paralyzed from a stroke, sleeps in the first bedroom at the top of the stairs. She is totally helpless, so a nurse remains at her side twenty-four hours a day. Socorro is fed intravenously, and shits into a sack that's attached to her side. Socorro clutches a rosary in her gnarled hands and mumbles to herself. No one can make out what she's saying. Socorro's eyes are glazed, she sits in her wheelchair and trembles ever so slightly . . . . I imagine she's already left her body, that she exists on some high spiritual plane. *(Pause)* In my movie, they kill the nurse first. They never touch my grandmother. In fact, they seem to be afraid of her. After the massacre, she's the only survivor left—mumbling in her wheelchair and clutching the rosary beads in her disfigured hands. *(Pause)* I sleep in the second bedroom. I hear them kill the nurse, quietly and efficiently. She makes one low sound. I lie in my bed, sweating, staring at the door. I hear the leaves rustling outside the screened window—the night is humming, alive with cicadas chirping and clicking. It is unbearably hot, even in the middle of the night. I am unable to move, sweating under my thin blanket. I hear soft movements in the next room. They are coming for me, I am sure of it. I go over the movie again and again, the movie I call *My Father's House*. *(Pause)* I often imagine the face of my killer. He is a feline guerrilla, with sharp cheekbones, copper skin, and blue-black hair. His sharp eyes pierce the darkness; he carefully bends his sullen face towards mine. My father sleeps in the third bedroom. *(Pause)* For a brief moment, I am sure the young man is actually going to kiss me. But I am wrong.

POSTCARD FROM BONGBONG:

Frisquito:

Happy Belated Birthday—I didn't forget! Thanks for sending the telescope. I'm writing a song about it in my head. Picked up a secondhand alto sax and am taking lessons. *Okay lang!* There are days I am actually happy, with my telescope and my saxophone. You'd be so proud. Do you know I'm only five feet two inches tall? Without my platform shoes, of course . . . and of course I know you've known all along.

love,

B.

After this postcard is read, the band strikes up opening chords for the song "Tenement Lover."

Tenement Lover

schoolboys keep it up all night
cool . . . cruel . . . school . . . boys
keep it up all night

but I need you
to make things right
tenement lover (4x)

listen to the night
listen to the night
the night is long and hot
and stifling
I wait for you
I wait for you
I wait for you
so hot and stifling

there's a woman
in the elevator, afraid
shrinking in the shadows
a young man shot
on the roof, afraid
shrinking in the shadows
but I don't care
I wait for you
tenement lover (4x)

tenement tenement
tenement torment
tenement tenement
tenement torment

I like the way you kiss
all my dark places
I like the way you fill
all my empty spaces
tenement lover
(Guitar solo)

schoolboys keep it up all night
cool . . . cruel . . . school . . . boys
keep it up all night
but I need you
to make things right

there's a woman in the elevator,
dead
and she doesn't even live here . . .
a young man shot
on the roof, dead
bleeding in the shadows . . .

but I don't care
I wait for you
I'm up on the roof
of the city
my arms are open wide
there's blood on my hands
blood in the air
blood
everywhere

tenement lover
tenement torment
tenement lover
tenement torment . . .

BONGBONG'S DREAM *(Spoken by the Narrator)*: In his dream, he learned how to fly. He floated and glided and went swimming in the clouds, which turned out to be his glittery blue sweater. Dancing girls did the rumba in the heavens, serenaded by smiling Chinese deities. A ghostly gangster choir sang *Stardust* as Bongbong flew by, propelled by the force of his exuberant joy. He was ascending higher and higher; faster and faster he flew up, into a tunnel of fog. Was that dot up above his friend Frisquito, waving frantically to him? Bongbong flapped and kicked, as if by doing so he could reach Frisquito. The dot became smaller and smaller, then vanished. Bongbong finally woke up, gasping for breath.

BONGBONG'S LAST LETTER:

Dear Frisquito,

I'm staying in this strange land just a little while longer. Are you surprised? Never is forever, you once said, *di ba?* Never say never. And so I wear my hat. And so—

love.

While the band begins the final song, the Beachcomber/Waiter reappears on the other side of the barbed wire. He looks around the deserted "beach," picking up some of the Sunbather's scattered belongings. He tries on her sunglasses, then settles down in her lounge chair and sips her unfinished drink.

THE FINAL SONG:

Ming the Merciless

dancing on the edge
of a razorblade, ming
king of the lionmen
sing   bring us to

the planet of no
return . . .

king of the lionmen,
come dancing in my tube.

sing, ming, sing.
blink sloe-eyed fantasy
and touch me where
there's always hot water
in this house.

o flying angel
o pterodactyl
your rocket glides
like a bullet

you are the asian nightmare
the yellow peril
the domino theory
the current
fashion trend

o ming
merciless ming
the silver edges
of your cloak
cut hearts in two
the blood-red dimensions
that trace
american galaxies

cinema life
cinema death
cinema of ethnic
prurient interest

your rocket glides
like a bullet
and touches me
where

there's always
hot water
in this house.

Lights out.

END OF PLAY

As the Crow Flies

Flies

The Sound of a Voice

David Henry Hwang

David Henry
Hwang

I was born in 1957 and grew up in a second-generation Chinese-American family in Los Angeles.

There was always a part of me that did things because they weren't expected of me. In terms of society, what I was supposed to be doing as an Asian American was becoming at least a professional, if not a math or a science professional. My parents hoped I would get into law or medicine or business.

I did toy with those options—that was part of me trying to be a good son. But I have no proficiency for math, so it wasn't even an option. And I have no hand-eye coordination, so the idea of me as a doctor was rather terrifying.

I was always more interested in doing something involving words. I was attracted to creating a world that could appear before me. The whole idea of being an artist appealed to me, partly because it was something I wasn't supposed to be.

When I was very young, twelve or thirteen, I thought my grandmother was dying, and I decided to get her family stories down on paper. I'd sit with her and do these oral histories, and then I wrote a twelve-year-old's equivalent of a novel. It was distributed to all the members of my family and highly praised, and that was it.

As a student at Stanford University I tried to write prose. I wasn't crazy about my prose—the only time it was good was when I wrote in the first person. I was always more interested in voices and hearing people talk, and when I started seeing plays it was a complete thrill for me. Every time I went to a bookstore and found another play by Pinter or Shepard it was a new excitement, like being in love. With this passion I managed to teach myself a lot, and John L'Heureux, my writing professor, was also very helpful.

In the summer of 1978, after my sophomore year, I went home to Los Angeles to spend the holiday. I saw this ad in the *Los Angeles Times*: "Study playwriting with Sam Shepard." It was for the first Padua Hills Playwrights Festival and, incredibly, only two playwriting students applied. We both got in and worked with Shepard, Irene Fornes, Murray Mednick. It was great.

Shepard affected me as a playwright and as a teacher. One of the first plays I ever read was *Geography of a Horse Dreamer*. I saw his plays at the Magic Theatre in San Francisco, and between that and studying with him at Padua and, in 1980, at the Bay Area Playwrights Festival, I started writing *FOB* and *Family Devotions*, which I dedicated to Sam.

I think of *FOB*, *Family Devotions* and *The Dance and the Railroad* as my Chinese-American trilogy. After that I went through a period where I had exhausted what I wanted to say about what it meant to be an Asian living in this country, the whole ethnicity of that. It was time to move on and see what else interested me.

I was attracted to a lot of Japanese literature, and I'd always been interested in Japanese movies. So I found a Kawabata story, *The House of Sleeping Beauties*, and adapted it into a play. It was a one-act, and I needed another to make a whole evening of it.

The Sound of a Voice is modeled on those movies based on Japanese ghost stories, like the stories Lafcadio Hearn collected.  They always involve an element of tragic love, erotic undertones and often a sense of ambiguity as to whether the characters are humans or spirits.

I wrote *Sound of a Voice* when I was very pessimistic about the state of male-female relationships. I think there's a sense in it of an almost inherent mistrust between the man and the woman, which symbolizes the way, in general, we don't really know one another.

The male character comes in with the presupposition that the woman is a witch, and everything she does can be interpreted along those lines. It's unclear whether she's somebody with a great deal of passion and concern, or an ordinary person who happens to be eccentric, or a witch.

The man's attitude could be taken as a metaphor for misogyny. In this culture to be a very attractive or beautiful woman is a double-edged sword. On the one hand men are attracted to you and on the other hand they want to kill you—literally. Thinking that a woman is a witch because men are enchanted with her is very much part of the misogynistic mindset.

As the Crow Flies was also written as a companion piece. It had something to do with the relationship between my grandmother and the person who had been cleaning house for her once a week for many years.

My grandmother is extremely stoic, kind of a tough cookie, and she does this thing that a lot of older Chinese people do. If I talk to her in English, it's no problem. But if one of my Caucasian friends talks to her in English, my grandmother never seems to understand. To the outside world she's like an odalisque, impenetrable.

So I thought, well, she's had this black cleaning lady for years and there must be some relationship, some form of understanding that's developed there. And this person who cleaned for her also happened to have two identities. She had one name for work, and at home she put on a wig, used another name, and became a different person. This is actually true. I didn't make it up, it was just a matter of accurate reporting.

One theme I trace through all my work is this kind of fluidity of identity. In a lot of my plays, from *FOB* to *M. Butterfly*, people become other people. It has a lot to do with the nature vs. nurture question. To what degree do you have an inherited identity, and to what degree is your personality shaped by the influences and environment around you?

This question is intimately related to my own desire to know myself. I happened to be born Chinese-American in the United States. Would I be different if I was born in China? Or if I had a different skin color in this country? I also think it's interesting to explore racism and stereotyping between different minority groups in this culture, because that's really where the future lies. If we're becoming a culture of many different ethnicities, then the way these ethnic groups relate to one another will be increasingly important—at least as important as the way all these ethnicities combined relate to white America.

I find it fascinating that the term "Asian" exists only in the West. People who live in Asian countries see themselves as Chinese or Japanese or Korean—just as people in France and Germany consider themselves French or German first, not European.

Asian is really our term, and I like it—first, because I think the experiences of Asians in this country are rather similar. Secondly, because I don't see the point of being nationalistic, and the concept of "Asian" stops nationalism dead. A person in Japan and a person in China would most likely not have the same close friendship as Philip Gotanda and I.

The Asian-American theatre movement has been important to me. Let's make an analogy between artistic development and one's personal development: if you grow up as a minority in this country there's a residual negativism that you take into your system, simply because of the racism in the air. You get to a point where you feel a certain amount of self-loathing and wonder if you don't measure up to certain things. One of the only ways to remedy that is for minority people to get together, segregate themselves for a while, and realize that they all have common experiences. You can sort of repair the damage that way.

But once that's done I believe there's an obligation, at least if one is going to remain engaged in the American experiment, to reintegrate yourself into the larger society. In the long run, if the ethnic theatres do their jobs properly, they should phase out their own existence. I think the future is not in monoethnic theatre, but in multicultural theatres that will do a black play, an Asian play, a white play, whatever.

Our country's in a transitional phase now. Over the next twenty or thirty years we're really going to see the emergence of minorities, with Caucasians becoming the plurality rather than the majority. That realignment is going to be scary and hard, but this place is such a great laboratory. You have people from all these different cultures who interact intimately: some hold on to their cultures, some don't, some hate other ethnic groups, some couldn't care less—it's such an interesting scheme of things. And within all the attitudes we find here there's so much to discover about how people of different nationalities and cultures have always looked at each other, throughout history.

It's so important to me that we're all engaged in this social experiment, that we don't give up on it, that we keep criticizing America and trying to change it. I mean, if not here, where?

Biographical Information

In 1988 David Henry Hwang became the first Asian-American dramatist to earn the coveted Tony Award. It was for M. *Butterfly*, a hit Broadway play based on the true story of a love affair between a French diplomat and a Chinese opera actor and spy. Theatres in two dozen countries have optioned productions of M. *Butterfly*, and a film version (scripted by Hwang) is also in the works.

Hwang's playwriting career began in 1979, with the Obie-winning *FOB*. He went on to complete his "Chinese-American trilogy" by writing *The Dance and the Railroad* and *Family Devotions* (both in 1981), and his later plays include *The House of Sleeping Beauties* (1983), *Rich Relations* (1986) and *1000 Airplanes on the Roof* (1988).

Most of Hwang's plays premiered at the Public Theater in New York, and have gone on to subsequent productions in the U.S., Europe and Asia. His many awards include a CINE Golden Eagle for the cable-television version of *The Dance and the Railroad*, and playwriting fellowships from the Rockefeller Foundation, the Guggenheim Foundation and the National Endowment for the Arts.

A resident of New York City, Hwang serves as co-dramaturge (with Philip Kan Gotanda) of the Asian American Theatre Company in San Francisco. He is writing the libretto for Philip Glass's opera *The Voyage*, scheduled to premiere at the Metropolitan Opera in 1992, and is also working on a "multicultural farce."

As the Crow Flies

About the Play

As the Crow Flies was first produced in 1986 at the Los Angeles Theatre Center, on a double bill with *The Sound of a Voice*. Reza Abdoh was the director.

Characters

HANNAH, a black woman in her 60s.
MRS. CHAN, a Chinese woman in her 70s, sometimes called Popo (Grandma).
P.K., a Chinese man in his 70s, sometimes called Gung Gung (Grandfather).
SANDRA, a black woman in her 40s.

Time and Place

The living room of an upper middle-class home. The present.

As the Crow Flies

A living room in an upper middle-class home, owned by Mrs. Chan, a Chinese woman in her seventies, and her husband, P.K. Up right, a door leads out to the front driveway. Stage left is a door leading to the rest of the house. Mrs. Chan sits in a large chair, center stage, looking downstage out into a garden. Around her, Hannah, a black woman in her late sixties, cleans. She has been their cleaning woman for over a decade.

HANNAH: I guess I never told you this before, Mrs. Chan, but I think the time is right now. See, I'm really two different folks. You've been knowin' me as Hannah Carter, 'cuz when I'm over here cleanin', that's who I am. But at night, or when I'm outside and stuff, I turn into Sandra Smith. *(Beat)* Is that all clear?

CHAN: Um. Yeah.

HANNAH: You got all that?

CHAN: When you are here, you are Hannah Carter—

HANNAH: Right.

CHAN: And, then, you go outside, and you are . . . someone . . . someone . . .

HANNAH: Sandra Smith.

CHAN: Um. Okay.

Pause.

HANNAH: You don't have any questions 'bout that?

CHAN: Hannah Carter, Sandra Smith—I understand.

HANNAH: Well, you know how you can tell the two apart?

CHAN: No. Because I have not seen Sandra—Sandra . . .

HANNAH: Smith. Well, when I'm Sandra Smith, see, I look different. First of all, I'm a lot younger.

CHAN: Good.

HANNAH: And, you know, since I'm younger, well, guess I'm looser, too. What I mean by that, is, when I talk, well, I use different words. Young words. And, Mrs. Chan, since I'm younger, my hair color's a lot different too. And I don't clean floors. 'Cuz young people nowadays, they don't clean floors. They stay up around the clock, and make themselves into lazy good-for-nothings, and drink a lot, and dance themselves into a state. Young people—I just don't know what's got into them. But whatever it is, the same thing's gotten into Sandra Smith. (*Pause*) You don't think this is all a little strange?

CHAN: No.

HANNAH: Well, that's the first time . . . I remember when I told Mrs. Washburn about Sandra Smith—she just fell right over.

CHAN: So what? So you have two different people.

HANNAH: That's right. Living inside me.

CHAN: So what? My uncle had six!

HANNAH: Six people?

CHAN: Maybe even seven. Who can keep count?

HANNAH: Seven? All in one guy?

CHAN: Way back in China—my second uncle—he had seven, maybe even eight people—inside here. I don't . . . is hard to remember all their name.

HANNAH: I can believe that.

CHAN: Chan Yup Lee—he was, uh, I think, the businessman. He runs Uncle's import-export association. Good man. Very stingy. I like him. Then, I think there was another: ah, C.Y. Sing—he is the family man. Then, one man, Fat-Fingers Lew. Introduce this sport—what is the name? Ball goes through big hoop.

HANNAH: Basketball?

CHAN: Yes, yes—introduce that to our village. Then, there is Big Ear Tong—collects debt for C.Y.'s company. Never talks, only fight. Then, also, one who has been to America—Morty Fong. He all the time warns us about Communists. And, then, oh, maybe two or three others that I hardly ever meet.

HANNAH: This is all one guy?

CHAN: Mmmmm.

HANNAH: Isn't that somethin'?

CHAN: No.

HANNAH: Huh?

CHAN: Whatever you can tell me—man with six persons inside, man with three heads, man who sees a flying ghost, a sitting ghost, a ghost disguise to look like his dead wife—none of these are so unusual.

HANNAH: No?

CHAN: I have lived a long time.

HANNAH: Well, so have I, Mrs. Chan, so have I. And I'm still scared of Sandra Smith.

CHAN: Scare? Why scare? Happens all the time.

HANNAH: I don't want Sandra comin' round to any of my houses that I clean.

CHAN: Aaah—do not worry.

HANNAH: Whaddya mean? Sandra's got no respect for authority.

CHAN: Do not worry. She will not come into any house.

HANNAH: What makes you so sure?

CHAN: You have to know how ghosts think. You say, Sandra appears outdoors. Therefore, she is the outside ghost. She cannot come inside.

HANNAH: Yeah? They got rules like that? In ghost-land?

CHAN: Yes—there are rules everyplace! Have you ever been someplace where there were none?

HANNAH: Well, no, but—

CHAN: You see? Ghosts cannot kill a man if there is a goldfish in the room. They will think the fish is gold, and take it instead. They cannot enter a house if there is a raised step in the doorway. Ghosts do not look, so they trip over it instead.

HANNAH: These ghosts don't sound like they got a lot on the ball.

CHAN: Some ghosts, they are smart. But most ghosts, they are like most people. When alive, they were stupid. After death, they remain the same.

HANNAH: Well, I don't think Sandra's got much respect for those rules. That's probably why she showed up at Mrs. Washburn's.

CHAN: Inside the house?

HANNAH: 'Fraid so.

CHAN: Oh. Mrs. Washburn—does she have a goldfish?

HANNAH: No, no—I don't think so.

CHAN: There—you see?

HANNAH: Anyway, Mrs. Chan, I just thought I oughta tell you about her, on account of what happened to Mrs. Washburn. I been working for all you people ten, sometimes twenty years. All my clients—they're gettin' up there. We're all startin' to show our age. Can't compete with the young girls no more.

CHAN: I never try—even when I was one.

HANNAH: Well, the older I get, the more I see of Sandra, so I just thought I oughta be warnin' you.

CHAN: I am not afraid of Sandra Smith.

HANNAH: Well, good then. Good for you.

CHAN: She comes here, I will fight her. Not like these Americans. So stupid. Never think of these things. Never think of ghost. Never think of death. Never prepare for anything. Always think, life goes on and on, forever. And so, always, it ends.

HANNAH: Okay. Glad to hear it. Guess I'll go take the slime off the shower walls.

Hannah exits, into the house. Chan just stares downstage, from her chair. Silence. P.K. enters from the driveway, golf clubs slung over his shoulder.

P.K.: Hi, Popo!

CHAN: Hello.

P.K.: Do you have a beer?

CHAN: Look in 'frigerator.

P.K.: Just return from a good game of golf!

CHAN: Ah! What are you talking about?

P.K.: Eighteen holes, Popo!

CHAN: Ai! You cannot remember anything anymore!

P.K.: So? I remember that I go to golf!

CHAN: How can this be? You do not drive!

P.K.: What do you mean? I drive the Eldorado.

CHAN: You cannot drive the Eldorado.

P.K.: I do!

CHAN: Hanh! We sell it many years ago!

P.K.: What?

CHAN: Yes! Remember? We sell it! To John, your nephew.

P.K.: Huh? How much did he pay?

CHAN: Who cares?

P.K.: I want to know!

CHAN: I always tell you, John buys the car; you always ask me, how much does he pay?

P.K.: It is important! It is worth—lots of money!

CHAN: Ah, not so much money.

P.K.: No! Lots!

CHAN: Not after Humphrey breaks the back window by trying to lower top while driving.

P.K.: Yes! I tell Humphrey—cannot lower while driving. He says, "Of course! Can! This is a luxury car!" How come we sell the car?

CHAN: Ah! You cannot remember anything!

P.K.: No. Gung Gung cannot remember anything anymore.

CHAN: We sell, because you can no longer drive.

P.K.: I can! I can!

CHAN: You cannot pass the test.

P.K.: Can Humphrey pass the test?

CHAN: Of course! Of course, he passes it.

P.K.: How can? He is the one who lowers top while driving!

CHAN: Gung Gung! Because he is young, so he can pass the test!

P.K.: Young, but not so smart.

CHAN: Stupid.

P.K.: Sometimes, stupid.

CHAN: Stupid does not matter. Many stupid people drive.

    Pause.

P.K.: So I did not go to golf?

CHAN: No! How can you go to golf? You cannot go anyplace.

P.K. *(Points to clubs)*: Then, what are these?

CHAN: You just put them on your shoulder, then walk outside. Two hour later, you return.

P.K.: Where did I go?

CHAN: I don't know! You tell me!

P.K.: I cannot remember anything, anymore. I thought that I go to play eighteen-hole golf. But there is no golf course. So perhaps I walk into those hills. Maybe I shoot a few balls in the hills. Maybe I sink a putt into a gopher hole.

Pause.

CHAN: Gung Gung.

P.K.: Yes, Popo?

CHAN: I saw a ghost today.

P.K.: Popo! A ghost?

CHAN: Yes—a warning ghost.

P.K.: Which is this?

CHAN: They warn that another ghost will soon come. Bigger. More dangerous. Fatter.

P.K.: Oh! Popo! Why do they send this warning ghost?

CHAN: Because, they are stupid! This is how, they become dead to begin with. Because when they were living, they were too stupid to listen to the warning ghost!

P.K.: Popo! Will you die? *(He starts to cry)* What will Gung Gung do without you?

CHAN: No.

P.K.: Without Popo, I will be completely all lost.

CHAN: No, Gung Gung.

P.K.: I will walk around all day, not know where I am going, not know where I come from, only saying, "Popo? Where is Popo? Where is—?"

CHAN: No! Will you listen to me? You ask the question, then you will not listen to the answer! Talk, talk, talk! If I die, leave you alone, I would be lucky!

P.K.: You mean, you will not die?

CHAN: No, I will not die.

P.K.: How can this be?

CHAN: They are stupid enough to send the warning ghost. This is how I know, they will not defeat me.

P.K.: But, when the ghost come, no one can resist.

CHAN: Who says this?

P.K.: Ummm . . .

CHAN: See? Maybe, Gung Gung, *you* cannot resist.

P.K.: No. I cannot resist.

CHAN: But you have no responsibilities. I have. I have responsibility. I cannot leave you alone, Gung Gung. And also, I must watch the grandchildren grow to adults.

P.K.: Yes—this would be good.

CHAN: So, you see, I cannot die.

P.K.: This makes me so happy.

CHAN: I will defeat the ghost.

P.K.: Yes! Popo! You can do it! Popo is very smart!

CHAN: Yeah, yeah, yeah, we all know this already.

P.K.: I am fortunate to marry such a smart wife.

CHAN: Not smart. Smart is not enough.

P.K.: More than smart.

CHAN: Fight. Fight is more important. I am willing to fight. I like to fight.

Pause.

P.K.: Why do I carry these golf clubs?

CHAN: I do not know! You ask so many times already!

P.K.: Oh—I suppose—I must go to golf.

Pause.

CHAN: Yes—you must go to golf.

P.K.: Okay. I will leave now. Take the Eldorado. Bye, Popo.

CHAN: Bye, Gung Gung.

P.K.: You will have a cold can of beer in the 'frigerator, for when I return?

CHAN: I will, Gung Gung. I will.

P.K. starts to exit out the upstage door.

Gung Gung!

P.K.: Yes, Popo?

CHAN: Have a good game, okay, Gung Gung?

P.K.: I will have a good game, okay, Popo. *(He exits)*

CHAN: I arrive in America one day, June 16, 1976. Many times, I have come here before, to visit children, but on this day, I arrive to stay. All my friends, all the Chinese in the Philippine, they tell me, "We thought you are stupid when you send all your children to America. We even feel sorry for you, that you will grow old all alone—no family around you." This is what they tell me.

The day I arrive in America, I do not feel sorry. I do not miss the Philippine, I do not look forward live in America. Just like, I do not miss China, when I leave it many years ago—go live in Philippine. Just like, I do not miss Manila, when Japanese take our home during wartime, and we are all have to move to Baguio, and live in haunted house. It is all same to me. Go, one home to the next, one city to another, nation to nation, across ocean big and small.

We are born traveling. We travel—all our lives. I am not looking for a home. I know there is none. The day I was marry, my mother put many gold bracelets on my arm, and so many necklaces that the back of my head grows sore. "These," she tells me. "These are for the times when you will have to run."

The upstage door opens. Hannah is standing there, dressed as Sandra Smith.
Sandra wears a bright orange fright wig and a tight dress, sports huge sunglasses,
and swings a small purse.

SANDRA: Well, hello there! Howdy, howdy, howdy!

CHAN: Hi.

SANDRA: Say, you seen Hannah? Hannah Carter? I understand she works here on
Wednesdays.

CHAN: I think, she just leave.

SANDRA: Oh, well, that's a shame. I usually don't get to visit where she works. We
were supposed to go for dinner at Chicken on Fire, but, looks like we're just
not connecting. Damn! Always happens, whenever I try to meet her at one
of these houses.

CHAN: So, would you like to go home, now?

SANDRA: Mmmm. Guess I could, but I wouldn't mind enjoying some of your
hospitality.

CHAN: What is this, hospitality?

SANDRA: You know. What you show your guests.

CHAN: We do not have guests here! Only relatives, and, ah, servants.

SANDRA: Well, what do you do when someone comes over?

CHAN: They tell me what they want. Then, they leave.

SANDRA: No time to socialize?

CHAN: What is, socialize?

SANDRA: You know. You're not gonna offer me a tea, coffee, cake, Sanka?

CHAN: No.

SANDRA: I can't hardly believe this house.

CHAN: People—they are like cats. If you feed them, they will always return.

SANDRA: What ever happened to old-fashioned manners?

CHAN: My manners—they are very old. We act like this for centuries.

SANDRA: My name's Sandra. Sandra Smith.

CHAN: This is no surprise. Are you finish, now? Hannah is not here.

SANDRA: No—I can see that. *(Pause)* You know, I've known Hannah—well, ever since
she was a little girl. She wasn't very pretty. No one is Louisville paid much attention to her. Yeah, she's had five husbands and all, okay, that's true, but my
personal guess is that most of 'em married her because she was a hard-working
woman who could bring home the bacon week after week. Certain men will
hold their noses for a free lunch. Hannah thinks the same thing, though she
hardly ever talks about it. How can she think anything else when all five of
them left her as soon as they got a whiff of some girl with pipe cleaners for
legs? Hard for her to think she's much more than some mule, placed on this
earth to work her back. She spends most of her life wanderin' from one beautiful
house to the next, knowing intimately every detail, but never layin' down her
head in any of 'em. She's what they call a good woman. Men know it, rich

folks know it. Everyplace is beautiful, 'cept the place where she lives. Home is a dark room, she knows it well, knows its limits. She knows she can't travel nowhere without returnin' to that room once the sun goes down. Home is fixed, it does not move, even as the rest of the world circles 'round and 'round, picking up speed.

CHAN: You are a ghost.

SANDRA: I have a good time, if that's what you mean.

CHAN: I was warned that you would come.

SANDRA: By Hannah? She's always tellin' people about me. Like I was some kinda celebrity or somethin'.

CHAN: I fight ghosts. I chase them.

SANDRA: Can't chase anything, unless you get it runnin' from ya first.

CHAN: In Baguio, we live in a haunted house.

SANDRA: In where?

CHAN: Baguio. In the Philippine.

SANDRA: I never been there.

CHAN: During the war, we live in a haunted house. I chase the ghost out, with pots and pan. So, I know I can defeat them.

SANDRA: Hannah—she lives in a haunted house right now.

CHAN: Yes—haunted with you.

SANDRA: I show her how to make her life a little easier. Someone's gotta do it, after all her sixty-some-odd years. How 'bout you? Anything I can help you with?

CHAN: Ha! I do not need a thing!

SANDRA: I'm not sure if I believe that, Mrs. . . . Mrs. . . . whatever. Hannah sees you sittin' here, day after day—

CHAN: I am old! Of course I sit!

SANDRA: —starin' out into that garden—

CHAN: So?

SANDRA: First off, it's mostly dirt.

CHAN: This way, easier to take care of.

SANDRA: But you stare like there's somethin' out there.

CHAN: Yes! The sun is out there!

SANDRA: Lookin' at the sun, Mrs.—ma'am? Gotta be careful you don't burn your eyeballs out.

CHAN: I only look outside because—sky, clouds, sun—they are all there—interesting to watch.

SANDRA: Real pretty, huh?

CHAN: Yes. Sometimes pretty.

SANDRA: Looks like home.

CHAN: What is this? All the time, you talk about home, home, home?

SANDRA: Just like you do.

CHAN: I never talk about home. Barely talk at all.

SANDRA: You think, you keep your lips buttoned, that means all your secrets are safe inside? If they're strong enough, things make themselves known, one way or another. Hannah knows, she's not stupid. She'd never tell anyone but me. But me, I'd tell anybody. *(Pause)* Want me to tell you?

CHAN: Tell me what?

SANDRA: What you're lookin' at out there?

Pause.

CHAN: I can defeat you. I defeat ghost before.

SANDRA: Honey, it's not a fight no more. I've been around fifteen years. I already know you. You know me. We see the same thing. Out there. *(Pause)* There's a crow sitting on a window sill. And two kids who chase it down a steep ravine. Their path grows darker and darker, but the crow continues, and the kids don't tire, even when the blisters start to show on their feet. Mud, sleet, rain, and snow, all try to make the kids give up the chase. The crow caws—mountains fall in its wake, but still the children continue. And then it becomes dark, so dark, and the crow throws disasters at their feet. Floods, droughts, wars. The children see nothing, now. They follow the crow only by the catastrophes it leaves in its path. Where there is famine, the crow must have been. Where there are earthquakes, it has rested. They run on faith now, passing through territories uncharted, following the sound of their suffering. And it is in this way that they pass through their lives. Hardly noticing that they've entered. Without stopping to note its passing. Just following a crow, with single dedication, forgetting how they started, or why they're chasing, or even what may happen if they catch it. Running without pause or pleasure, past the point of their beginning.

Over the next section, Mrs. Chan's dress slowly rises into the air. She wears a white slip beneath. She stands up from the chair, for the first time in the play, and walks over to Sandra.

I see it in the distance.

CHAN: It is waiting for me.

SANDRA: I cannot stop my running.

CHAN: I cannot rest, even for a second.

SANDRA: There's a field out in the distance.

CHAN: There's a wooden gate in that field.

SANDRA: There is a crow sitting on that gate.

CHAN: It caws.

SANDRA: It caws.

CHAN: And disaster comes.

SANDRA: Once again.

CHAN: Nothing new.

SANDRA: Nothing blue.

CHAN: Only the scent of home.

SANDRA: I don't know why I follow it.

CHAN: I don't care to know.
SANDRA: Not now.
CHAN: Not here.
SANDRA: Not ever. Perhaps someday.
CHAN: Maybe to remember.
SANDRA: Why I run.
CHAN: Why I chase.
SANDRA: Until I am so—
CHAN: So tired.
SANDRA: Another disaster.
CHAN: Another lonely child.
SANDRA: We follow the scent of home.

Sandra removes her wig, glasses, tight dress. She too wears a white slip. She is Hannah again. Mrs. Chan moves towards the door. Hannah ever so slowly lowers herself into Mrs. Chan's chair. Hannah sits in it, beams.

HANNAH: Ooooh. Nice home, Mrs. Chan.
CHAN: I see it.
HANNAH: So do I, so do I.
CHAN: I see all the way past those mountains.
HANNAH: Welcome home, Mrs. Chan.
CHAN: Welcome home, Hannah.

Mrs. Chan exits through the garden. Hannah looks around her like a kid with a new toy. Upstage, P.K. enters with golf clubs. He cannot see Hannah in the chair.

P.K.: Hi, Popo! (Pause) Where is my beer?

Hannah closes her eyes, a smile on her face.

You leave a beer in the 'frigerator? (Pause) Popo? Popo?

P.K. is walking towards the chair as lights fade to black.

END OF PLAY

The Sound
of a Voice

About the Play

Part of a double bill called *Sound and Beauty*, *The Sound of a Voice* premiered at the Public Theater in 1983, under the direction of John Lone. It was published in *The Best Short Plays 1985*.

Characters

MAN, 50s, Japanese.
WOMAN (Hanako), 40s or 50s, Japanese.

Place

Woman's house, in a remote corner of a forest.

The Play

The Sound of a Voice

Scene 1

Evening. Woman warms tea for man. Man rubs himself, trying to get warm.

MAN: You are very kind to take me in.
WOMAN: This is a remote corner of the world. Guests are rare.
MAN: The tea—you pour it well.
WOMAN: No.
MAN: The sound it makes—in the cup—very soothing.
WOMAN: That is the tea's skill, not mine. *(She hands the cup to him)* May I get you
   something else? Rice, perhaps?
MAN: No.
WOMAN: And some vegetables?
MAN: No, thank you.
WOMAN: Fish? *(Pause)* It is at least two days walk to the nearest village. I saw no horse.
   You must be very hungry. You would do a great honor to dine with me. Guests
   are rare.
MAN: Thank you.

*Woman gets up, leaves. Man gets up, walks to kitchen door, listens. The room
is sparsely furnished, except for one shelf on which stands a vase of brightly colored flowers. The flowers stand out in sharp contrast to the starkness of the room.*

111

He crosses to the vase of flowers. He touches them. Quickly, he takes one of the flowers, hides it in his clothes. The woman reenters. She carries a tray with food.

WOMAN: Please. Eat. It will give me great pleasure.

MAN: This—this is magnificent.

WOMAN: Eat.

MAN: Thank you. *(He motions for the woman to join him)*

WOMAN: No, thank you.

MAN: This is wonderful. The best I've tasted.

WOMAN: You are reckless in your flattery, sir. But anything you say, I will enjoy hearing. It's not even the words. It's the sound of a voice, the way it moves through the air.

MAN: How long has it been since you last had a visitor?

Pause.

WOMAN: I don't know.

MAN: Oh?

WOMAN: I lose track. Perhaps five months ago, perhaps ten years, perhaps yesterday. I don't consider time when there is no voice in the air. It's pointless. Time begins with the entrance of a visitor, and ends with his exit.

MAN: And in between? You don't keep track of the days? You can't help but notice—

WOMAN: Of course I notice.

MAN: Oh.

WOMAN: I notice, but I don't keep track. *(Pause)* May I bring out more?

MAN: More? No. No. This was wonderful.

WOMAN: I have more.

MAN: Really—the best I've had.

WOMAN: You must be tired. Did you sleep in the forest last night?

MAN: Yes.

WOMAN: Or did you not sleep at all?

MAN: I slept.

WOMAN: Where?

MAN: By a waterfall. The sound of the water put me to sleep. It rumbled like the sounds of a city. You see, I can't sleep in too much silence. It scares me. It makes me feel that I have no control over what is about to happen.

WOMAN: I feel the same way.

MAN: But you live here—alone?

WOMAN: Yes.

MAN: It's so quiet here. How can you sleep?

WOMAN: Tonight, I'll sleep. I'll lie down in the next room, and hear your breathing through the wall, and fall asleep shamelessly. There will be no silence.

MAN: You're very kind to let me stay here.

WOMAN: This is yours. *(She unrolls a mat)*

MAN: Did you make it yourself?

WOMAN: Yes. There is a place to wash outside.

MAN: Thank you.

WOMAN: Good night.

MAN: Good night. *(He starts to leave)*

WOMAN: May I know your name?

MAN: No. I mean, I would rather not say. If I gave you a name, it would only be made up. Why should I deceive you? You are too kind for that.

WOMAN: Then what should I call you? Perhaps—"Man Who Fears Silence"?

MAN: How about, "Man Who Fears Women"?

WOMAN: That name is much too common.

MAN: And you?

WOMAN: Hanako.

MAN: That's your name?

WOMAN: It's what you may call me.

MAN: Good night, Hanako. You are very kind.

WOMAN: You are very smart. Good night.

Man exits. Woman picks up the dishes and teapot, returns them offstage to kitchen. She goes to the vase. She picks up the flowers, studies them. She carries them out of the room with her. Man reenters. He glimpses the spot where the vase used to sit. He listens at the various screens, then suddenly hears a sound. He prepares to draw his sword, then hears a shakuhachi (an end-blown bamboo flute). He sits on the mat, looks at the flower, puts it away. Then he sits on guard with his sword ready at his side.

Scene 2

Dawn. Man is packing. Woman enters with food.

WOMAN: Good morning.

MAN: Good morning, Hanako.

WOMAN: You weren't planning to leave?

MAN: I have quite a distance to travel today.

WOMAN: Please. *(She offers him food)*

MAN: Thank you.

WOMAN: May I ask where you're traveling to?

MAN: It's far.

WOMAN: I know this region well.

MAN: Oh? Do you leave the house often?

WOMAN: I used to. I used to travel a great deal. I know the region from those days.

MAN: You probably wouldn't know the place I'm headed.

WOMAN: Why not?

MAN: It's new. A new village. It didn't exist in "those days."

Pause.

WOMAN: I thought you said you wouldn't deceive me.

MAN: I didn't. You don't believe me, do you?

WOMAN: No.

MAN: Then I didn't deceive you, did I? I'm traveling. That much is true.

WOMAN: Are you in such a hurry?

MAN: Traveling is a matter of timing. Catching the light.

Woman exits. Man finishes eating, puts down his bowl. Woman reenters with the vase of flowers.

Where did you find those? They don't grow native around these parts, do they?

WOMAN: No, they've all been brought in by visitors. Such as yourself. They were left here. In my custody.

MAN: But—they look so fresh, so alive.

WOMAN: I take care of them. They remind me of the people and places outside this house.

MAN: May I touch them?

WOMAN: Certainly.

MAN: These have just blossomed.

WOMAN: No, they were in bloom yesterday. If you'd noticed them before, you would know that.

MAN: You must have received these very recently. I would guess—within five days.

WOMAN: I don't know. But I wouldn't trust your estimate. It's all in the amount of care you show to them. I create a world which is outside the realm of what you know.

MAN: What do you do?

WOMAN: I can't explain. Words are too inefficient. It takes hundreds of words to describe a single act of caring. With hundreds of acts, words become irrelevant. *(Pause)* But perhaps you can stay.

MAN: How long?

WOMAN: As long as you'd like.

MAN: Why?

WOMAN: To see how I care for them.

MAN: I *am* tired.

WOMAN: Rest.

MAN: The light?

WOMAN: It will return.

Day. Man is carrying chopped wood. He is stripped to the waist. Woman enters.

WOMAN: You're very kind to do that for me.

MAN: I enjoy it, you know. Chopping wood. It's clean. No questions. You take your ax, you stand up the log, you aim—pow!—you either hit it or you don't. Success or failure.

WOMAN: You seem to have been very successful today.

MAN: Why shouldn't I be? It's a beautiful day. I can see to those hills. The trees are cool. The sun is gentle. Ideal. If a man can't be successful on a day like this, he might as well kick the dust up into his own face.

Man notices woman staring at him. Man pats his belly, looks at her.

Protection from falls.

WOMAN: What?

Man touches his belly, showing some fat.

Oh. Don't be silly.

Man begins slapping the fat on his belly to a rhythm.

MAN: Listen—I can make music—see? That wasn't always possible. But now—that I've developed this—whenever I need entertainment . . . *(He continues slapping)*

WOMAN: You shouldn't make fun of your body.

MAN: Why not? I saw you. You were staring.

WOMAN: I wasn't making fun. I was just—stop that!

He stops.

MAN: Then why were you staring?

WOMAN: I was . . .

MAN: Laughing?

WOMAN: No.

MAN: Well?

WOMAN: I was—your body. It's . . . strong.

Pause.

MAN: People say that. But they don't know. I've heard that age brings wisdom. That's a laugh. The years don't accumulate here. They accumulate here. *(He pats his stomach)* But today is a day to be happy, right? The woods. The sun. Blue. It's a happy day. I'm going to chop wood.

WOMAN: There's nothing left to chop. Look.

MAN: Oh. I guess . . . that's it.

WOMAN: Sit. Here.

MAN: But . . .

WOMAN: There's nothing left. Learn to love it.

MAN: Don't be ridiculous.

WOMAN: Touch it.

MAN: It's flabby.

WOMAN: It's strong.

MAN: It's weak.

WOMAN: And smooth.

MAN: Do you mind if I put on my shirt?

WOMAN: Of course not. Shall I get it for you?

MAN: No. No. Just sit there. (*Picks up his shirt. He pauses, studies his body*) You think it's cute, huh?

WOMAN: I think you should learn to love it.

Man pats his belly.

MAN *(To belly)*: You're okay, sir. You hang onto my body like a great horseman.

WOMAN: Not like that.

MAN *(Still to belly)*: You're also faithful. You'll never leave me for another man.

WOMAN: No.

MAN: What do you want me to say?

Woman leans over to man. She touches his belly.

Scene 4

Night. Flowers are gone from stand. Man is alone, sleeping on the mat. Suddenly, he starts, awakened by the sound of the shakuhachi. He sits up and grabs his sword, then relaxes as he recognizes the instrument. He crosses to a screen and listens, then returns to the mat and sits. He takes out the stolen flower. He stares into it.

Scene 5

Day. Woman is cleaning while man exercises. She is on her hands and knees, scrubbing the floor.

MAN: I heard your playing last night.

WOMAN: My playing?

MAN: Shakuhachi.

WOMAN: Oh.

MAN: You played very softly. I had to strain to hear it. Next time don't be afraid. Play out. Fully. Clear. It must've been very beautiful, if only I could've heard it clearly. Why don't you play for me sometime?

WOMAN: I'm very shy about it.

MAN: Why?

WOMAN: I play for my own satisfaction. That's all. It's something I developed on my own. I don't know if it's at all acceptable by outside standards.

MAN: Play for me. I'll tell you.

WOMAN: No, I'm sure you're too knowledgeable in the arts.

MAN: Who? Me?

WOMAN: You being from the city and all.

MAN: I'm ignorant, believe me.

WOMAN: I'd play, and you'd probably bite your cheek.

MAN: Ask me a question about music. Any question. I'll answer incorrectly. I guarantee it.

WOMAN (*Looking at the floor*): Look at this.

MAN: What?

WOMAN: A stain.

MAN: Where?

WOMAN: Here? See? I can't get it out.

MAN: Oh. I hadn't noticed it before.

WOMAN: I notice it every time I clean.

MAN: Here. Let me try.

WOMAN: Thank you.

MAN: Ugh. It's tough.

WOMAN: I know.

MAN: How did it get here?

WOMAN: It's been there as long as I've lived here.

MAN: I hardly stand a chance. (*Pause*) But I'll try. One—two—three—four! One—two—three—four! See, you set up . . . gotta set up . . . a rhythm—two—three—four. Used to practice with a rhythm. One—two—three—four. Yes, remember. Like battle . . . like fighting, one—two—three—four. One—two—three—four. (*The stain starts to fade away*) Look . . . there it goes . . . got the sides . . . the edges . . . fading away . . . fading quick . . . towards the center to the heart . . . two—three—four. One—two—three—four—dead!

WOMAN: Dead.

MAN: I got it! I got it! A little rhythm! All it took! Four! Four!

WOMAN: Thank you.

MAN: I didn't think I could do it . . . but there—it's gone—I did it!

WOMAN: Yes. You did.

MAN: And you—you were great.

WOMAN: No—I just watched.

MAN: We were a team! You and me!

WOMAN: I only provided encouragement.

MAN: You were great! You were!

Man grabs woman. Pause.

WOMAN: It's gone. Thank you. Would you like to hear me play shakuhachi?

MAN: Yes I would.

WOMAN: I don't usually play for visitors. It's so . . . I'm not sure. I developed it—all by myself—in times when I was alone. I heard nothing . . . . The air began to be oppressive—stale. So I learned to play shakuhachi. I learned to make sounds on it. I tried to make these sounds resemble the human voice. The shakuhachi became my weapon. It kept me from choking on many a silent evening.

MAN: I'm here. You can hear my voice.

WOMAN: Speak again.

MAN: I will.

Scene 6

Night. Man is sleeping. He starts. He lifts his head up. He listens. The shakuhachi melody rises up once more. The time, however, it becomes louder and more clear than before. He gets up. He cannot tell from what direction the music is coming. It seems to come from all directions at once, as omnipresent as the air. Slowly, he moves toward the wall with the sliding panel through which the woman enters and exits. He puts his ear against it, thinking the music may be coming from there. He slides the door open just a crack, ever so carefully. He peeks through the crack. As he does, the upstage wall of the set becomes transparent, and through the scrim we are able to see what he sees. Woman is carrying the vase of flowers in front of her as she moves slowly through the cubicles upstage of the scrim. She is transformed. She is beautiful. She wears a brightly colored kimono. Man observes this scene for a long time. He then slides the door shut. The scrim returns to opaque. The music continues. He returns to his mat. He picks up the stolen flower. It is brown and wilted, dead. He looks at it, throws it down. The music slowly fades out.

Scene 7

Morning. Man is practicing sword maneuvers. He practices with the feel of a man whose spirit is willing but flesh is inept. He tries to execute deft movements but is dissatisfied with his efforts. Suddenly, he feels something buzzing around his neck—a mosquito. He slaps his neck, but misses it. He sees it flying near him. He swipes at it with his sword. He keeps missing. Finally, he thinks he's hit it. He runs over, kneels down to recover the fallen insect. He picks up the two halves of the mosquito on two different fingers. Woman enters the room. She looks as she normally does. She is carrying a vase of flowers, which she places on its shelf.

MAN: Look.

WOMAN: I'm sorry?

MAN: Look.

WOMAN: What?

He brings over the two halves of the mosquito to show her.

MAN: See?

WOMAN: Oh.

MAN: I hit it—chop!

WOMAN: These are new forms of target practice?

MAN: Huh? Well—yes—in a way.

WOMAN: You seem to do well at it.

MAN: Thank you. For last night. I heard your shakuhachi. It was very loud, strong—good tone.

WOMAN: Did you enjoy it? I wanted you to enjoy it. If you wish, I'll play it for you every night.

MAN: Every night!

WOMAN: If you wish.

MAN: No—I don't—I don't want you to treat me like a baby.

WOMAN: What? I'm not.

MAN: Oh, yes. Like a baby who you must feed in the middle of the night or he cries. Waaah! Waaah!

WOMAN: Stop that!

MAN: You need your sleep.

WOMAN: I don't mind getting up for you. (*Pause*) I would enjoy playing for you. Every night. While you sleep. It will make me feel . . . like I'm shaping your dreams. I go through long stretches when there is no one in my dreams. It's terrible. During those times, I avoid my bed as much as possible. I paint. I weave. I play shakuhachi. I sit on mats and rub powder into my face. Anything to keep from facing a bed with no dreams. It is like sleeping on ice.

MAN: What do you dream of now?

WOMAN: Last night—I dreamt of you. I don't remember what happened. But you were very funny. Not in a mocking way. I wasn't laughing at you. But you made me laugh. And you were very warm. I remember that. (*Pause*) What do you remember about last night?

MAN: Just your playing. That's all. I got up, listened to it, and went back to sleep. (*Gets up, resumes practicing with his sword*)

WOMAN: Another mosquito bothering you?

MAN: Just practicing. Ah! Weak! Too weak! I tell you, it wasn't always like this. I'm telling you, there were days when I could chop the fruit from a tree without ever taking my eyes off the ground. (*Continuing to practice with his sword*) You ever use one of these?

WOMAN: I've had to pick one up, yes.

MAN: Oh?

WOMAN: You forget . . . I live alone . . . out here . . . there is . . . not much to sustain me but what I manage to learn myself. It wasn't really a matter of choice.

MAN: I used to be very good, you know. Perhaps I can give you some pointers.

WOMAN: I'd really rather not.

MAN: C'mon—a woman like you—you're absolutely right. You need to know how to defend yourself.

WOMAN: As you wish.

MAN: Do you have something to practice with?

WOMAN: Yes. Excuse me. *(She exits. She reenters with two wooden sticks)* Will these do?

MAN: Fine. *(He takes one)* Nice. Now, show me what you can do.

WOMAN: I'm sorry?

MAN: Run up and hit me.

WOMAN: Please.

MAN: Go on—I'll block it.

WOMAN: I feel so . . . undignified.

MAN: Go on!

She taps him playfully.

Not like that! C'mon!

WOMAN: I'll try to be gentle.

MAN: What?

WOMAN: I don't want to hurt you.

MAN: You won't. Hit me!

Woman charges at man, quickly, deftly. She scores a hit.

WOMAN: Did I hurt you?

MAN: No—let's try that again.

They square off again. Woman rushes forward. Man blocks an apparent strike. She rushes in for another. She scores.

WOMAN: Did I hurt you? I'm sorry.

MAN: No.

WOMAN: I hurt you.

MAN: Don't be ridiculous!

WOMAN: Do you wish to hit me?

MAN: No.

WOMAN: Do you want me to try again?

MAN: No. Just practice there—by yourself—let me see you run through some maneuvers.

WOMAN: Must I?

MAN: Yes! Go!

Woman goes to an open area.

My greatest strength always was as a teacher.

Woman executes a series of movements. Her whole manner is transformed. Man watches with increasing amazement. Her movements end. She regains her submissive manner.

WOMAN: I'm so embarrassed. My skills—they're so—inappropriate. I look like a man.

MAN: Where did you learn that?

WOMAN: There is much time to practice here.

MAN: But you—the techniques . . .

WOMAN: I don't know what's fashionable in the outside world. *(Pause)* Are you unhappy?

MAN: No.

WOMAN: Really?

MAN: I'm just . . . surprised.

WOMAN: You think it's unbecoming for a woman.

MAN: No, no. Not at all.

WOMAN: You want to leave.

MAN: No!

WOMAN: All visitors do. I know. I've met many. They say they'll stay. And they do. For a while. Until they see too much. Or they learn something new. There are boundaries outside of which visitors do not want to see me step. Only who knows what those boundaries are? Not I. They change with every visitor. You have to be careful not to cross them, but you never know where they are. And one day, inevitably, you step outside the lines. The visitor knows. You don't. You didn't know that you'd done anything different. You thought it was just another part of you. The visitor sneaks away. The next day, you learn that you had stepped outside his heart. I'm afraid you've seen too much.

MAN: There are stories.

WOMAN: What?

MAN: People talk.

WOMAN: Where? We're two days from the nearest village.

MAN: Word travels.

WOMAN: What are you talking about?

MAN: There are stories about you. I heard them. They say that your visitors never leave this house.

WOMAN: That's what you heard?

MAN: They say you imprison them.

WOMAN: Then you were a fool to come here.

MAN: Listen.

WOMAN: Me? Listen? You. Look! Where are these prisoners? Have you seen any?

MAN: They told me you were very beautiful.

WOMAN: Then they are blind as well as ignorant.

MAN: You are.

WOMAN: What?

MAN: Beautiful.

WOMAN: Stop that! My skin feels like seaweed.

MAN: I didn't realize it at first. I must confess. I didn't. But over these few days— your face has changed for me. The shape of it. The feel of it. The color. All changed. I look at you now and I am no longer sure you are the same woman who had poured tea for me just a week ago. And because of that I remember—how little I know about a face that changes in the night. *(Pause)* Have you heard those stories?

WOMAN: I don't listen to old wives' tales.

MAN: But have you heard them?

WOMAN: Yes. I've heard them. From other visitors—young—hot-blooded—or old—who came here because they were told great glory was to be had by killing the witch in the woods.

MAN: I was told that no man could spend time in this house without falling in love.

WOMAN: Oh? So why did you come? Did you wager gold that you could come out untouched? The outside world is so flattering to me. And you—are you like the rest? Passion passing through your heart so powerfully that you can't hold on to it?

MAN: No! I'm afraid!

WOMAN: Of what?

MAN: Sometimes—when I look into the flowers, I think I hear a voice—from inside—a voice beneath the petals. A human voice.

WOMAN: What does it say? "Let me out"?

MAN: No. Listen. It hums. It hums with the peacefulness of one who is completely imprisoned.

WOMAN: I understand that if you listen closely enough, you can hear the ocean.

MAN: No. Wait. Look at it. See the layers? Each petal—hiding the next. Try and see where they end . . . . You can't. Follow them down, further down, around and as you come down—faster and faster—the breeze picks up. The breeze becomes a wail. And in that rush of air—you can hear a voice.

Woman grabs flower from man.

WOMAN: So, you believe I water and prune my lovers? How can you be so foolish? *(She throws the flower to the ground)* Do you come only to leave again? To take a chunk of my heart, then leave with your booty on your belt, like a prize? You say that I imprison hearts in these flowers? Well, bits of my heart are trapped with travelers across this land. I can't even keep track. So kill me. If you came here to destroy a witch, kill me now. I can't stand to have it happen again.

Man begins to pull out sword—cannot use it.

MAN: I won't leave you.

WOMAN: I believe you.

Scene 8

Day. Woman is modeling her kimono.

WOMAN: Do you like it?

MAN: Yes, it's beautiful.

WOMAN: I wanted to wear something special today.

MAN: It's beautiful. *(He takes out his sword)* Excuse me. I must practice.

WOMAN: Shall I get you something?

MAN: No.

WOMAN: Some tea, maybe?

MAN: No, thank you. *(He resumes swordplay)*

WOMAN: Perhaps later today—perhaps we can go out—just around here. We can look for flowers.

MAN: All right.

WOMAN: We don't have to.

MAN: No. Let's.

WOMAN: I just thought if . . .

MAN: Fine. Where do you want to go?

WOMAN: There are very few recreational activities around here, I know.

MAN: All right. We'll go this afternoon.

Pause.

WOMAN: Can I get you something?

MAN: What?

WOMAN: You might be . . .

MAN: I'm not hungry or thirsty or cold or hot.

WOMAN: Then what are you?

MAN: Practicing.

Man resumes practicing; woman exits. Man sits down. He examines his sword, thinks. He stands up. He places the sword on the ground with the tip pointed directly upward. He keeps it from falling by placing the tip under his chin. He experiments with different degrees of pressure. Woman reenters. She sees him in this precarious position.

WOMAN: Don't do that!

MAN: What?

WOMAN: You can hurt yourself!

MAN: I was practicing!

WOMAN: You were playing!

MAN: I was practicing!

WOMAN: It's dangerous.

MAN: What do you take me for—a child?

WOMAN: Sometimes wise men do childish things.

MAN: I knew what I was doing!

WOMAN: It scares me.

MAN: Don't be ridiculous.

WOMAN: Don't! Don't do that!

MAN: Get back!

WOMAN: But . . .

MAN: Sssssh!

WOMAN: I wish . . .

MAN: Listen to me! The slightest shock, you know—the slightest shock—surprise—it might make me jerk or—something—and then . . . . So you must be perfectly still and quiet.

WOMAN: But I . . .

MAN: Sssssh! *(Silence)* I learned this exercise from a friend—I can't even remember his name—good swordsman—many years ago. He called it his meditation position. He said, like this, he could feel the line between this world and the others because he rested on it. If he saw something in another world that he liked better, all he would have to do is let his head drop, and he'd be there. Simple. No fuss. One day, they found him with the tip of his sword run clean out the back of his neck. He was smiling. I guess he saw something he liked. Or else he'd fallen asleep.

WOMAN: Stop that.

MAN: Stop what?

WOMAN: Tormenting me.

MAN: I'm not.

WOMAN: Take it away!

MAN: You don't have to watch, you know.

WOMAN: Do you want to die that way—an accident?

MAN: I was doing this before you came in.

WOMAN: If you do, all you need to do is tell me.

MAN: What?

WOMAN: I can walk right over. Lean on the back of your head.

MAN: Don't try to threaten—

WOMAN: Or jerk your sword up.

MAN: —or scare me. You can't threaten . . .

WOMAN: I'm not. But if that's what you want.

MAN: You wouldn't do it.

WOMAN: Oh?

MAN: Then I'd be gone. You wouldn't let me leave that easily.

WOMAN: Yes I would.

MAN: You'd be alone.

WOMAN: No. I'd follow you. Forever. *(Pause)* Now let's stop this nonsense.

MAN: No! I can do what I want! Don't come any closer!

WOMAN: Then release your sword.

MAN: Come any closer and I'll drop my head.

Woman slowly approaches man. She grabs the sword. She pulls it out from under his chin.

WOMAN: There will be no more of this.

She exits with the sword. Man starts to follow her, then stops. He touches under his chin. On his finger, he finds a drop of blood.

Scene 9

Night. Man is leaving the house. He is just about out when he hears the shakuhachi. Woman appears in the doorway to the outside.

WOMAN: It's time for you to go?

MAN: Yes. I'm sorry.

WOMAN: You're just going to sneak out? A thief in the night? A frightened child?

MAN: I care about you.

WOMAN: You express it strangely.

MAN: I leave in shame because it is proper. *(Pause)* I came seeking glory.

WOMAN: To kill me? You can say it. You'll be surprised at how little I blanch. As if you'd said, "I came for a bowl of rice," or "I came seeking love," or "I came to kill you."

MAN: Weakness. All weakness. Too weak to kill you. Too weak to kill myself. Too weak to do anything but sneak away in shame.

Woman brings out man's sword.

WOMAN: Were you even planning to leave without this?

He takes sword.

Why not stay here?

MAN: I can't live with someone who's defeated me.

WOMAN: I never thought of defeating you. I only wanted to take care of you. To make you happy. Because that made me happy and I was no longer alone.

MAN: You defeated me.

WOMAN: Why do you think that way?

MAN: I came here with a purpose. The world was clear. You changed the shape of your face, the shape of my heart—rearranged everything—created a world where I could do nothing.

WOMAN: I only tried to care for you.

MAN: I guess that was all it took.

Pause.

WOMAN: You still think I'm a witch. Just because old women gossip. You are so cruel. Once you arrived, there were only two possibilities: I would die or you would leave. *(Pause)* If you believe I'm a witch, then kill me. Rid the province of one more evil.

MAN: I can't—

WOMAN: Why not? If you believe that about me, then it's the right thing to do.

MAN: You know I can't.

WOMAN: Then stay.

MAN: Don't try to force me!

WOMAN: I won't force you to do anything. (*Pause*) All I wanted was an escape—for both of us. The sound of a human voice—the simplest thing to find, and the hardest to hold on to. This house—my loneliness is etched into the walls. Kill me, but don't leave. Even in death, my spirit would rest here and be comforted by your presence.

MAN: Force me to stay.

WOMAN: I won't.

Man starts to leave.

Beware.

MAN: Of what?

WOMAN: The ground on which you walk is weak. It could give way at any moment. The crevice beneath is dark.

MAN: Are you talking about death? I'm ready to die.

WOMAN: Fear for what is worse than death.

MAN: What?

WOMAN: Falling. Falling through the darkness. Waiting to hit the ground. Picking up speed. Waiting for the ground. Falling faster. Falling alone. Waiting. Falling. Waiting. Falling.

Man leaves. Woman goes out through the door to her room. Man reenters. He looks for her in the main room. He goes to the mat, sees the shakuhachi. He puts down his sword, takes off his bundle and coat. He goes into her room. He comes out. He goes to the mat, picks up the shakuhachi, clutches it to him. He moves everything else off the mat, sits, and puts the shakuhachi to his mouth. He begins to blow into it. He tries to make sounds.

The upstage scrim lights up. We see the woman. She has hung herself with a rope suspended from the roof. Around her swirl the thousands of petals from the flowers. They fill the upstage area like a blizzard of color.

Man continues to attempt to play. Lights fade to black.

END OF PLAY

And the Soul
Shall Dance

Wakako Yamauchi

Wakako Yamauchi

I was born in California during the latter part of the Depression. I'm a farm kid from the Imperial Valley, like the girl in *And the Soul Shall Dance.*

My parents are from Japan, and we lived in a community that was largely Japanese. On weekends we went to a Japanese Buddhist church and spoke Japanese, then during the week I went to an American school and studied the three Rs. It was hard when I went into the first grade because I didn't know any English.

There weren't many neighbors around us, and the ones we had were a half mile away. I did a lot of reading as a child because we were isolated. My father couldn't resist those people who came around selling magazines, and he also bought a series of large volumes called the Book of Knowledge.

Like all children my ambitions changed from year to year. I wanted to write, I wanted to paint. But those things were almost unattainable for minorities at that time. I suppose my parents thought I'd be like other Nisei, the children of Issei (Japanese-born Americans). They would go to high school and work in the fruit stands, or if they became professionals they would service the Japanese community as doctors or accountants.

If I were realistic I probably would have planned on marrying a farmer, working on the farm, raising a family in the Valley. It was very important for Depression kids to do something practical, something to make a living. Art is the lowest-paid and most difficult profession in any society, and so not many of us thought about it seriously. And there was so much prejudice against Japanese Americans, even before the war. You just tried to live quietly, and not call attention to yourself.

128

Wakako Yamauchi

My education came to a halt with World War II. At the time we had a boardinghouse in Oceanside, a town just north of San Diego. My father had suffered an enormous loss when his last lettuce crop failed. In Oceanside he did some day work for other farmers while my mother got the boardinghouse going. We had to buy all the beds and linens and dishes to get started—it was very expensive. When the war broke out we were just coming out of debt. Then we lost everything.

I didn't quite graduate from high school because we were sent, like all other Japanese Americans, to internment camp. We went to the Camp in Poston, Arizona in 1941, when I was 17. It was a terrible place. You couldn't run away from it because you'd die in the desert—*if* you escaped the bullets from the sentries. How did living there affect me? When you're young, you're resilient. You just have to go on with your life.

But I felt very bitter there, and very closed in. It was so bad that I tried very hard to get transferred out. I went on a work leave for about a year to Salt Lake City, then came back to Camp, and I got out again to work in Chicago.

Then, just as the war was ending, I found out my father was dying, so I had to go back to Camp. By the time I returned he had already died. It was very strange. It was around the time the Camps were closing and I couldn't get a lift from the guard post, which was quite a long way from our barracks. I was walking along the road and I heard some people talking, and that's how I figured out my father must

be dead. He died of bleeding ulcers, right after Hiroshima was bombed. I think he just didn't want to start over again.

My mother and two sisters and I were in one of the last groups to leave Camp. We didn't know where to go, so we went to San Diego and lived there for a while. Then I went up to Los Angeles to attend art school.

I didn't start writing until many years later. I never intended to become a writer. I was trying to be an artist, and I thought I could at least get a job in a commercial art studio doing layout, design, something like that.

Later I got married, dropped everything, and had a little girl. When she grew up I decided to take a correspondence course in short-story writing from UC Berkeley. That's when I learned a little bit about character, point of view, and other basics.

The first version of *And the Soul Shall Dance* was a short story, one of the first stories I wrote. I couldn't sell it to white magazines, but in 1974 four young men up in San Francisco put together an anthology of Asian-American writers. They selected *Soul* for the book, and when it came out Mako, the artistic director of East West Players, contacted me. He wanted me to turn it into a play.

I had never written a play, but at the time I was going through a divorce and felt I wanted to really put my heart into something. Then I broke my leg, and had to stay in bed. So I sent my daughter out for some books on playwriting and that's when I started to write the script for *Soul*. Though I rewrote it about six times, it wasn't that hard to do.

The play is based on a memory, but I embellished it. Like Masako and her family, we had a childless couple as neighbors, and they were always drinking and carousing. Our farm was so isolated that sometimes you could hear the neighbors talking and laughing across the fields.

I didn't consciously decide I was going to write the play from the point of view of the women. But my mother was a feminist in her time, and she always made me feel that I was somebody. Japanese men were very chauvinistic, especially in those days, but women had a way of adapting things, of handling the men. That's one of the things I wanted to show, that feeling we had: "You can step on us, but you haven't got us yet!"

I think that if you want to touch people you have to make them care about your characters. I guess, somehow or another, I did that in this play. When I think about it now, I know the character of Emiko, the unhappy wife, isn't very well drawn. But I guess she must touch an experience that many people have had, the experience of being where you don't want to be.

Soul premiered at East West Players in 1977, codirected by Mako and Alberto Isaac. I was very surprised that my very first play was so successful. It really opened up a lot of doors for me. I've had more plays produced, and some of my early stories, the same ones rejected by white magazines, have been published in college texts. I think there's more interest in the Asian-American experience, but I still don't think it's broken open. There are some people like Philip Gotanda and David Hwang who've broken the barrier and gone into mainstream theatres, but it still isn't that easy. It isn't that easy for any playwright.

I can only write what I feel. *And the Soul Shall Dance* comes out of a feeling. It comes out of looking back and wondering "What happened then?" and coming to my own conclusions.

Biographical Information

Wakako Yamauchi is the author of ten plays and the recipient of four Rockefeller Foundation playwriting grants. Her works for the stage include *The Music Lesson* (premiered at the Public Theater in 1980), *12-1-A* (first produced at Asian American

Theatre in 1982), and *The Memento* (originally seen at the Pan Asian Repertory Theatre in 1984). Her new play *The Chairman's Wife* is scheduled for production by both East West Players and Pan Asian Rep in 1990.

A prose writer also, Yamauchi's short stories and plays have been collected in numerous anthologies and textbooks, among them *Worlds of Literature* (W.W. Norton, 1989) and *Minority Women Writers* (Houghton Mifflin, 1979).

She lives in Gardena, California.

About the Play

Originally a short story published in 1974, *And the Soul Shall Dance* received its first professional production in Los Angeles in 1977 by the East West Players, under the codirection of Mako and Alberto Isaac. It has since been seen at Pan Asian Repertory Theatre, Asian American Theatre, Cal State Asian American Theatre, Kaui Community Theatre and University of Hawaii. The play was published by *West Coast Plays* in 1982.

A ninety-minute version produced by Hollywood Television Theatre aired over the Public Broadcasting System in 1978. It was shown again in 1987, on cable television's Arts & Entertainment channel.

Characters

MURATA, 40, Issei farmer.
HANA, Issei wife of Murata.
MASAKO, 11, Nisei daughter of the Muratas.
OKA, 45, Issei farmer.
EMIKO, 30, wife of Oka.
KIYOKO, 14, Oka's daughter.

Time and Place

The play takes place on and between two small farms in Southern California's Imperial Valley in the early 1930s.

And the Soul Shall Dance

ACT ONE

Scene 1

Interior of the Murata house, afternoon. The set is spare. There is a kitchen table, four chairs, a bed, and on the wall, a calendar indicating the year and month: June, 1935. There is a doorway leading to the other room. Props are: a bottle of sake, two cups, a dish of chiles, a phonograph, and two towels hanging on pegs on the wall. A wide wooden bench sits outside.

The bathhouse has just burned to the ground due to the carelessness of Masako, Nisei daughter, eleven. Offstage there are sounds of Murata, forty, Issei farmer, putting out the fire.

Inside the house Hana Murata, Issei wife, in a drab house dress, confronts Masako, who is wearing a summer dress of the era. Masako is sullen and somewhat defiant. Hana breaks the silence.

HANA: How could you be so careless, Masako? You know you should be extra careful with fire. How often have I told you? Now the whole bathhouse is gone. I told you time and again, when you stoke a fire, you should see that everything is swept into the fireplace.

Murata enters. He's dressed in old work clothes. He suffers from heat and exhaustion.

133

MURATA (*Coughing*): Shack went up like a matchbox. . . . This kind of weather dries everything . . . just takes a spark to make a bonfire out of dry timber.

HANA: Did you save any of it?

MURATA: No. Couldn't . . .

HANA (*To Masako*): How many times have I told you . . .

Masako moves nervously.

MURATA: No use crying about it now. *Shikata ga nai.* It's gone now. No more bathhouse. That's all there is to it.

HANA: But you've got to tell her. Otherwise she'll make the same mistake. You'll be building a bathhouse every year.

Murata removes his shirt and wipes off his face. He throws his shirt on a chair and sits at the table.

MURATA: *Baka!* Ridiculous!

MASAKO: I didn't do it on purpose. (*She goes to the bed, opens a book*)

HANA (*Follows Masako*): I know that but you know what this means? It means we bathe in a bucket . . . inside the house. Carry water in from the pond, heat it on the stove. . . . We'll use more kerosene.

MURATA: Tub's still there. And the fireplace. We can still build a fire under the tub.

HANA (*Shocked*): But no walls! Everyone in the country can see us!

MURATA: Wait till dark then. Wait till dark.

HANA: We'll be using a lantern. They'll still see us.

MURATA: Angh! Who? Who'll see us? You think everyone in the country waits to watch us take a bath? Hunh! You know how stupid you sound? Ridiculous!

HANA (*Defensively*): It'll be inconvenient.

Hana is saved by a rap on the door. Oka, Issei neighbor, forty-five, enters. He is short and stout, dressed in faded work clothes.

OKA: Hello! Hello! Oi! What's going on here? Hey! Was there some kind of fire?

Hana rushes to the door to let Oka in. He stamps the dust from his shoes and enters.

HANA: Oka-san! You just wouldn't believe . . . . We had a terrible thing happen.

OKA: Yeah. Saw the smoke from down the road. Thought it was your house. Came rushing over. Is the fire out?

Murata half rises and sits back again. He's exhausted.

MURATA (*Gesturing*): Oi, oi. Come in . . . sit down. No big problem. It was just our bathhouse.

OKA: Just the *furoba*, eh?

MURATA: Just the bath.

HANA: Our Masako was careless and the *furoba* caught fire. There's nothing left of it but the tub.

Masako looks up from her book, pained. She makes a very small sound.

OKA: Long as the tub's there, no problem. I'll help you with it. *(He starts to roll up his sleeves. Murata looks at him)*

MURATA: What . . . now? Now?

OKA: Long as I'm here.

HANA: Oh, Papa. Aren't we lucky to have such friends?

MURATA *(To Hana)*: Hell, we can't work on it now. The ashes are still hot. I just now put the damned fire out. Let me rest awhile. *(To Oka)* Oi, how about a little sake? *(Gesturing to Hana)* Make sake for Oka-san.

Oka sits at the table. Hana goes to prepare the sake. She heats it, gets out the cups and pours it for the men.

I'm tired . . . I am *tired.*

HANA: Oka-san has so generously offered his help . . .

Oka is uncomfortable. He looks around and sees Masako sitting on the bed.

OKA: Hello, there, Masako-chan. You studying?

MASAKO: No, it's summer vacation.

MURATA *(Sucking in his breath)*: Kids nowadays . . . no manners . . .

HANA: She's sulking because I had to scold her.

Masako makes a small moan.

MURATA: Drink Oka-san.

OKA *(Swallowing)*: Ahhh, that's good.

MURATA: Eh, you not working today?

OKA: No . . . no . . . I took the afternoon off today. I was driving over to Nagatas' when I saw this big black cloud of smoke coming from your yard.

HANA: It went up so fast . . .

MURATA: What's up at Nagatas'? *(To Hana)* Get the chiles out. Oka-san loves chiles.

Hana opens a jar of chiles and puts them on a plate. She serves the men and gets her mending basket and walks to Masako. Masako makes room for her on the bed.

OKA *(Helping himself)*: Ah, chiles. *(Murata looks at him, the question unanswered)* Well, I want to see him about my horse. I'm thinking of selling my horse.

MURATA: Sell your horse!

OKA *(Scratches his head)*: The fact is, I need some money. Nagata-san's the only one around made money this year, and I'm thinking he might want another horse.

MURATA: Yeah, he made a little this year. And he's talking big . . . big! Says he's leasing twenty more acres this fall.

OKA: Twenty acres?

MURATA: Yeah. He might want another horse.

OKA: Twenty acres, eh?

MURATA: That's what he says. But you know his old woman makes all the decisions.

Oka scratches his head.

HANA: They're doing all right.

MURATA: Henh. Nagata-kun's so hen-pecked, it's pathetic. *Peko-peko. (He makes motions of a hen pecking)*

OKA *(Feeling the strain)*: I better get over there.

MURATA: Why the hell you selling your horse?

OKA: I need cash.

MURATA: Oh, yeah. I could use some too. Seems like everyone's getting out of the depression but the poor farmers. Nothing changes for us. We go on and on planting our tomatoes and summer squash and eating them. . . . Well, at least it's healthy.

HANA: Papa, do you have lumber?

MURATA: Lumber? For what?

HANA: The bath.

MURATA *(Impatiently)*: Don't worry about that. We need more sake now.

Hana rises to serve him.

OKA: You sure Nagata-kun's working twenty more acres?

MURATA: Last I heard. What the hell; if you need a few bucks, I can loan you . . .

OKA: A few hundred. I need a few hundred dollars.

MURATA: Oh, a few hundred. But what the hell you going to do without a horse? Out here a man's horse is as important as his wife.

OKA *(Seriously)*: I don't think Nagata will buy my wife.

The men laugh, but Hana doesn't find it so funny. Murata glances at her. She fills the cups again. Oka makes a half-hearted gesture to stop her. Masako watches the pantomime carefully. Oka swallows his drink in one gulp.

I better get moving.

MURATA: What's the big hurry?

OKA: Like to get the horse business done.

MURATA: Ehhhh . . . relax. Do it tomorrow. He's not going to die, is he?

OKA *(Laughing)*: Hey, he's a good horse. I want to get it settled today. If Nagata-kun won't buy, I got to find someone else. You think maybe Kawaguchi . . . ?

MURATA: Not Kawaguchi . . . . Maybe Yamamoto.

HANA: What is all the money for, Oka-san? Does Emiko-san need an operation?

OKA: Nothing like that . . .

HANA: Sounds very mysterious.

OKA: No mystery, Mrs. No mystery. No sale, no money, no story.

MURATA *(Laughing)*: That's a good one. "No sale, no money, no . . . . " Eh, Mama.

He points to the empty cups. Hana fills the cups and goes back to Masako.

HANA *(Muttering)*: I see we won't be getting any work done today. *(To Masako)* Are you reading again? Maybe we'd still have a bath if you—

MASAKO: I didn't do it on purpose.

MURATA *(Loudly)*: I sure hope you know what you're doing, Oka-kun. What'd you do without a horse?

OKA: I was hoping you'd lend me yours now and then . . . *(He looks at Hana)* I'll pay for some of the feed.

MURATA *(Emphatically waving his hand)*: Sure! Sure!

OKA: The fact is, I need that money. I got a daughter in Japan and I just got to send for her this year.

Coming to life, Hana puts down her mending and sits at the table.

HANA: A daughter? You have a daughter in Japan? Why, I didn't know you had children. Emiko-san and you . . . I thought you were childless.

OKA *(Scratching his head)*: We are. I was married before.

MURATA: You son-of-a-gun!

HANA: Is that so? How old is your daughter?

OKA: Kiyoko must be . . . fifteen now. Yeah, fifteen.

HANA: Fifteen! Oh, that *would* be too old for Emiko-san's child. Is Kiyoko-san living with relatives in Japan?

OKA *(Reluctantly)*: Yeah, with grandparents. With Shizue's parents. Well, the fact is, Shizue, that's my first wife, and Emiko were sisters. They come from a family with no sons. I was a boy when I went to work for the family . . . as an apprentice . . . they're blacksmiths. Later I married Shizue and took on the family name—you know, *yoshi*—because they had no sons. My real name is Sakakihara.

MURATA: Sakakihara! That's a great name!

HANA: A magnificent name!

OKA: No one knows me by that here.

MURATA: Should have kept that . . . Sakakihara.

OKA *(Muttering)*: I don't even know myself by that name.

HANA: And Shizue-san passed away and you married Emiko-san?

OKA: Oh, yeah. Well, Shizue and I lived with the family for a while and we had the baby . . . that's, you know, Kiyoko . . . . *(The liquor has affected him and he's become less inhibited)* Well, while I was serving apprentice with the family, they always looked down their noses at me. After I married, it got worse. . . . That old man . . . angh! He was terrible! Always pushing me around, making me look bad in front of my wife and kid. That old man was mean . . . ugly!

MURATA: Yeah, I heard about that apprentice work—*detchi-boko*. . . . Heard it was damned humiliating.

OKA: That's the God's truth!

MURATA: Never had to do it myself. I came to America instead. They say *detchi-boko* is bloody hard work.

OKA: The work's all right. I'm not afraid of work. It's the humiliation! I hated them! Pushing me around like I was still a boy. . . . Me, a grown man! And married to their daughter! *(Murata groans in sympathy)* Well, Shizue and I talked it over and we decided the best thing was to get away. We thought if I came to America and made some money . . . you know, send her money until we had enough, I'd go back and we'd leave the family . . . you know, move to another province . . . start a small business, maybe in the city, a noodle shop or something.

MURATA: That's everyone's dream. Make money, go home and live like a king.

OKA: I worked like a dog. Sent every penny to Shizue. And then she died. She died on me!

Hana and Murata observe a moment of silence in respect for Oka's anguish.

HANA: And you married Emiko-san.

OKA: I didn't marry her. They married her to me! Right after Shizue died.

HANA: But Oka-san, you were lucky . . .

OKA: Before the body was cold! No respect! By proxy. The old man wrote me they were arranging a marriage by proxy for me and Emiko. They said she'd grown to be a beautiful woman and would serve me well.

HANA: Emiko-san *is* a beautiful woman.

OKA: And they sent her to me. Took care of everything! Immigration, fare, everything.

HANA: But she's your sister-in-law—Kiyoko's aunt. It's good to keep the family together.

OKA: That's what I thought. But hear this: Emiko was the favored one. Shizue was not so pretty, not so smart. They were grooming Emiko for a rich man—his name was Yamoto—lived in a grand house in the village. They sent her to schools, you know, the culture thing: tea ceremony, you know, all that. They didn't even like me, and suddenly they married her to me.

MURATA: Yeah. You don't need all that formal training to make it over here. Just a strong back.

HANA: And a strong will.

OKA: It was all arranged. I couldn't do anything about it.

HANA: It'll be all right. With Kiyoko coming . . .

OKA *(Dubiously)*: I hope so . . . I never knew human beings could be so cruel. You know how they mistreated my daughter? You know after Emiko came over, things got from bad to worse and I *never* had enough money to send to Kiyoko.

MURATA: They don't know what it's like here. They think money's picked off the ground here.

OKA: And they treated Kiyoko so bad. They told her I forgot about her. They told her I didn't care—they said I abandoned her. Well, she knew better. She wrote to me all the time and I always told her I'd send for her . . . soon as I got the money. *(He shakes his head)* I just got to do something this year.

HANA: She'll be happier here. She'll know her father cares.

OKA: Kids tormented her for not having parents.

MURATA: Kids are cruel.

HANA: Masako will help her. She'll help her get started at school. She'll make friends . . . she'll be all right.

OKA: I hope so. She'll need friends. *(He considers he might be making a mistake after all)* What could I say to her? Stay there? It's not what you think over here? I can't help her? I just have to do this thing. I just have to do this one thing for her.

MURATA: Sure . . .

HANA: Don't worry. It'll work out fine.

Murata gestures to Hana. She fills the cups.

MURATA: You talk about selling your horse, I thought you were pulling out.

OKA: I wish I could. But there's nothing else I can do.

MURATA: Without money, yeah . . .

OKA: You can go into some kind of business with money, but a man like me . . . no education . . . there's no kind of job I can do. I'd starve in the city.

MURATA: Dishwashing, maybe. Janitor . . .

OKA: At least here we can eat. Carrots, maybe, but we can eat.

MURATA: All the carrots we been eating 'bout to turn me into a rabbit.

They laugh. Hana starts to pour more wine for Oka but he stops her.

OKA: I better not drink any more. Got to drive to Nagata-san's yet. *(He rises and walks over to Masako)* You study hard, don't you? You'll teach Kiyoko English, eh? When she gets here . . .

HANA: Oh, yes. She will.

MURATA: Kiyoko-san could probably teach her a thing or two.

OKA: She won't know about American ways . . .

MASAKO: I'll help her.

HANA: Don't worry, Oka-san. She'll have a good friend in our Masako.

They move toward the door.

OKA: Well, thanks for the sake. I guess I talk too much when I drink. *(He scratches his head and laughs)* Oh. I'm sorry about the fire. By the way, come to my house for your bath . . . until you build yours again.

HANA *(Hesitantly)*: Oh, uh . . . thank you. I don't know if . . .

MURATA: Good! Good! Thanks a lot. I need a good hot bath tonight.

OKA: Tonight, then.

MURATA: We'll be there.

HANA *(Bowing)*: Thank you very much. Sayonara.

OKA *(Nodding)*: See you tonight.

Oka leaves. Hana faces her husband as soon as the door closes.

HANA: Papa, I don't know about going over there.

MURATA *(Surprised)*: Why?

HANA: Well, Emiko-san . . .

MURATA *(Irritated)*: What's the matter with you? We need a bath and Oka's invited us over.

HANA *(To Masako)*: Help me clear the table.

Masako reluctantly leaves her book and begins to clear the table.

Papa, you know we've been neighbors already three, four years and Emiko-san's never been very hospitable.

MURATA: She's shy, that's all.

HANA: Not just shy . . . she's strange. I feel like she's pushing me off . . . she makes me feel like—I don't know—like I'm prying or something.

MURATA: Maybe you are.

HANA: And never puts out a cup of tea . . . . If she had all that training in the graces . . . why, a cup of tea . . .

MURATA: So if you want tea, ask for it.

HANA: I can't do that, Papa. She's strange . . . I don't know . . . *(To Masako)* When we go there, be very careful not to say anything wrong.

MASAKO: I never say anything anyway.

HANA *(Thoughtfully)*: Would you believe the story Oka-san just told? Why, I never knew . . .

MURATA: There're lot of things you don't know. Just because a man don't . . . talk about them, don't mean he don't feel . . . don't think about . . .

HANA *(Looking around)*: We'll have to take something. . . . There's nothing to take. . . . Papa, maybe you can dig up some carrots.

MURATA: God, Mama, be sensible. They got carrots. Everybody's got carrots.

HANA: Something . . . maybe I should make something.

MURATA: Hell, they're not expecting anything.

HANA: It's not good manners to go empty-handed.

MURATA: We'll take the sake.

Hana grimaces. Masako sees the record player.

MASAKO: I know, Mama. We can take the Victrola! We can play records for Mrs. Oka. Then nobody has to talk.

Murata laughs. Fade-out.

Scene 2

That evening. We see the exterior wall of the Okas' weathered house. There is a workable screen door and a large screened window. Outside there is a wide wooden bench that can accommodate three or four people. There is one separate chair and a lantern stands against the house.

The last rays of the sun light the area in a soft golden glow. This light grows gray as the scene progresses and it is quite dark at the end of the scene.

Through the screened window, Emiko Oka, Issei woman, thirty, can be seen walking erratically back and forth. She wears a drab cotton dress but her grace and femininity come through. Her hair is in a bun, in the style of Issei women of the era.

Oka sits cross-legged on the bench. He wears a yukata *[summer robe] and fans himself with a round Japanese fan.*

The Muratas enter. Murata carries towels and a bottle of sake. Hana carries the Victrola, and Masako a package containing their yukatas.

OKA *(Standing to receive the Muratas)*: Oh, you've come. Welcome!
MURATA: Yah . . . . Good of you to ask us.
HANA *(Bowing)*: Yes, thank you very much. *(To Masako)* Say "hello," Masako.
MASAKO: Hello.
HANA: And "thank you."
MASAKO: Thank you.

Oka makes motion of protest. Emiko stops her pacing and watches from the window.

HANA *(Glancing briefly at the window)*: And how is Emiko-san this evening?
OKA *(Turning toward the house)*: Emi! Emiko!
HANA: That's all right. Don't call her out. She must be busy.
OKA *(Half rising)*: Emiko!

Emiko comes to the door. Hana starts a deep bow toward the door.

MURATA: *Konbanwa* [Good evening]!
HANA: *Konbanwa*, Emiko-san. I feel so bad about this intrusion. Your husband has told you, our bathhouse was destroyed by fire and he graciously invited us to come use yours.

Emiko shakes her head.

OKA: I didn't have a chance to . . .
HANA *(Recovering and nudging Masako)*: Say hello to Mrs. Oka.
MASAKO: Hello, Mrs. Oka.

Hana lowers the Victrola onto the bench.

OKA: What's this? You brought a phonograph?
MASAKO: It's a Victrola.
HANA *(Laughing indulgently)*: Yes. Masako wanted to bring this over and play some records.
MURATA *(Extending the wine)*: Brought a little sake too.
OKA *(Taking the bottle)*: Ah, now that I like. Emiko, bring out the cups.

He waves at his wife, but she doesn't move. He starts to ask again, but decides to get them himself. He enters the house and returns with two cups. Emiko seats herself on the single chair. The Muratas unload their paraphernalia; Oka pours the wine, the men drink, Hana chatters and sorts the records. Masako stands by, helping her.

HANA: Yes, our Masako loves to play records. I like records too . . . and Papa, he . . .

MURATA *(Watching Emiko)*: They take me back home. The only way I can get there . . . in my mind.

HANA: Do you like music, Emiko-san? *(Emiko looks vague but smiles faintly)* Oka-san, you like them, don't you?

OKA: Yeah. But I don't have a player. No chance to hear them.

MURATA: I had to get this for them. They wouldn't leave me alone until I got it. Well . . . a phonograph . . . what the hell, they got to have *some* fun.

HANA: We don't have to play them, if you'd rather not . . .

OKA: Play. Play them.

HANA: I thought we could listen to them and relax. *(She extends some records to Emiko)* Would you like to look through these, Emiko-san?

Emiko doesn't respond. She pulls out a sack of Bull Durham and starts to roll a cigarette. Hana pushes Masako to her.

Take these to her.

Masako moves toward Emiko with the records. Masako stands watching her as she lights her cigarette.

Some of these are very old. You might know them, Emiko-san. *(She sees Masako watching Emiko)* Masako, bring those over here. *(She laughs uncomfortably)* You might like this one, Emiko-san . . . *(She starts the player)* Do you know it?

The record whines out "Kago No Tori." Emiko listens with her head cocked. She smokes her cigarette. She becomes wrapped in nostalgia and memories of the past. Masako watches her carefully.

MASAKO *(Whispering)*: Mama, she's crying.

Startled, Hana and Murata look toward Emiko.

HANA *(Pinching Masako)*: Shhh. The smoke is in her eyes.

MURATA: Did you bring the record I like, Mama?

Emiko rises abruptly and enters the house.

MASAKO: They were tears, Mama.

HANA: From yawning, Masako. *(Regretfully, to Oka)* I'm afraid we've offended her.

OKA *(Unaware)*: Hunh? Aw . . . no . . . pay no attention . . . no offense . . .

Masako looks toward the window. Emiko stands forlornly and slowly drifts into a dance.

HANA: I'm very sorry. Children, you know . . . they'll say anything, anything that's on their minds.

MURATA *(Notices Masako watching Emiko through the window and tries to divert her attention)*: The needles. Masako, where're the needles?

MASAKO (*Still watching*): I forgot them.

Hana sees what's going on. Oka is unaware.

HANA: Masako, go take your bath now. Masako . . .

Masako reluctantly picks up her towel and leaves.

OKA: Yeah, yeah . . . take your bath.

MURATA (*Sees Emiko still dancing*): Change the record, Mama.

OKA (*Still unaware*): That's kind of sad.

MURATA: No use to get sick over a record. We're supposed to enjoy.

Hana stops the record. Emiko disappears from the window. Hana selects a lively ondo [folk dance]—"Tokyo Ondo."

HANA: We'll find something more fun.

The three begin to tap their feet to the music.

Can't you just see the festival? The dancers, the bright kimonos, the paper lanterns bobbing in the wind, the fireflies . . . how nostalgic. . . . Oh, how nostalgic . . .

From the side of the house, Emiko appears. Her hair is down, she wears an old straw hat. She dances in front of the Muratas. They're startled. After the first shock, they watch with frozen smiles. They try to join Emiko's mood but something is missing. Oka is grieved. He finally stands as though he's had enough. Emiko, now close to the door, ducks into the house.

That was pretty . . . very nice . . .

Oka settles down and grunts. Murata clears his throat and Masako returns from her bath.

MURATA: You're done already? (*He's glad to see her*)

MASAKO: I wasn't very dirty. The water was too hot.

MURATA: Good! Just the way I like it.

HANA: Not dirty?

MURATA (*Picking up his towel*): Come on, Mama . . . scrub my back.

HANA (*Laughing embarrassedly*): Oh, oh . . . well . . . (*She stops the player*) Masako, now don't forget . . . crank the machine and change the needle now and then.

MASAKO: I didn't bring them.

HANA: Oh. Oh . . . all right. I'll be back soon . . . don't forget . . . crank.

She leaves with her husband. Oka and Masako are alone. Oka is awkward and falsely hearty.

OKA: So! So you don't like hot baths, eh?

MASAKO: Not too hot.

OKA (*Laughing*): I thought you like it real hot. Hot enough to burn the house down. That's a little joke.

Masako busies herself with the records to conceal her annoyance.

I hear you're real good in school. Always top of the class.

MASAKO: It's a small class. Only two of us.

OKA: When Kiyoko comes, you'll help her in school, yeah? You'll take care of her . . . a favor for me, eh?

MASAKO: Okay.

OKA: You'll be her friend, eh?

MASAKO: Okay.

OKA: That's good. That's good. You'll like her. She's a nice girl too. (*He stands, yawns, and stretches*) I'll go for a little walk now. (*He touches his crotch to indicate his purpose*)

Masako turns her attention to the records and selects one—"The Soul Shall Dance"—and begins to sway to the music. The song draws Emiko from the house. She looks out the window, sees Masako is alone and begins to slip into a dance.

EMIKO: Do you like that song, Masa-chan?

Masako is startled and draws back. She remembers her mother's warning. She doesn't know what to do. She nods.

That's one of my favorite songs. I remember in Japan I used to sing it so often . . . my favorite song . . . (*She sings along with the record*)
    Akai kuchibiru
    Kappu ni yosete
    Aoi sake nomya
    Kokoro ga odoru . . .
Do you know what that means, Masa-chan?

MASAKO: I think so . . . . The soul will dance?

EMIKO: Yes, yes, that's right.
    The soul shall dance.
    Red lips against a glass
    Drink the green . . .

MASAKO: Wine?

EMIKO (*Nodding*): Drink the green wine.

MASAKO: Green? I thought wine is purple.

EMIKO (*Nodding*): Wine is purple . . . but this is a green liqueur. (*She holds up one of the china cups as though it were crystal, and looks at it as though the light were shining through it and she sees the green liquid*) It's good . . . it warms your heart.

MASAKO: And the soul dances.

EMIKO: Yes.

MASAKO: What does it taste like? The green wine . . .

EMIKO: Oh, it's like . . . it's like . . .

The second verse starts. "Kurai yoru no yume/ Setsunasa yo/ Aoi sake nomya/ Yume mo odoru . . . ."

MASAKO: In the dark night . . .

EMIKO: Dreams are unbearable . . . insufferable . . . *(She turns sad)*

MASAKO: Drink the . . .

EMIKO *(Nodding)*: Drink the green wine . . .

MASAKO: And the dreams will dance.

EMIKO *(Softly)*: I'll be going back one day . . .

MASAKO: To where?

EMIKO: My home . . . Japan . . . my real home. I'm planning to go back.

MASAKO: By yourself?

EMIKO *(Nodding)*: Oh, yes. It's a secret. You can keep a secret?

MASAKO: Uh-huh. I have lots of secrets . . . all my own . . .

The music stops. Emiko sees Oka approaching and disappears into the house. Masako attends to the record and does not know Emiko is gone.

Secrets I never tell anyone.

OKA: Secrets? What kind of secrets? What did she say?

MASAKO: Oh. Nothing.

OKA: What did you talk about?

MASAKO: Nothing. . . . Mrs. Oka was talking about the song. She was telling me what it meant . . . about the soul.

OKA *(Scoffing)*: Heh! What does she know about soul? *(Calming down)* Ehhh . . . some people don't have them . . . souls.

MASAKO *(Timidly)*: I thought . . . I think everyone has a soul. I read in a book . . .

OKA *(Laughing)*: Maybe . . . maybe you're right. I'm not an educated man, you know . . . I don't know too much about books. When Kiyoko comes you can talk to her about it. Kiyoko is very . . .

From inside the house, we hear Emiko begin to sing loudly at the name Kiyoko as though trying to drown it out. Oka stops talking. Then resumes.

Kiyoko is very smart. You'll have a good time with her. She'll learn your language fast. How old did you say you are?

MASAKO: Almost twelve.

By this time Oka and Masako are shouting, trying to be heard above Emiko's singing.

OKA: Kiyoko is fifteen . . . . Kiyoko . . .

Oka is exasperated. He rushes into the house seething. Masako hears Oka's muffled rage: "Behave yourself," and "kitchigai" come through. Masako slinks to the window and looks in. Oka slaps Emiko around. Masako reacts to the violence. Oka comes out. Masako returns to the bench in time. He pulls his fingers through his hair and sits next to Masako. She very slightly draws away.

Want me to light a lantern?

MASAKO *(Shaken)*: No . . . ye— . . . okay . . .

OKA: We'll get a little light here . . .

He lights the lantern as the Muratas return from their bath. They are in good spirits.

MURATA: Ahhhh . . . . Nothing like a good hot bath.

HANA: So refreshing . . .

MURATA: A bath should be taken hot and slow. Don't know how Masako gets through so fast.

HANA: She probably doesn't get in the tub.

MASAKO: I do.

Everyone laughs.

Well I do.

Emiko comes out. She has a large purple welt on her face. She sits on the separate chair, hands folded, quietly watching the Muratas. They look at her with alarm. Oka engages himself with his fan.

HANA: Oh! Emiko-san . . . what . . . ah-ah . . . whaa . . . *(She draws a deep breath)* What a nice bath we had . . . such a lovely bath. We do appreciate your hos . . . pitality. Thank you so much.

EMIKO: Lovely evening, isn't it?

HANA: Very lovely. Very. Ah, a little warm, but nice . . . . Did you get a chance to hear the records? *(Turning to Masako)* Did you play the records for Mrs. Oka?

MASAKO: Ye— . . . no . . . . The needle was . . .

EMIKO: Yes, she did. We played the records together.

MURATA: Oh, you played the songs together?

EMIKO: Yes . . . yes . . .

MURATA: That's nice. . . . Masako can understand pretty good, eh?

EMIKO: She understands everything . . . everything I say.

MURATA *(Withdrawing)*: Oh, yeah? Eh, Mama, we ought to be going . . . *(He closes the player)* Hate to bathe and run but . . .

HANA: Yes, yes. Tomorrow is a busy day. Come, Masako.

EMIKO: Please . . . stay a little longer.

MURATA: Eh, well, we got to be going.

HANA: Why, thank you, but . . .

EMIKO: It's still quite early.

OKA *(Indicating he's ready to say good-bye)*: Enjoyed the music. And the sake.

EMIKO: The records are very nice. Makes me remember Japan. I sang those songs . . . those very songs . . . . Did you know I used to sing?

HANA *(Politely)*: Why, no . . . no. I didn't know that. You must have a very lovely voice.

EMIKO: Yes.

HANA: No, I didn't know that. That's very nice.

EMIKO: Yes, I sang. My parents were very strict . . . they didn't like it. They said it was frivolous. Imagine?

HANA: Yes, I can imagine. Things were like that . . . in those days singing was not considered proper for nice . . . I mean, only for women in the profess— . . .

MURATA: We better get home, Mama.

HANA: Yes, yes. What a shame you couldn't continue with it.

EMIKO: In the city I did do some classics: the dance, and the *koto*, and the flower, and of course, the tea . . . *(She makes the proper gesture for the different disciplines)* All those. Even some singing . . . classics, of course.

HANA *(Politely)*: Of course.

EMIKO: All of it is so disciplined . . . so disciplined. I was almost a *natori*.

HANA: Oh! How nice.

EMIKO: But everything changed.

HANA: Oh!

EMIKO: I was sent here to America. *(She glares at Oka)*

HANA: Oh, too bad . . . I mean, too bad about your *natori*.

MURATA *(Loudly to Oka)*: So did you see Nagata today?

OKA: Oh, yeah. Yeah.

MURATA: What did he say? Is he interested?

OKA: Yeah. Yeah. He's interested.

MURATA: He likes the horse, eh?

OKA: Ah . . . yeah.

MURATA: I knew he'd like him. I'd buy him myself if I had the money.

OKA: Well, I have to take him over tomorrow. He'll decide then.

MURATA: He'll buy . . . he'll buy. You'd better go straight over to the ticket office and get that ticket. Before you—ha-ha—spend the money.

OKA: Ha-ha. Yeah.

HANA: It'll be so nice when Kiyoko-san comes to join you. I know you're looking forward to it.

EMIKO *(Confused)*: Oh . . . oh . . .

HANA: Masako is so happy. It'll be good for her too.

EMIKO: I had more freedom in the city . . . I lived with an aunt and she let me . . . . She wasn't so strict.

Murata and Masako have their gear together and stand ready to leave.

MURATA: Good luck on the horse tomorrow.

OKA: Yeah, thanks.

HANA *(Bowing)*: Many, many thanks.

OKA *(Nodding toward the sake)*: Thanks for the sake.

HANA *(Bowing again)*: Good night, Emiko-san. We'll see you again soon. We'll bring the records too.

EMIKO *(Softly)*: Those songs . . . those very songs . . .

MURATA: Let's go, Mama.

> *The Muratas pull away. Light follows them and grows dark on the Okas. The*
> *Muratas begin walking home.*

HANA: That was uncomfortable.

MASAKO: What's the matter with—

HANA: Shhhh!

MURATA: I guess Oka has his problems.

MASAKO: Is she really *kitchigai?*

HANA: Of course not. She's not crazy. Don't say that word, Masako.

MASAKO: I heard Mr. Oka call her that.

HANA: He called her that?

MASAKO: I . . . I think so.

HANA: You heard wrong, Masako. Emiko-san isn't crazy. She just likes her drinks.
She had too much to drink tonight.

MASAKO: Oh.

HANA: She can't adjust to this life. She can't get over the good times she had in
Japan. Well, it's not easy . . . but one has to know when to bend . . . like the
bamboo. When the winds blow, bamboo bends. You bend or crack. Remember
that, Masako.

MURATA *(Laughing wryly)*: Bend, eh? Remember that, Mama.

HANA *(Softly)*: You don't know . . . it isn't ever easy.

MASAKO: Do you want to go back to Japan, Mama?

HANA: Everyone does.

MASAKO: Do you, Papa?

MURATA: I'll have to make some money first.

MASAKO: I don't. Not me. Not Kiyoko . . .

HANA: After Kiyoko-san comes, Emiko will have company and things will straighten
out. She has nothing to live on but memories. She doesn't have any friends.
At least I have my friends at church . . . at least I have that. She must get awful
lonely.

MASAKO: I know that. She tried to make friends with me.

HANA: She did? What did she say?

MASAKO: Well, sort of . . .

HANA: What did she say?

MASAKO: She didn't say anything. I just felt it. Maybe you should be her friend,
Mama.

MURATA: Poor woman. We could have stayed longer.

HANA: But you wanted to leave. I tried to be friendly. You saw that. It's not easy
to talk to Emiko. She either closes up, you can't pry a word from her, or else
she goes on and on . . . all that . . . that . . . about the *koto* and tea and the
flower . . . I mean, what am I supposed to say? She's so unpredictable. And the
drinking . . .

MURATA: All right, all right, Mama.

MASAKO: Did you see her black eye?

HANA (*Calming down*): She probably hurt herself. She wasn't very steady.

MASAKO: Oh, no. Mr. Oka hit her.

HANA: I don't think so.

MASAKO: He hit her. I saw him.

HANA: You saw that? Papa, do you hear that? She saw them. That does it. We're not going there again.

MURATA: Aww . . . Oka wouldn't do that. Not in front of a kid.

MASAKO: Well, they didn't do it in front of me. They were in the house.

MURATA: You see . . .

HANA: That's all right. You just have to fix the bathhouse. Either that or we're going to bathe at home . . . in a bucket. We're not going . . . we'll bathe at home. (*Murara mutters to himself*) What?

MURATA: I said all right, it's the bucket then. I'll get to it when I can.

Hana passes Murata and walks ahead.

Scene 3

Same evening. Lights cross-fade to the exterior of the Oka house. The Muratas have just left. Emiko sits on the bench. Her back is to Oka. Oka, still standing, looks at her contemptuously as she takes the bottle and one of the cups to pour herself a drink.

OKA: Nothing more disgusting than a drunk woman. (*Emiko ignores him*) You made a fool of yourself. *Washi baka ni shite!* You made a fool of me!

Emiko doesn't move.

EMIKO: One can only make a fool of oneself.

OKA: You learn that in the fancy schools, eh? (*Emiko examines the pattern on her cup*) Eh? Eh? Answer me! (*Emiko ignores him*) I'm talking to you. Answer me! (*Menacing*) You don't get away with that. You think you're so fine . . .

Emiko looks off into the horizon. Oka turns her roughly around.

When I talk, you listen!

Emiko turns away again. Oka pulls the cup from her hand.

Goddamnit! What'd you think my friends think of you? What kind of ass they think I am? (*He grabs her shoulders*)

EMIKO: Don't touch me . . . don't touch me.

OKA: Who the hell you think you are? "Don't touch me, don't touch me." Who the hell! High and mighty, eh? Too good for me, eh? Don't put on the act for me . . . I know who you are.

EMIKO: Tell me who I am, Mister Smart Peasant.

OKA: Shut your fool mouth, goddamnit! Sure! I'll tell you. I know all about you . . .
Shizue told me. The whole village knows.

EMIKO: Shizue!

OKA: Yeah! Shizue. Embarrassed the hell out of her, your own sister.

EMIKO: Embarrassed? I have nothing to be ashamed of. I don't know what you're
talking about.

OKA *(Derisively)*: You don't know what I'm talking about. I know. The whole village
knows. They're all laughing at you. At me! Stupid Oka got stuck with a secondhand woman. I didn't say anything because . . .

EMIKO: I'm not secondhand!

OKA: Who you trying to fool? I know. Knew long time ago . . . . Shizue wrote me
all about your affairs in Tokyo. The men you were mess—

EMIKO: Affairs? Men?

OKA: That man you were messing with . . . I knew all along. I didn't say anything
because you . . . I . . .

EMIKO: I'm not ashamed of it.

OKA: You're not ashamed! What the hell! Your father thought he was pulling a fast
one on me . . . thought I didn't know nothing . . . thought I was some kind
of dumb ass . . . I didn't say nothing because Shizue's dead . . . Shizue's dead.
I was willing to give you a chance.

EMIKO *(Laughing)*: A chance?

OKA: Yeah! A chance! Laugh! Give a *joro* another chance. Sure, I'm stupid . . . dumb.

EMIKO: I'm not a whore. I'm true . . . he knows I'm true.

OKA: True! Ha!

EMIKO: You think I'm untrue just because I let . . . let you . . . . There's only one
man for me.

OKA: Let me *(Obscene gesture)* you? I can do what I want with you. Your father palmed
you off on me—like a dog or cat—an animal . . . couldn't do nothing with you.
Even that rich dumb Yamato wouldn't have you. Your father—greedy father—so
proud . . . making big plans for you . . . for himself. Ha! The whole village
laughing at him . . . *(Emiko hangs her head)* Shizue told me. And she was working like a dog . . . trying to keep your goddamn father happy . . . doing my work
and yours.

EMIKO: My work?

OKA: Yeah, your work too! She killed herself working! She killed herself . . . *(He
has tender memories of his dull, uncomplaining wife)* Up in the morning getting
the fires started, working the bellows, cleaning the furnace, cooking, and late
at night working with the sewing . . . tending the baby. . . . *(He mutters)* The
goddamn family killed her. And you . . . you out there in Tokyo with the fancy clothes, doing the *(He sneers)* dance, the tea, the flower, the *koto*, and the . . .
(Obscene gesture)

EMIKO *(Hurting)*: Achhhh . . .

OKA: Did you have fun? Did you have fun on your sister's blood? *(Emiko doesn't answer)* Did you? He must have been a son-of-a-bitch. . . . What would make that goddamn greedy old man send his prize mare to a plow horse like me? What kind of bum was he that your father—

EMIKO: He's not a bum . . . he's not a bum.

OKA: Was he Korean? Was he *Etta?* That's the only thing I could figure.

EMIKO: I'm true to him. Only him.

OKA: True? You think he's true to you? You think he waits for you? Remembers you? *Aho!* Think he cares?

EMIKO *(Nodding quietly)*: He does.

OKA: And waits ten years? *Baka!* Go back to Japan and see. You'll find out. Go back to Japan. *Kaire!*

EMIKO: In time.

OKA: In time? How about now?

EMIKO: I can't now.

OKA: Ha! Now! Go now! Who needs you? Who needs you? You think a man waits ten years for a woman? You think you're some kind of . . . of . . . diamond . . . treasure . . . he's going to wait his life for you? Go to him. He's probably married with ten kids. Go to him. Get out! Goddamn *joro* . . . . Go! Go!

He sweeps Emiko off the bench.

EMIKO *(Hurting)*: Ahhhh! I . . . I don't have the money. Give me money to—

OKA: If I had money I would give it to you ten years ago. You think I been eating this *kuso* for ten years because I like it?

EMIKO: You're selling the horse. . . . Give me the—

OKA *(Scoffing)*: That's for Kiyoko. I owe you nothing.

EMIKO: Ten years, you owe me.

OKA: Ten years of what? Misery? You gave me nothing. I give you nothing. You want to go, pack your bag and start walking. Try cross the desert. When you get dry and hungry, think about me.

EMIKO: I'd die out there.

OKA: Die? You think I didn't die here?

EMIKO: I didn't do anything to you.

OKA: No, no you didn't. All I wanted was a little comfort and . . . you . . . no, you didn't. No. So you die. We all die. Shizue died. If she was here, she wouldn't treat me like this. . . . *(He thinks of his poor dead wife)* Ah, I should have brought her with me. She'd be alive now. We'd be poor but happy . . . like . . . like Murata and his wife . . . and the kid . . .

EMIKO: I wish she were alive too. I'm not to blame for her dying. I didn't know . . . I was away. I loved her. I didn't want her to die . . . I . . .

OKA *(Softening)*: I know that. I'm not blaming you for that . . . . And it's not my fault what happened to you either . . .

Emiko is silent and he mistakes that for a change in attitude. He is encouraged.

You understand that, eh? I didn't ask for you. It's not my fault you're here in this desert . . . with . . . with me . . .

Emiko weeps. Oka reaches out.

I know I'm too old for you. It's hard for me too . . . but this is the way it is. I just ask you be kinder . . . understand it wasn't my fault. Try make it easier for me . . . for yourself too.

Oka touches her and she shrinks from his touch.

EMIKO: Ach!

OKA (*Humiliated again*): Goddamn it! I didn't ask for you! *Aho!* If you were smart you'd done as your father said . . . cut out that *saru shibai* with the *Etta* . . . married the rich Yamoto. Then you'd still be in Japan. Not here to make my life so miserable. (*Emiko is silent*) And you can have your *Etta* . . . and anyone else you want. Take them all on . . . (*He is worn out. It's hopeless*) God, why do we do this all the time? Fighting, fighting all the time. There must be a better way to live . . . there must be another way.

Oka waits for a response, gives up, and enters the house. Emiko watches him leave and pours herself another drink. The storm has passed, the alcohol takes over. She turns to the door Oka disappeared into.

EMIKO: Because I must keep the dream alive . . . the dream is all I live for. I am only in exile now. Because if I give in, all I've lived before . . . will mean nothing . . . will be for nothing. . . . Because if I let you make me believe this is all there is to my life, the dream would die . . . I would die . . . (*She pours another drink and feels warm and good*)

Fade-out.

END OF ACT ONE

ACT TWO

Scene 1

Muratas' kitchen, afternoon. The calendar reads September. Masako is at the kitchen table with several books. She thumbs through a Japanese magazine. Hana is with her, sewing.

MASAKO: Do they always wear kimonos in Japan, Mama?
HANA: Most of the time.
MASAKO: I wonder if Kiyoko will be wearing a kimono like this?

HANA (*Peering into Masako's magazine*): They don't dress like that . . . not for everyday.

MASAKO: I wonder what she's like.

HANA: Probably a lot like you. What do you think she's like?

MASAKO: She's probably taller.

HANA: Mr. Oka isn't tall.

MASAKO: And pretty . . .

HANA (*Laughing*): Mr. Oka . . . . Well, I don't suppose she'll look like her father.

MASAKO: Mrs. Oka is pretty.

HANA: She isn't Kiyoko-san's real mother, remember.

MASAKO: Oh. That's right.

HANA: But they are related. Well, we'll soon see.

MASAKO: I thought she was coming in September. It's already September.

HANA: Papa said Oka-san went to San Pedro a few days ago. He should be back soon with Kiyoko-san.

MASAKO: Didn't Mrs. Oka go too?

HANA (*Glancing toward the Oka house*): I don't think so. I see lights in their house at night.

MASAKO: Will they bring Kiyoko over to see us?

HANA: Of course. First thing, probably. You'll be very nice to her, won't you?

MASAKO (*Leaves the table and finds another book*): Sure. I'm glad I'm going to have a friend. I hope she likes me.

HANA: She'll like you. Japanese girls are very polite, you know.

MASAKO: We have to be or our mamas get mad at us.

HANA: Then I should be getting mad at you more often.

MASAKO: It's often enough already, Mama. (*She opens a hardback book*) Look at this, Mama . . . I'm going to show her this book.

HANA: She won't be able to read at first.

MASAKO: I love this story. Mama, this is about people like us—settlers—it's about the prairie. We live in a prairie, don't we?

HANA: Prairie? Does that mean desert?

MASAKO: I think so.

HANA (*Nodding and looking bleak*): We live in a prairie.

MASAKO: It's about the hardships and the floods and droughts and how they have nothing but each other.

HANA (*Nodding*): We have nothing but each other. But these people—they're white people.

MASAKO (*Nodding*): Sure, Mama. They come from the East. Just like you and Papa came from Japan.

HANA: We come from the Far Far East. That's different. White people are different from us.

MASAKO: I know that.

HANA: White people among white people . . . that's different from Japanese among white people. You know what I'm saying?

MASAKO: I know that. How come they don't write books about us . . . about Japanese people?

HANA: Because we're nobodies here.

MASAKO: If I didn't read these, there'd be nothing for me . . .

HANA: Some of the things you read, you're never going to know.

MASAKO: I can dream though.

HANA (*Sighing*): Sometimes the dreaming makes the living harder. Better to keep your head out of the clouds.

MASAKO: That's not much fun.

HANA: You'll have fun when Kiyoko-san comes. You can study together, you can sew, and sometimes you can try some of those fancy American recipes.

MASAKO: Mama, you have to have chocolate and cream and things like that.

HANA: We'll get them.

We hear the putt-putt of Oka's old car. Masako and Hana pause and listen. Masako runs to the window.

MASAKO: I think it's them!

HANA: The Okas?

MASAKO: It's them! It's them!

Hana stands and looks out. She removes her apron and puts away her sewing.

HANA: Two of them. Emiko-san isn't with them. Let's go outside.

Oka and Kiyoko, fourteen, enter. Oka is wearing his going-out clothes: a sweater, white shirt, dark pants, but no tie. Kiyoko walks behind him. She is short, chunky, broad-chested and very self-conscious. Her hair is straight and banded into two shucks. She wears a conservative cotton dress, white socks and two-inch heels. Oka is proud. He struts in, his chest puffed out.

OKA: Hello, hello . . . . We're here. We made it! (*He pushes Kiyoko forward*) This is my daughter, Kiyoko. (*To Kiyoko*) Murata-san . . . remember I was talking about? My friends . . .

KIYOKO (*Barely audible as she speaks a standard formal greeting, bowing deeply*): Hajime mashite yoroshiku onegai shimasu . . .

HANA (*Also bowing formally*): I hope your journey was pleasant.

OKA (*While the women are still bowing, he pushes Kiyoko toward Masako*): This is Masako-chan; I told you about her . . .

Masako is shocked at Kiyoko's appearance. The girl she expected is already a woman. She stands with her mouth agape and withdraws noticeably. Hana rushes in to fill the awkwardness.

HANA: Say hello, Masako. My goodness, where are your manners? (*She laughs apologetically*) In this country they don't make much to-do about manners. (*She stands back to examine Kiyoko)* My, my, I didn't picture you so grown up. My, my . . . . Tell me, how was your trip?

OKA *(Proudly)*: We just drove in from Los Angeles just this morning. We spent the night in San Pedro and the next two days we spent in Los Angeles . . . you know, Japanese town.

HANA: How nice!

OKA: Kiyoko was so excited. Twisting her head this way and that—couldn't see enough with her big eyes. *(He imitates her fondly)* She's from the country, you know . . . just a big country girl. Got all excited about the Chinese dinner— we had a Chinese dinner. She never ate it before.

Kiyoko covers her mouth and giggles.

HANA: Chinese dinner!

OKA: Oh, yeah. Duck, *pakkai*, chow mein, seaweed soup . . . the works!

HANA: A feast!

OKA: Oh, yeah. Like a holiday. Two holidays. Two holidays in one.

HANA *(Pushes Masako forward)*: Two holidays in one! Kiyoko-san, our Masako has been looking forward to meeting you.

KIYOKO *(Bowing again)*: Hajime mashite . . .

HANA: She's been thinking of all sorts of things she can do with you: sewing, cooking . . .

MASAKO: Oh, Mama.

Kiyoko covers her mouth and giggles.

HANA: It's true, Kiyoko-san. She's been looking forward to having a best friend.

Kiyoko giggles again and Masako pulls away.

OKA: Kiyoko, you shouldn't be so shy. The Muratas are my good friends and you should feel free with them. Ask anything, say anything . . . right?

HANA: Of course, of course. *(She is slightly annoyed with Masako)* Masako, go in and start the tea.

Masako enters the house.

I'll call Papa. He's in the yard. Papa! Oka-san is here! *(To Kiyoko)* Now tell me, how was your trip? Did you get seasick?

KIYOKO *(Bowing and nodding)*: Eh [Yes]. A little . . .

OKA: Tell her. Tell her how sick you got.

Kiyoko covers her mouth and giggles.

HANA: Oh, I know, I know. I was too. That was a long time ago. I'm sure things are improved now. Tell me about Japan . . . what is it like now? They say it's so changed . . . modern . . .

OKA: Kiyoko comes from the country . . . backwoods. Nothing changes much there from century to century.

HANA: Ah! That's true. That's why I love Japan. And you wanted to leave. It's unbelievable. To come here!

OKA: She always dreamed about it.

HANA: Well, it's not really that bad.

OKA: No, it's not that bad. Depends on what you make of it.

HANA: That's right. What you make of it. I was just telling Masako today . . .

Murata enters. He rubs his hands to take off the soil and comes in grinning. He shakes Oka's hand.

MURATA: *Oi, oi* . . .

OKA: Yah . . . I'm back. This is my daughter.

MURATA: No! She's beautiful!

OKA: Finally made it. Finally got her here.

MURATA *(To Kiyoko)*: Your father hasn't stopped talking about you all summer.

HANA: And Masako too.

KIYOKO *(Bowing)*: *Hajime mashite* . . .

MURATA *(Acknowledging with a short bow)*: Yah. How'd you like the trip?

OKA: I was just telling your wife—had a good time in Los Angeles. Had a couple of great dinners, took in the cinema—Japanese pictures, bought her some American clothes.

HANA: Oh, you bought that in Los Angeles.

MURATA: Got a good price for your horse, eh? Lots of money, eh?

OKA: Nagata's a shrewd bargainer. Heh. It don't take much money to make her happy. She's a country girl.

MURATA: That's all right. Country's all right. Country girl's the best.

OKA: Had trouble on the way back.

MURATA: Yeah?

OKA: Fan belt broke.

MURATA: That'll happen.

OKA: Lucky I was near a gasoline station. We were in the mountains. Waited in a restaurant while it was getting fixed.

HANA: Oh, that was good.

OKA: Guess they don't see Japanese much. Stare? Terrible! Took them a long time to wait on us. Dumb waitress practically threw the food at us. Kiyoko felt bad.

HANA: Ah! That's too bad . . . too bad. That's why I always pack a lunch when we take trips.

MURATA: They'll spoil the day for you . . . those barbarians!

OKA: Terrible food too. Kiyoko couldn't swallow the dry bread and bologna.

HANA: That's the food they eat!

MURATA: Let's go in . . . have a little wine. Mama, we got wine? This is a celebration.

HANA: I think so . . . a little . . .

They enter the house talking. Masako has made the tea, and Hana begins to serve the wine.

How is your "mother"? Was she happy to see you?

KIYOKO: Oh, she . . . yes . . .

HANA: I just know she was surprised to see you so grown up. Of course, you remember her from Japan, don't you?

KIYOKO *(Nodding)*: Eh. I can barely remember. I was very young . . .

HANA: Of course. But you do, don't you?

KIYOKO: She was gone most of the time . . . at school in Tokyo. She was very pretty, I remember that.

HANA: She's still very pretty.

KIYOKO: *Eh.* She was always laughing. She was much younger then.

HANA: Oh now, it hasn't been that long ago.

Masako leaves the room to go outside. The following dialogue continues muted as light goes dim in the house and focuses on Masako. Emiko enters, is drawn to the Murata window and listens.

OKA: We stayed at an inn on East First Street. *Shizuokaya.* Whole inn filled with Shizuoka people . . . talking the old dialect. Thought I was in Japan again.

MURATA: That right?

OKA: Felt good. Like I was in Japan again.

HANA *(To Kiyoko)*: Did you enjoy Los Angeles?

KIYOKO *(Nodding)*: Eh.

OKA: That's as close as I'll get to Japan.

MURATA: *Mattakuna!* That's for sure.

Outside Masako becomes aware of Emiko.

MASAKO: Why don't you go in?

EMIKO: Oh. Oh. Why don't you?

MASAKO: They're all grownups in there. I'm not grown up.

EMIKO *(Softly)*: All grownups. . . . Maybe I'm not either. *(Her mood changes)* Masa-chan, do you have a boyfriend?

MASAKO: I don't like boys. They don't like me.

EMIKO: Oh, that will change. You will change. I was like that too.

MASAKO: Besides, there're none around here . . . Japanese boys . . . . There are some at school, but they don't like girls.

HANA *(Calling from the kitchen)*: Masako . . .

Masako doesn't answer.

EMIKO: Your mother is calling you.

MASAKO *(Answering her mother)*: Nani [What]?

HANA *(From the kitchen)*: Come inside now.

EMIKO: You'll have a boyfriend one day.

MASAKO: Not me.

EMIKO: You'll fall in love one day. Someone will make the inside of you light up, and you'll know you're in love. *(She relives her own experience)* Your life will change . . . grow beautiful. It's good, Masa-chan. And this feeling you'll remember the rest of your life . . . will come back to you . . . haunt you . . . keep you alive . . . five, ten years . . . no matter what happens . . . keep you alive.

HANA *(From the kitchen)*: Masako . . . . Come inside now.

Masako turns aside to answer and Emiko slips away.

MASAKO: What, Mama?

HANA *(Coming outside)*: Come inside. Don't be so unsociable. Kiyoko wants to talk to you.

MASAKO *(Watching Emiko leave)*: She doesn't want to talk to me. You're only saying that.

HANA: What's the matter with you? Don't you want to make friends with her?

MASAKO: She's not my friend. She's your friend.

HANA: Don't be so silly. She's only fourteen.

MASAKO: Fifteen. They said fifteen. She's your friend. She's an old lady.

HANA: Don't say that.

MASAKO: I don't like her.

HANA: Shhh! Don't say that.

MASAKO: She doesn't like me either.

HANA: Ma-chan. Remember your promise to Mr. Oka? You're going to take her to school, teach her the language, teach her the ways of Americans.

MASAKO: She can do it herself. You did.

HANA: That's not nice, Ma-chan.

MASAKO: I don't like the way she laughs. *(She imitates Kiyoko holding her hand to her mouth and giggling and bowing)*

HANA: Oh, how awful! Stop that. That's the way the girls do in Japan. Maybe she doesn't like your ways either. That's only a difference in manners. What you're doing now is considered very bad manners. *(She changes tone)* Ma-chan . . . just wait—when she learns to read and speak, you'll have so much to say to each other. Come on, be a good girl and come inside.

MASAKO: It's just old people in there, Mama. I don't want to go in.

Hana calls Kiyoko away from the table and speaks confidentially to her.

HANA: Kiyoko-san, please come here a minute. Maybe it's better for you to talk to Masako alone.

Kiyoko leaves the table and walks to Hana outside.

Masako has a lot of things to tell you about . . . what to expect in school and things . . .

MURATA (*Calling from the table*): Mama, put out something . . . chiles . . . for Oka-san.

> *Hana leaves the two girls and enters the house. Kiyoko and Masako stand awkwardly, Kiyoko glancing shyly at Masako.*

MASAKO: Do you like it here?
KIYOKO (*Nodding*): Eh.

> *There's an uncomfortable pause.*

MASAKO: School will be starting next week . . .
KIYOKO (*Nodding*): Eh.
MASAKO: Do you want to walk to school with me?
KIYOKO (*Nodding*): Ah.
MASAKO (*Rolls her eyes and tries again*): I leave at 7:30.
KIYOKO: Ah.

> *There's a long pause. Masako finally gives up and moves offstage.*

MASAKO: I have to do something.

> *Kiyoko watches her leave and uncertainly moves back to the house. Hana looks up at Kiyoko coming in alone, sighs, and quietly pulls out a chair for her. Fade-out.*

Scene 2

> *November, night. Interior of the Murata house. Lamps are lit. The family is at the kitchen table. Hana sews, Masako does her homework, Murata reads the paper. They're dressed in warm robes and having tea. Outside, thunder rolls in the distance and lightning flashes.*

HANA: It'll be *ohigan* [an autumn festival] soon.
MURATA: Something to look forward to.
HANA: We will need sweet rice for *omochi* [rice cakes].
MURATA: I'll order it next time I go to town.
HANA (*To Masako*): How is school? Getting a little harder?
MASAKO: Not that much. Sometimes the arithmetic is hard.
HANA: How is Kiyoko-san doing? Is she getting along all right?
MASAKO: She's good in arithmetic. She skipped a grade already.
HANA: Already? That's good news. Only November and she skipped a grade! At this rate she'll be through before you.
MASAKO: Well, she's older.
MURATA: Sure, she's older, Mama.
HANA: Has she made any friends?
MASAKO: No. She follows me around all day. She understands okay, but she doesn't talk. She talks like, you know . . . she says "ranchi" for lunch and "ranchi" for

ranch too, and like that. Kids laugh and copy behind her back. It's hard to understand her.

HANA: You understand her, don't you?

MASAKO: I'm used to it.

Murata smiles secretly.

HANA: You should tell the kids not to laugh; after all, she's trying. Maybe you should help her practice those words . . . show her what she's doing wrong.

MASAKO: I already do. Our teacher told me to do that.

MURATA (*Looking up from his paper*): You ought to help her all you can.

HANA: And remember when you started school you couldn't speak English either.

MASAKO: I help her.

Murata rises and goes to the window. The night is cold. Lightning flashes and the wind whistles.

MURATA: Looks like a storm coming up. Hope we don't have a freeze.

HANA: If it freezes, we'll have another bad year. Maybe we ought to start the smudge pots.

MURATA (*Listening*): It's starting to rain. Nothing to do now but pray.

HANA: If praying is the answer, we'd be in Japan now . . . rich.

MURATA (*Wryly*): We're not dead yet. We still have a chance. (*Hana glares at this small joke*) Guess I'll turn in.

HANA: Go to bed . . . go to bed. I'll sit up and worry.

MURATA: If worrying was the answer, we'd be around the world twice and in Japan. Come on, Mama. Let's go to bed. It's too cold tonight to be mad.

There's an urgent knock on the door. The family react to it.

Dareh da! (*Goes to the door and pauses*) Who is it!

KIYOKO (*Weakly*): It's me . . . help me . . .

Murata opens the door and Kiyoko enters. She's dressed in a kimono with a shawl thrown over. Her legs are bare except for a pair of straw zori. Her hair is stringy from the rain and she trembles from the cold.

MURATA: My God! Kiyoko-san! What's the matter?

HANA: Kiyoko-san! What is it?

MURATA: What happened?

KIYOKO (*Gasping*): They're fighting . . . they're fighting.

MURATA: Ah . . . don't worry . . . those things happen. No cause to worry. Mama, make tea for her. Sit down and catch your breath. I'll take you home when you're ready.

HANA: Papa, I'll take care of it.

MURATA: Let me know when you're ready to go home.

HANA: It must be freezing out there. Try to get warm. Try to calm yourself.

MURATA: Kiyoko-san . . . don't worry.

AND THE SOUL SHALL DANCE

Hana waves Masako and Murata off. Murata leaves. Masako goes to her bed in the kitchen.

HANA: Papa, I'll take care of it.

KIYOKO *(Looking at Murata's retreating form)*: I came to ask your help.

HANA: You ran down here without a lantern? You could have fallen and hurt yourself.

KIYOKO: I don't care . . . I don't care.

HANA: You don't know, Kiyoko-san. It's treacherous out there . . . snakes, spiders . . .

KIYOKO: I must go back . . . I . . . I . . . you . . . please come with me.

HANA: First, first, we must get you warm. . . . Drink your tea.

KIYOKO: But they might kill each other. They're fighting like animals. Help me stop them!

HANA *(Goes to the stove to warm a pot of soup)*: I cannot interfere in a family quarrel.

KIYOKO: It's not a quarrel . . . it's a . . .

HANA: That's all it is. A family squabble. You'll see. Tomorrow . . .

KIYOKO *(Rises and puts her hand on Hana's arm)*: Not just a squabble . . . please!

She starts toward the door but Hana restrains her.

HANA: Now listen. Listen to me, Kiyoko-san. I've known your father and mother a little while now. I suspect it's been like this for years. Every family has some kind of trouble.

KIYOKO: Not like this . . . not like this.

HANA: Some have it better—some worse. When you get married, you'll understand. Don't worry. Nothing will happen. *(She takes a towel from the wall and dries Kiyoko's hair)* You're chilled to the bone. You'll catch your death . . .

KIYOKO: I don't care . . . I want to die.

HANA: Don't be silly. It's not that bad.

KIYOKO: They started drinking early in the afternoon. They make some kind of brew and hide it somewhere in the desert.

HANA: It's illegal to make it. That's why they hide it. That home brew is poison to the body . . . and the mind too.

KIYOKO: It makes them crazy. They drink it all the time and quarrel constantly. I was in the other room studying. I try so hard to keep up with school.

HANA: We were talking about you just this evening. Masako says you're doing so well . . . you skipped a grade?

KIYOKO: It's hard . . . hard . . . I'm too old for the class and the children . . . *(She remembers all her problems and starts to cry again)*

HANA: It's always hard in a new country.

KIYOKO: They were bickering and quarreling all afternoon. Then something happened. All of a sudden I saw them on the floor . . . hitting and . . . and . . . . He was hitting her in the stomach, the face . . . . I tried to stop them, but they were so . . . drunk.

HANA: There, there . . . . It's probably all over now.

KIYOKO: Why does it happen like this? Nothing is right. Everywhere I go . . . Masa-chan is so lucky. I wish my life was like hers. I can hardly remember my real mother.

HANA: Emiko-san is almost a real mother to you. She's blood kin.

KIYOKO: She hates me. She never speaks to me. She's so cold. I want to love her but she won't let me. She hates me.

HANA: I don't think that's true, Kiyoko-san.

KIYOKO: I know it's true.

HANA: No. I don't think you have anything to do with it. It's this place. She hates it. This place is so lonely and alien.

KIYOKO: Then why didn't she go back? Why did they stay here?

HANA: You don't know. It's not so simple. Sometimes I think—

KIYOKO: Then why don't they make the best of it here? Like you?

HANA: That isn't easy either. Believe me. *(She goes to the stove to stir the soup)* Sometimes . . . sometimes the longing for homeland fills me with despair. Will I never return again? Will I never see my mother, my father, my sisters again? But what can one do? There are responsibilities here . . . children . . . *(She draws a sharp breath)* And another day passes . . . another month . . . another year. Eventually everything passes. *(She takes the soup to Kiyoko)* Did you have supper tonight?

KIYOKO *(Bowing gratefully)*: Ah. When my . . . my aunt gets like this, she doesn't cook. No one eats. I don't get hungry anymore.

HANA: Cook for yourself. It's important to keep your health.

KIYOKO: I left Japan for a better life here . . .

HANA: It isn't easy for you, is it? But you must remember your filial duty.

KIYOKO: It's so hard.

HANA: But you can make the best of it here, Kiyoko-san. And take care of yourself. You owe that to yourself. Eat. Keep well. It'll be better, you'll see. And sometimes it'll seem worse. But you'll survive. We do, you know . . . we do . . . *(She looks around)* It's getting late.

KIYOKO *(Apprehensively)*: I don't want to go back.

HANA: You can sleep with Masako tonight. Tomorrow you'll go back. And you'll remember what I told you.

She puts her arms around Kiyoko, who is overcome with self-pity and begins to weep quietly.

Life is never easy, Kiyoko-san. Endure. Endure. Soon you'll be marrying and going away. Things will not always be this way. And you'll look back on this . . . this night and you'll—

There is a rap on the door. Hana exchanges glances with Kiyoko and goes to answer it. She opens it a crack. Oka has come looking for Kiyoko. He's dressed in an overcoat and holds a wet newspaper over his head.

OKA: Ah! I'm sorry to bother you so late at night . . . the fact is . . .

HANA: Oka-san . . .

OKA *(Jovially)*: Good evening, good evening . . . *(He sees Kiyoko)* Ah . . . there you are . . . . Did you have a nice visit?

HANA *(Irritated)*: Yes, she's here.

OKA *(Still cheerful)*: Thought she might be. Ready to come home now?

HANA: She came in the rain.

OKA *(Ignoring Hana's tone)*: That's foolish of you, Kiyoko. You might catch cold.

HANA: She was frightened by your quarreling. She came for help.

OKA *(Laughing with embarrassment)*: Oh! Kiyoko, that's nothing to worry about. It's just we had some disagreement . . .

HANA: That's what I told her, but she was frightened all the same.

OKA: Children are—

HANA: Not children, Oka-san. Kiyoko. Kiyoko was terrified. I think that was a terrible thing to do to her.

OKA *(Rubbing his head)*: Oh, I . . . I . . .

HANA: If you had seen her a few minutes ago . . . hysterical . . . shaking . . . crying . . . wet and cold to the bone . . . out of her mind with worry.

OKA *(Rubbing his head)*: Oh . . . I . . . don't know what she was so worried about.

HANA: You. You and Emiko fighting like you were going to kill each other.

OKA *(There's nothing more to hide. He lowers his head in penitence)*: Aaaaaachhhhhhh . . .

HANA: I know I shouldn't tell you this, but there're one or two things I have to say: You sent for Kiyoko-san and now she's here. You said yourself she had a bad time in Japan, and now she's having a worse time. It isn't easy for her in a strange new country; the least you can do is try to keep her from worrying . . . especially about yourselves. I think it's terrible what you're doing to her . . . terrible!

OKA *(Bowing in deep humility)*: I am ashamed . . .

HANA: I think she deserves better. I think you should think about that.

OKA *(Still in his bow)*: I thank you for this reminder. It will never happen again. I promise.

HANA: I don't need that promise. Make it to Kiyoko-san.

OKA *(To Kiyoko)*: Come with Papa now. He did a bad thing. He'll be a good papa from now. He won't worry his little girl again. All right? All right?

They move to the door.

KIYOKO: Thank you so much.

Hana puts Murata's robe around Kiyoko, who tries to return it.

OKA: Madam. I thank you again.

HANA *(To Kiyoko)*: That's all right. You can bring it back tomorrow. *(Aside to Kiyoko)* Remember . . . remember what we talked about. *(Loudly)* Good night, Oka-san.

They leave. Hana goes to Masako, who lies on the bed, and covers her. Murata appears from the bedroom. He's heard it all. He and Hana exchange a glance and together they retire to their room. Fade-out.

Scene 3

The next morning. The Murata house and yard. Hana and Murata have already left the house to examine the rain damage in the fields. Masako prepares to go to school. She puts on a coat and picks up her books and lunch bag. Meanwhile, Kiyoko slips quietly into the yard. She wears a coat and carries Murata's robe. She sets it on the outside bench. Masako walks out and is surprised to see Kiyoko.

MASAKO: Hi. I thought you'd be . . . sick today.

KIYOKO: Oh. I woke up late.

MASAKO *(Scrutinizing Kiyoko's face)*: Your eyes are red.

KIYOKO *(Averting her eyes)*: Oh. I . . . got . . . sand in it. Yes.

MASAKO: Do you want to use eye drops? We have eye drops in the house.

KIYOKO: Oh . . . no. That's all right.

MASAKO: That's what you call bloodshot.

KIYOKO: Oh.

MASAKO: My father gets it a lot. When he drinks too much.

KIYOKO: Oh . . .

MASAKO *(Notices Kiyoko doesn't have her lunch)*: Where's your lunch bag?

KIYOKO: I . . . forgot it.

MASAKO: Did you make your lunch today?

KIYOKO: Yes. Yes, I did. But I forgot it.

MASAKO: Do you want to go back and get it?

KIYOKO: No, that's all right.

They are silent for a while.

We'll be late.

MASAKO: Do you want to practice your words?

KIYOKO *(Thoughtfully)*: Oh . . .

MASAKO: Say, "My."

KIYOKO: My?

MASAKO: Eyes . . .

KIYOKO: Eyes.

MASAKO: Are . . .

KIYOKO: Are.

MASAKO: Red.

KIYOKO: Red.

MASAKO: Your eyes are red. *(Kiyoko doesn't repeat it)* I . . . *(Kiyoko doesn't cooperate)* Say, "I."

KIYOKO: I.

MASAKO: Got . . .

KIYOKO: Got.

MASAKO: Sand . . . *(Kiyoko balks)* Say, "I."

KIYOKO *(Sighing)*: I.

MASAKO: Reft . . .

KIYOKO: Reft.

MASAKO: My . . .

KIYOKO: My.

MASAKO: Runch . . .

KIYOKO: Run . . . lunch. *(She stops)* Masako-san, you are mean. You are hurting me.

MASAKO: It's a joke! I was just trying to make you laugh!

KIYOKO: I cannot laugh today.

MASAKO: Sure you can. You can laugh. Laugh! Like this! *(She makes a hearty laugh)*

KIYOKO: I cannot laugh when you make fun of me.

MASAKO: Okay, I'm sorry. We'll practice some other words then, okay? *(Kiyoko doesn't answer)* Say, "Okay."

KIYOKO *(Reluctantly)*: Okay . . .

MASAKO: Okay, then . . . um . . . um . . . *(She still teases and talks rapidly)* Say . . . um . . . "She sells sea shells on the sea shore."

Kiyoko turns away indignantly.

Aw, come on, Kiyoko! It's just a joke. Laugh!

KIYOKO *(Imitating sarcastically)*: Ha-ha-ha! Now you say, "*Kono kyaku wa yoku kaki ku kyaku da* [This guest eats a lot of persimmons]!"

MASAKO: Sure! I can say it! *Kono kyaku waki ku kyoku kaku* . . .

KIYOKO: That's not right.

MASAKO: *Koki kuki kya* . . .

KIYOKO: No.

MASAKO: Okay, then. You say, "Sea sells she shells . . . shu . . . sss . . ."

They both laugh, Kiyoko with her hands over her mouth. Masako takes Kiyoko's hands from her mouth.

Not like that! Like this! *(She gives a big belly laugh)*

KIYOKO: Like this? *(She imitates Masako)*

MASAKO: Yeah, that's right! You're not mad anymore?

KIYOKO: I'm not mad anymore.

MASAKO: Okay. You can share my lunch today because we're . . .

KIYOKO: "Flends?"

Masako looks at Kiyoko, they giggle and move on. Hana and Murata come in from assessing the storm's damage. They are dressed warmly. Hana is depressed. Murata tries hard to be cheerful.

MURATA: It's not so bad, Mama.

HANA: Half the ranch is flooded . . . at least half.

MURATA: No-no. A quarter, maybe. It's sunny today . . . it'll dry.

HANA: The seedlings will rot.

MURATA: No, no. It'll dry. It's all right—better than I expected.

HANA: If we have another bad year, no one will lend us money for the next crop.

MURATA: Don't worry. If it doesn't drain by tomorrow, I'll replant the worst places. We still have some seed left. Yeah, I'll replant . . .

HANA: More work.

MURATA: Don't worry, Mama. It'll be all right.

HANA *(Quietly)*: Papa, where will it end? Will we always be like this—always at the mercy of the weather—prices—always at the mercy of the gods?

MURATA *(Patting Hana's back)*: Things will change. Wait and see. We'll be back in Japan by . . . in two years . . . guarantee . . . . Maybe sooner.

HANA *(Dubiously)*: Two years . . .

MURATA *(Finds the robe on the bench)*: Ah, look, Mama. Kiyoko-san brought back my robe.

HANA *(Sighing)*: Kiyoko-san . . . poor Kiyoko-san . . . and Emiko-san.

MURATA: Ah, Mama. We're lucky. We're lucky, Mama.

Hana smiles sadly at Murata. Fade-out.

Scene 4

*The following spring, afternoon. Exterior of the Oka house. Oka is dressed to go out. He wears a sweater, long-sleeved white shirt, dark pants, no tie. He puts his foot on the bench to wipe off his shoe with the palm of his hand. He straightens his sleeve, removes a bit of lint, and runs his fingers through his hair. He hums under his breath. Kiyoko comes from the house. Her hair is frizzled with a permanent wave, she wears a gaudy new dress and a pair of new shoes. She carries a movie magazine—*Photoplay *or* Modern Screen.

OKA *(Appreciatively)*: Pretty. Pretty.

KIYOKO *(Turning for him)*: It's not too *hadeh?* I feel strange in colors.

OKA: Oh no. Young girls should wear bright colors. There's time enough to wear gray when you get old. Old-lady colors. *(Kiyoko giggles)* Sure you want to go to the picture show? It's such a nice day . . . shame to waste in a dark hall.

KIYOKO: Where else can we go?

OKA: We can go to the Muratas.

KIYOKO: All dressed up?

OKA: Or Nagatas. I'll show him what I got for my horse.

KIYOKO *(Laughing)*: Oh, I love the pictures.

OKA: We don't have many nice spring days like this. Here the season is short. Summer comes in like a dragon . . . right behind . . . breathing fire . . . like a dragon. You don't know the summers here. They'll scare you. *(He tousles Kiyoko's hair and pulls a lock of it. It springs back. He shakes his head in wonder)* Goddamn. Curly hair. Never thought curly hair could make you so happy.

KIYOKO *(Giggling)*: All the American girls have curly hair.

OKA: Your friend Masako like it?

KIYOKO *(Nodding)*: She says her mother will never let her get a permanent wave.

OKA: She said that, eh? Bet she's wanting one.

KIYOKO: I don't know about that.

OKA: Bet she's wanting some of your pretty dresses too.

KIYOKO: Her mother makes all her clothes.

OKA: Buying is just as good. Buying is better. No trouble that way.

KIYOKO: Masako's not so interested in clothes. She loves the pictures, but her mother won't let her go. Someday, can we take Masako with us?

OKA: If her mother lets her come. Her mother's got a mind of her own . . . a stiff back.

KIYOKO: But she's nice.

OKA *(Dubiously)*: Oh, yeah. Can't be perfect, I guess. Kiyoko, after the harvest I'll have money and I'll buy you the prettiest dress in town. I'm going to be lucky this year. I feel it.

KIYOKO: You're already too good to me . . . dresses, shoes, permanent wave . . . movies . . .

OKA: That's nothing. After the harvest, just wait . . .

KIYOKO: Magazines . . . . You do enough. I'm happy already.

OKA: You make me happy too, Kiyoko. You make me feel good . . . like a man again . . . . *(That statement bothers him)* One day you're going to make a young man happy. *(Kiyoko giggles)* Someday we going to move from here.

KIYOKO: But we have good friends here, Papa.

OKA: Next year our lease will be up and we got to move.

KIYOKO: The ranch is not ours?

OKA: No. In America, Japanese cannot own land. We lease and move every two, three years. Next year we going to go someplace where there's young fellows. There's none good enough for you here. *(He watches Kiyoko giggle)* Yeah. You going to make a good wife. Already a good cook. I like your cooking.

KIYOKO *(A little embarrassed)*: Shall we go now?

OKA: Yeah. Put the magazine away.

KIYOKO: I want to take it with me.

OKA: Take it with you?

KIYOKO: Last time, after we came back, I found all my magazines torn in half.

OKA *(Looking toward the house)*: Torn?

KIYOKO: This is the only one I have left.

OKA *(Not wanting to deal with it)*: All right. All right.

The two prepare to leave when the door opens. Emiko stands there, her hair is unkempt and she looks wild. She holds an empty can in one hand, the lid in the other.

EMIKO: Where is it?

Oka tries to make a hasty departure.

KIYOKO: Where is what?

Oka pushes Kiyoko ahead of him, still trying to make a getaway.

EMIKO: Where is it? Where is it? What did you do with it?

Emiko moves toward Oka. He can't ignore her and he stops.

OKA (*With false unconcern to Kiyoko*): Why don't you walk on ahead to the Muratas?
KIYOKO: We're not going to the pictures?
OKA: We'll go. First you walk to the Muratas. Show them your new dress. I'll meet you there.

Kiyoko picks up a small package and exits. Oka sighs and shakes his head.

EMIKO (*Shaking the can*): Where is it? What did you do with it?
OKA (*Feigning surprise*): With what?
EMIKO: You know what. You stole it. You stole my money.
OKA: *Your* money?
EMIKO: I've been saving that money.
OKA: Yeah? Well, where'd you get it? Where'd you get it, eh? You stole it from me! Dollar by dollar . . . . You stole it from me! Out of my pocket!
EMIKO: I saved it!
OKA: From my pocket!
EMIKO: It's mine! I saved for a long time . . . . Some of it I brought from Japan.
OKA: *Bakayuna!* What'd you bring from Japan? Nothing but some useless kimonos.

Oka starts to leave but Emiko hangs on to him.

EMIKO: Give back my money! Thief!
OKA (*Swings around and balls his fists but doesn't strike*): Goddamn! Get off me!
EMIKO (*Now pleading*): Please give it back . . . please . . . please . . .

She starts to stroke him. Oka pulls her hands away and pushes her from him.

Oni!
OKA (*Seething*): Oni? What does that make you? *Oni baba?* Yeah, that's what you are . . . a devil!
EMIKO: It's mine! Give it back . . .
OKA: The hell! You think you can live off me and steal my money too? How stupid you think I am?
EMIKO (*Tearfully*): But I've paid . . . I've paid . . .
OKA: With what?
EMIKO: You know I've paid.
OKA (*Scoffing*): You call that paying?

EMIKO: What did you do with it?

OKA: I don't have it.

EMIKO: It's gone? It's gone?

OKA: Yeah! It's gone. I spent it. The hell! Every last cent.

EMIKO: The new clothes . . . the curls . . . restaurants . . . pictures . . . shoes . . . .
My money . . . my going-home money . . .

OKA: You through?

EMIKO: What will I do? What will—

OKA: I don't care what you do. Walk. Use your feet. Swim to Japan. I don't care.
I give you no more than you gave me. Now I don't want anything. I don't care
what you do. (He walks away)

*Emiko still holds the empty can. Offstage we hear Oka's car door slam and the
sound of his old car starting off. Accustomed to crying alone, she doesn't utter
a sound. Her shoulders begin to shake, her dry soundless sobs turn to a silent
laugh. She wipes the dust gently from the can as though comforting a friend. Her
movements become sensuous, her hands move on to her own body, around her
throat, over her breasts, to her hips, caressing, soothing, reminding her of her lover's
hands. Fade-out.*

Scene 5

*Same day, late afternoon. Exterior of the Murata house. The light is soft. Hana
is sweeping the yard; Masako hangs a glass wind chime on the exposed wall.*

HANA (Directing Masako): There . . . there. That's a good place.

MASAKO: Here?

HANA (Nodding): It must catch the slightest breeze. (Sighing and listening) It brings
back so much . . . . That's the reason I never hung one before. I guess it doesn't
matter much anymore . . .

MASAKO: I thought you liked to think about Japan.

HANA (Laughing sadly): I didn't want to hear that sound so often . . . get too used
to it. Sometimes you hear something too often, after a while you don't hear
it anymore . . . . I didn't want that to happen. The same thing happens to feelings too, I guess. After a while you don't feel anymore. You're too young to
understand that yet.

MASAKO: I understand, Mama.

HANA: Wasn't it nice of Kiyoko-san to give us the *furin*?

MASAKO: I love it. I don't know anything about Japan, but it makes me feel something
too.

HANA: Maybe someday when you're grown up, gone away, you'll hear it and
remember yourself as this little girl . . . remember this old house, the ranch,
and . . . your old mama . . .

MASAKO: That's kind of scary.

Emiko enters unsteadily. She carries a bundle wrapped in a furoshiki *[colorful scarf]. In the package are two beautiful kimonos.*

HANA: Emiko-san! What a pleasant surprise! Please sit down. We were just hanging the *furin*. It was so sweet of Kiyoko-san to give it to Masako. She loves it.

Emiko looks mildly interested. She acts as normal as she can throughout the scene, but at times drops her facade, revealing her desperation.

EMIKO: Thank you. *(She sets her bundle on the bench but keeps her hand on it)*

HANA: Your family was here earlier. *(Emiko smiles vaguely)* On their way to the pictures, I think. *(To Masako)* Make tea for us, Ma-chan.

EMIKO: Please don't . . .

HANA: Kiyoko-san was looking so nice—her hair all curly . . . . Of course, in our day, straight black hair was desirable. Of course, times change.

EMIKO: Yes.

HANA: But she did look fine. My, my, a colorful new dress, new shoes, a permanent wave—looked like a regular American girl. Did you choose her dress?

EMIKO: No . . . I didn't go.

HANA: You know, I didn't think so. Very pretty though. I liked it very much. Of course, I sew all Masako's clothes. It saves money. It'll be nice for you to make things for Kiyoko-san too. She'd be so pleased. I know she'd be pleased . . .

While Hana talks, Emiko plucks nervously at her package. She waits for Hana to stop talking.

Emiko-san, is everything all right?

EMIKO *(Smiling nervously)*: Yes.

HANA: Masako, please go make tea for us. See if there aren't any more of those crackers left. Or did you finish them? *(To Emiko)* We can't keep anything in this house. She eats everything as soon as Papa brings it home. You'd never know it, she's so skinny. We never have anything left for company.

MASAKO: We hardly ever have company anyway.

Hana gives her daughter a strong look, and Masako goes into the house. Emiko is lost in her own thoughts. She strokes her package.

HANA: Is there something you . . . I can help you with? *(Very gently)* Emiko-san?

EMIKO *(Suddenly frightened)*: Oh no. I was thinking . . . . Now that . . . now that . . . Masa-chan is growing up . . . older . . .

HANA *(Relieved)*: Oh, yes. She's growing fast.

EMIKO: I was thinking . . . *(She stops, puts the package on her lap and is lost again)*

HANA: Yes, she *is* growing. Time goes so fast. I think she'll be taller than me soon. *(She laughs weakly, stops and looks puzzled)*

EMIKO: Yes.

Emiko's depression pervades the atmosphere. Hana is affected by it. The two women sit in silence. A small breeze moves the wind chimes. For a moment light grows dim on the two lonely figures. Masako comes from the house with a tray of tea. The light returns to normal again.

HANA *(Gently)*: You're a good girl.

Masako looks first to Emiko then to her mother. She sets the tray on the bench and stands near Emiko, who seems to notice her for the first time.

EMIKO: How are you?

HANA *(Pours the tea and serves her)*: Emiko-san, is there something I can do for you?

EMIKO: There's . . . I was . . . I . . . Masa-chan will be a young lady soon . . .

HANA: Oh, well, now I don't know about "lady."

EMIKO: Maybe she would like a nice . . . nice . . . *(She unwraps her package)* I have kimonos . . . I wore in Japan for dancing . . . maybe she can . . . if you like, I mean. They'll be nice on her . . . she's so slim . . .

Emiko shakes out a robe. Hana and Masako are impressed.

HANA: Ohhhh! Beautiful!

MASAKO: Oh, Mama! Pretty!

Hana and Masako finger the material.

Gold threads, Mama.

HANA: Brocade!

EMIKO: Maybe Masa-chan would like them. I mean for her school programs . . . Japanese school . . .

HANA: Oh, no! Too good for country. People will be envious of us . . . wonder where we got them.

EMIKO: I mean for festivals . . . *Obon, Hana Matsuri* . . .

HANA: Oh, but you have Kiyoko-san now. You should give them to her. Has she seen them?

EMIKO: Oh . . . no . . .

HANA: She'll love them. You should give them to her . . . not our Masako.

EMIKO: I thought . . . I mean I was thinking of . . . if you could give me a little . . . if you could pay . . . manage to give me something for . . .

HANA: But these gowns, Emiko-san—they're worth hundreds.

EMIKO: I know, but I'm not asking for that. Whatever you can give . . . only as much as you can give.

MASAKO: Mama?

HANA: Masako, Papa doesn't have that kind of money.

EMIKO: Anything you can give . . . anything . . .

MASAKO: Ask Papa.

HANA: There's no use asking. I know he can't afford it.

EMIKO *(Looking at Masako)*: A little at a time.

MASAKO: Mama?

HANA *(Firmly)*: No, Masako. This is a luxury.

Hana folds the gowns and puts them away. Masako is disappointed. Emiko is devastated. Hana sees this and tries to find some way to help.

Emiko-san, I hope you understand . . . *(Emiko is silent, trying to gather her resources)* I know you can sell them and get the full price somewhere. Let's see . . . a family with a lot of growing daughters . . . someone who did well last year . . . . Nagatas have no girls . . . . Umedas have girls but no money . . . . Well, let's see . . . . Maybe not here in this country town. Ah . . . . You can take them to the city, Los Angeles, and sell them to a store . . . or Terminal Island . . . lots of wealthy fishermen there. Yes, that would be the place. Why, it's no problem, Emiko-san. Have your husband take them there. I know you'll get your money. He'll find a buyer. I know he will.

EMIKO: Yes. *(She finishes folding and ties the scarf. She sits quietly)*

HANA: Please have your tea. I'm sorry . . . I really would like to take them for Masako but it just isn't possible. You understand, don't you? *(Emiko nods)* Please don't feel so . . . so bad. It's not really a matter of life or death, is it? Emiko-san?

Emiko nods again. Hana sips her tea.

MASAKO: Mama? If you could ask Papa . . .

HANA: Oh, the tea is cold. Masako, could you heat the kettle?

EMIKO: No more. I must be going. *(She picks up her package and rises slowly)*

HANA *(Looking helpless)*: So soon? Emiko-san, please stay.

Emiko starts to go.

Masako will walk with you. *(She pushes Masako forward)*

EMIKO: It's not far.

HANA: Emiko-san? You'll be all right?

EMIKO: Yes . . . yes . . . yes . . . *(She goes)*

HANA *(Calling after her)*: I'm sorry, Emiko-san.

EMIKO: Yes . . .

Masako and Hana watch as Emiko leaves. The light grows dim as though a cloud passes over. Emiko is gone. Hana strokes Masako's hair.

HANA: Your hair is so black and straight . . . nice . . .

They stand close. The wind chimes tinkle; light grows dim. Light returns to normal. Murata enters. He sees this tableau of mother and child and is puzzled.

MURATA: What's going on here?

The two women part.

HANA: Oh . . . nothing . . . nothing . . .

MASAKO: Mrs. Oka was here. She had two kimo—

HANA *(Putting her hand on Masako's shoulder)*: It was nothing . . .

MURATA: Eh? What'd she want?

HANA: Later, Papa. Right now, I'd better fix supper.

MURATA *(Looking at the sky)*: Strange how that sun comes and goes. Maybe I didn't need to irrigate—looks like rain. *(He remembers and is exasperated)* Ach! I forgot to shut the water.

MASAKO: I'll do it, Papa.

HANA: Masako, that gate's too heavy for you.

MURATA: She can handle it. Take out the pin and let the gate fall all the way down. All the way. And put the pin back. Don't forget to put the pin back.

HANA: And be careful. Don't fall in the canal.

Masako leaves.

MURATA: What's the matter with that girl?

HANA: Nothing. Why?

MURATA: Usually have to beg her to do . . .

HANA: She's growing up.

MURATA: Must be that time of the month.

HANA: Oh, Papa, she's too young for that yet.

MURATA *(Genially as they enter the house)*: Got to start sometime. Looks like I'll be outnumbered soon. I'm outnumbered already.

Hana glances at him and quietly sets about preparations for supper. Murata removes his shirt and sits at the table with a paper. Light fades slowly.

Scene 6

Same evening. Exterior, desert. There is at least one shrub. Masako appears, walking slowly. From a distance we hear Emiko singing the song "And the Soul Shall Dance." Masako looks around, sees the shrub and crouches under it. Emiko appears. She's dressed in one of her beautiful kimonos tied loosely at her waist. She carries a branch of sage. Her hair is loose.

EMIKO: *Akai kuchibiru*
Kappu ni yosete
Aoi sake nomya
Kokoro ga odoru . . .
Kurai yoru no yume
Setsu nasa yo . . .

She breaks into a dance, laughs mysteriously, turns round and round, acting out a fantasy. Masako stirs uncomfortably. Emiko senses a presence. She stops, drops her branch and walks offstage, singing as she goes.

> *Aoi sake nomya*
> *Yume mo odoru . . .*

Masako watches as Emiko leaves. She rises slowly and picks up the branch Emiko has left. She looks at the branch, moves forward a step and looks off to the point where Emiko disappeared. Light slowly fades until only the image of Masako's face remains etched in the mind.

END OF PLAY

Pay the Chinaman

Laurence Yep

Laurence Yep

I'm a third-generation Chinese American, and a California native. My mother was raised in West Virginia, where my grandfather had a laundry. West Virginia was much more real to me than China because my mother told me stories about it.

I grew up in the Fillmore District of San Francisco, a predominately black neighborhood where my father ran a grocery store, but I went to a Catholic school in Chinatown. Even though I had friends in both neighborhoods I was always an outsider. When my school friends wanted to tell dirty jokes they spoke in Chinese so the nuns wouldn't understand. But I didn't know Chinese so I missed out on a good deal of humor when I was a kid. When my black friends in the Fillmore played war games I'd be the all-purpose "Oriental," the Japanese or the Korean.

In school the librarians would bring around these books about kids in the suburbs living a kind of *Leave It to Beaver* existence that seemed totally unreal to me. In my neighborhood nobody left their door unlocked, nobody had a bicycle. So I wound up reading a lot of science fiction instead, because science fiction talks about ordinary people taken out of our world and brought to another world, learning strange customs, new languages, and so on. That was what I was doing every time I got off and on the #30 Stockton bus.

Later I went to St. Ignatius, a prep school run by Jesuits, and a priest there got me interested in writing stories. I sold my first story when I was eighteen to a science fiction magazine, and I just kept on writing and publishing science fiction. I didn't realize until later that when I was writing these first-person narratives of aliens I was really writing about myself. I was developing this emotional vocabulary to talk about myself.

At a certain point I wanted to be as "All American" as any white kid—up until the 1960s. Then, in college at University of California, Santa Cruz, I started getting interested in my own history. It was a crazy period. There weren't even bibliographies of Asian-American subjects, so I just went to the library every week and dug up what I could find, then reported back to my professor.

A friend joined Harper & Row and asked me to write some science fiction for children. I did, and then I wrote *Dragonwings*, a children's book about an actual Chinese-American aviator who flew his own plane in 1909. It was the right book at the right time, and it won several children's literature awards.

I first got interested in playwriting in 1984. I was invited to participate in an experiment by the Bay Area Playwrights Festival at the Exploratorium, a San Francisco science museum. "Science Fiction on Stage" was a program designed to bring together science fiction writers, playwrights and directors to create science fiction theatre without special effects.

Working in theatre was a revelation to me. I was used to sitting in my study creating a world all by myself, so it was very interesting being in a workshop situation with an actor who'd react to my dialogue by telling me, "I'd never say that." If a character actually talked back to me while I was writing fiction, I'd think I was going schizo!

But it was nice to have a shared fantasy. When theatre goes right there's nothing quite like it. And when it goes bad, there's nothing quite like the embarrassment.

Kenneth Grantham, my director on the science fiction project, later invited me to join another group, California On Stage. We're a circle of professional writers, actors and directors dedicated to developing historical theatre about California. *Pay the Chinaman* came out of that.

The idea for the play began when I walked into a friend's house and her father shouted out, "Pay the Chinaman!" He was actually playing a card game, a form of solitaire.

He explained that up in the lumber camps in Northern California, where he was raised, the Chinese cooks would rent out card and board games to the lumberjacks for entertainment. Pay the Chinaman was one of the games they played. The phrase means pay up, pay the piper.

I found that phrase symbolic of Chinese immigrants who managed to manipulate the American environment and come out ahead. From there I just started thinking about survivors. And con men too: as a doctoral student in English, I read a lot of American novels, and one that lingered in my mind was Herman Melville's *The Confidence Man*. Actually, I named the town in *Pay the Chinaman* after the riverboat in *The Confidence Man*.

It seems to me that the con man is the perfect actor. I'm fascinated by the way actors can draw on some memory, some pain of their own to play a character, the way actors can listen to someone else's story and then take it into themselves, manipulate it and project it out to the audience. It seemed that a piece about con men would be a perfect vehicle for actors.

At the time I was also writing a novel about a crucial period in Chinese-American history, 1877 to 1893. The novel was going to be like a *Winesburg, Ohio* for Chinese Americans just before the deluge comes. I had about a dozen characters in my head, and the con man and young man were two of them.

I'd done quite a bit of historical research on that era, and discovered it was a savage time. There were really two Chinese Americas: the urban one that we still know, and the little Chinatowns spreading all over the West. In a period of about sixteen years most of those smaller Chinatowns were erased. Massacres occurred in some areas, in others the Chinese were just driven out. In Tacoma, Washington they were marched out to the sound of an American brass band marching behind them.

Given the way I grew up, I've always been interested in the figure of survivor. I think it's a multicultural, universal theme. I do a lot of lecturing around the country to groups of schoolteachers, and I had an interesting experience in Minnesota talking to Finnish Americans. I discovered they have their own literature, their own newspapers, their own drama, and they went through experiences very similar to what Chinese Americans went through. That's one of the things that keeps me writing: there are so many interesting stories that haven't been told.

I think multiculturalism is beginning to take root in parts of this country, thanks to educators with a certain level of savvy. But I would like to be able to have the experience on the mainland that I had while visiting Hawaii. In Hawaii, no one can assume anything by your appearance. I knew a violinist, half Hungarian and half Japanese, who had pale skin but Japanese features. On the mainland he is always asked what ethnicity he is; in Hawaii he's never asked, because everyone there is more than one thing.

I do think it's important to know your heritage, and honor it. It amazes me how few kids know their grandparents, how many are cut off from their pasts—but it makes sense if your parents move every five years because their corporation shifts them from city to city, and if you live in a society where the rate of change is frightening.

One of the things that's almost monstrous about the young man in *Pay the Chinaman* is that he denies his past, and any sense of having roots. It's almost as if he wants to erase himself, and if you erase yourself totally there's nothing but a hole there. If you always define yourself negatively, you never have a positive concept of what you are. You're always busy denying and fighting, and you never define your strengths.

It took me about twenty years to come to a realization that I could never be white. Then it took me another five years to realize I could never be totally Chinese, that instead I was an Asian American, a Chinese American, a person between two cultures. That's what I learned in Hawaii. You can be from more than one culture, and you can draw from the best of both.

Biographical Information

Before turning to playwriting Laurence Yep established a career as an award-winning author of children's literature and science fiction. Yep earned a Ph.D. in American literature from SUNY (State University of New York) at Buffalo, and began writing children's books in 1973. He now has more than a dozen novels for youth to his credit, many of which explore aspects of Chinese-American history and Chinese mythology. His most popular works include *Dragonwings* (recipient of a 1976 Newbery Honor), and *Dragon of the Lost Sea* (commended by the American Library Association in 1982).

Yep lives in San Francisco. He continues to write novels for young readers, and lectures nationwide on the topic of children's literature. He is the author of another one-act, *Fairy Bones*, and is working on a new play.

About the Play

Pay the Chinaman was developed under the aegis of California On Stage, a San Francisco writers' workshop led by director Kenneth Grantham. The Asian American Theatre premiered the play in 1987 at Zephyr Theatre, under the direction of Lane Nishikawa. Sharing the double bill was Yep's *Fairy Bones*, which is about the same period in Chinese-American history.

Characters

CON MAN
YOUNG MAN

Time

The summer of 1893.

Place

California.

Pay the Chinaman

The summer of 1893. A riverboat slip in the town of Fidele in the Sacramento delta on the bank of a river that could be straight out of Huckleberry Finn. A Chinese reed organ plays hollow, ghostly notes from offstage; but the feeling is of an American scene that has been possessed by alien spirits.

Wood lies stacked and there are a few sacks waiting to be shipped. There are crates of Chinese vegetables with a large destination tag written in both Chinese and English.

In the distance, two-story, whitewashed clapboard houses crowd one another on the narrow street as in any American town; but the store signs are bilingual and the English is cheerfully pompous: Fortunate Orchards. The store window has Chinese vegetables and perhaps a dried duck hanging there.

A fiftyish man in a flashy kung-fu outfit shuffles to the center of the stage. Around his neck is a carved wooden object that he will finger throughout the play. Resting on his shoulder is a bamboo pole. A basket hangs from either end. He sets the pole and baskets down carefully and arranges some of the crates as a table. Then, taking a board from one basket, he sets it across two other crates. Then he wraps his queue around his neck with a flourish. Producing a gong from the other basket, he begins to beat it.

CON MAN: The dragon sat high upon his throne; but Shifty Lee skinned him easy as a squirrel.

181

A nervous young man edges out in a hat and coat too big for him. On his shoulder is a pole. From one end hangs a small chest of drawers which contains his barber gear. A narrow stool and small stove hang from the other.

The Monkey King shook Heaven itself; but Young the Gent ran him down like a rabbit. They were mighty men and brave and true and I love to tell the tales. *(Waving to the young man)* Don't be shy, boy. Was the Dark Lord scared to look someone in the eye? Don't think too hard on that one. Of course, he didn't. He walked right up to monsters and tied them into knots. And what gave him his phenomenal strength? It all came from prayer, boy. Prayer. Clean living. The right food. And . . . *(With a flourish, removes a towel from one basket)* My magic elixir. Been drinking it for years. Give you a little demonstration in just a moment. *(Fakes a chop at the board)* Soon as I round up a crowd. *(To the audience)* It's a new age of wonders, folks. A new age. *(Beats the gong)*

YOUNG MAN: You're going to wear out that gong.

CON MAN: I'll wear out the town's ears first.

YOUNG MAN: Fellow came through last week with a gong just like that.

CON MAN: Is that a fact?

YOUNG MAN: Sold a tonic. Said it'd pep people right up.

CON MAN: And it didn't.

YOUNG MAN: Oh, it did. Folks got real excited when it took the enamel off their teeth.

They both consider the basket of tonic.

CON MAN *(Laying the towel back over the basket)*: He should have sold it as paint remover.

YOUNG MAN: Busted up so many boards that folks didn't complain. Only we don't get so het up when someone beats a gong now.

CON MAN *(Putting the gong in a basket)*: You don't know who to trust nowadays. Fellow like that makes it hard on someone with a tonic that's—

YOUNG MAN: A real boon to humanity.

CON MAN: Have we met before?

YOUNG MAN: You and that other fellow had a lot in common.

CON MAN: He even stole my pitch.

YOUNG MAN: I'd tell you where he went, but he busted three boards at the same time. *(Picking up the con man's board)* And his weren't sawn halfway through.

CON MAN *(Removing the board and setting it behind him)*: You examined his boards?

YOUNG MAN: Of course.

CON MAN: Pretty smart for a newcomer.

YOUNG MAN: How'd you know?

CON MAN: You'll learn how to take in your own clothes. We all do.

YOUNG MAN: My mother always did the sewing.

CON MAN: No wife?

YOUNG MAN: There's a girl, regular piece of silk, but her family wanted us to wait.

CON MAN: Wanted to see if you'd come back rich.

YOUNG MAN: Naw, wanted to see if I'd make it back period.

CON MAN: My wife just wouldn't take no for an answer. Not on anything. She was pregnant before she'd let me leave for America.

YOUNG MAN: Imagine that.

CON MAN: Been guesting over here thirty years now. But I've made it home five times.

YOUNG MAN: Not bad, old man.

CON MAN: Finally going to listen to my wife. Leaving the Golden Mountain for good now.

YOUNG MAN: The tonic business pays that well?

CON MAN: Can't complain. But it's time to go. Hate's boiling on the stove.

YOUNG MAN (*Ruefully*): Great time to come over.

CON MAN: Welcome to America—the land of the Golden Mountain. Demons don't let in many of your kind nowadays.

YOUNG MAN: Came in as a merchant's boy. Paper son. New name. New village. Whole new person.

CON MAN: Handy. You Yan-ping?

YOUNG MAN: No, Toi-Shan.

CON MAN (*Takes out a deck of cards*): That makes us sort of neighbors.

YOUNG MAN: Don't gamble. Even with neighbors.

CON MAN: Just a friendly game.

YOUNG MAN: And then you'll suggest playing for a little money—to keep it interesting.

CON MAN (*Setting the cards down*): Too hot to travel. Ever play Pay the Chinaman? Demons call it solitaire too.

YOUNG MAN: Forget it.

CON MAN: Come on. (*Beginning to lay out the cards on top of a crate*) You know how the cards go? Ace, two, three?

YOUNG MAN: I'm not that fresh off the boat.

CON MAN: I lay out twenty-eight cards like so. They come in waves. Seven at a time. But it's getting harder to come over. So it's only six the next time. Then five. Four. Three. Two. Then just one. And there they are. Guests of the land of the Golden Mountain.

YOUNG MAN: And the rest of these cards?

CON MAN: They're so fresh off the boat they go into my hand. You have to find the aces and bring them over to you.

YOUNG MAN: Back home in China.

CON MAN: Just so. And for every card you take from the Golden Mountain and send back home, I pay you.

YOUNG MAN: And for every card left on the Golden Mountain?

CON MAN: You pay me. The same for any cards left in your hand. I'll play a game. You watch. (*Playing the cards as he continues his patter*) Now we need to find the aces so we can cart them over to your side of the ocean. No, nothing showing. So we set the guests to digging. And we line them up; one in a red coat and then one in a black coat. Working folk and fancy folk. And so on. (*Plays for a while*) Following me so far?

YOUNG MAN: Kind of.

CON MAN: Now I take the remaining twenty-four cards in my hand.

YOUNG MAN: The FOBs.

CON MAN: Right. And I send the FOBs in three at a time. Where's a red eight? That'd set everyone to moving around. (*Lays out several sets of three*) Ah, there you are. (*Plays*) Finally an ace. (*Plays*) And another palace. And there's a third. They're crowding the docks now. They can see the palace roofs gleaming at home. Whoa, and a fourth. And now the guests are jamming into the boats. Steam's up. Anchors weighed. And they're sailing home—left, right, up, down, all around. (*Finishes the deck*) And I'm all alone; and you got all the company.

YOUNG MAN (*Skeptically*): I don't know.

CON MAN (*Collecting the cards and shuffling*): Got another game for you. (*Holding up his fists*) Little hand music.

YOUNG MAN: Forget it.

CON MAN (*Flashing fingers and fists while he talks*): Just passing the time. I'll even let you set the stakes.

YOUNG MAN: Seen it. But I never could get a hook into it.

CON MAN (*Holding up fists and unfolding fingers to the numbers*): It's easy. Nothing. Five. Ten. Now hold up a hand.

The young man holds up one hand.

Fifteen. Now the other.

The young man holds up both hands.

Twenty.

YOUNG MAN (*Tentatively as he closes the fingers of one hand*): Fifteen? (*Closing the fingers of the second hand*) Ten?

CON MAN (*Closing the fingers of one hand*): Five. (*Closing the fingers of his other hand*) And back to nothing.

YOUNG MAN: Nothing. (*Holding up the fingers of one hand again*) Five. (*Holding up the fingers of both hands*) Ten.

CON MAN (*Holding up one hand*): Fifteen. (*Holding up the other hand*) Twenty.

YOUNG MAN: We add up all four hands.

CON MAN: Right. And we take turns calling. Let's try it. I'll call. Twenty.

YOUNG MAN: That's wrong.

CON MAN: So it's your turn.

YOUNG MAN: Ten. I didn't call it either.

CON MAN: So it'd be my turn. Caller shows. Other player shows. Caller's right; his delight.

YOUNG MAN: But then they did a lot of drinking too.

CON MAN: You have been watching. (*He takes an earthenware jar from the second basket*)

Recognize this too? Tiger whiskey. Put the fur on you. *(Handing the jar to the*
young man)

YOUNG MAN: Never could afford it back in China.

CON MAN: Well, you're over here now. And the loser has to drink this.

YOUNG MAN: No money though.

CON MAN: You're setting the stakes.

YOUNG MAN *(Pouring a drink)*: As long as it stays friendly.

CON MAN: Suits me. You start.

YOUNG MAN: Ten.

CON MAN: Five.

YOUNG MAN: Fifteen. *(Winning)*

CON MAN: You shouldn't win if you're really curious about the taste. *(Taking a drink)*
You get to call again.

The young man pours a drink.

YOUNG MAN: Twenty.

CON MAN: Five.

YOUNG MAN: Ten. *(Winning a second time)* Hang the Butcher! I keep winning.

CON MAN: Let me explain something, boy. In this case, you win by losing.

YOUNG MAN: Never seen the luck. That necklace a charm?

CON MAN: Hardly.

YOUNG MAN *(Examines the necklace)*: It's a carving of a monkey. And there's a little
man inside the monkey. Is it all from one piece of wood?

CON MAN: It passes the time.

YOUNG MAN: There's an even smaller man inside the little one. Just how many little
men are inside there?

CON MAN: As far and as deep as you can see.

YOUNG MAN: That's an awful lot of carving even for someone who's bored.

CON MAN: Why are we palavering when there's whiskey to drink?

YOUNG MAN *(Pouring)*: My call. Fifteen.

CON MAN: Ten.

YOUNG MAN: Twenty. *(Winning)* I won again!

CON MAN: You're going to die of thirst if you keep this up. *(Takes a drink)* I can just
hear your innards. They're like little old men whispering from inside you.
Leathery old voices, dried and cracked: whiskey, whiskey, whiskey.

YOUNG MAN: What do you think my chances are?

CON MAN: You just won three times straight.

YOUNG MAN: Not the game. I mean here.

CON MAN *(Thoughtful pause)*: Afraid?

YOUNG MAN: Aren't you?

CON MAN: Never seen anyone so lucky.

YOUNG MAN: My call again. *(Pouring)* Five.

CON MAN: Ten.

YOUNG MAN: Fifteen.

CON MAN: Twenty.

The young man finally loses.

YOUNG MAN: Finally. *(Taking a drink)* Turn out, boys, the tarantulas are loose.

CON MAN: Jar's not going to last. Ought to see who's going to buy the next.

YOUNG MAN: Let's keep it friendly.

CON MAN: Where's the harm in losing a few dollars?

YOUNG MAN: I guess the loser is just buying the next jar. *(He pulls out a thick roll of money and extracts a dollar)*

CON MAN: Where'd you get all those greenbacks? That'd choke even a landlord.

YOUNG MAN *(Hurriedly putting the roll away)*: Most of this isn't mine. Going to open a real barber shop with my cousin.

CON MAN *(Suspiciously)*: Already? Most folks come over on credit.

YOUNG MAN: But then it takes them years to pay it off. Mortgaged the house, fields and brothers; but I bought my own ticket.

CON MAN: There's no moss on you.

YOUNG MAN: Provided I last.

CON MAN *(Pouring)*: My call. Twenty. *(He wins)*

YOUNG MAN: That's good!

CON MAN *(Pouring and then playing)*: Nothing.

YOUNG MAN: Ten. *(He wins, drinks, shakes the jar)* Almost empty. Let's make it five dollars.

CON MAN: Your friendship's pretty expensive.

YOUNG MAN: It's just for the next jar. Trust me.

CON MAN: Don't put much stock in that word.

YOUNG MAN: You and me, all us Chinese got to stick together.

The con man takes out a thick wad of bills. He pretends to be an agent as he counts out the money.

CON MAN: Oh, no, I wouldn't steer you wrong. You'll get rich if you go. Why do you think they call it the land of the Golden Mountain? Nuggets big as your fists right there in the dirt. Just scoop 'em up. Hell, here's a tip just 'cause I like you. You find yourself a nice hill and lay down and the nuggets roll right into your palms.

YOUNG MAN: Who said that?

CON MAN: Last man I trusted.

YOUNG MAN: Didn't you swallow the whale?

CON MAN: That was only the fin. You should have heard that agent talk. *(Pretending to be agent again)* You boys remind me of my brothers. Tell you what I'll do. Got a friend who owns a boat. I'll put the word in. Treat you and your little brother like kings. Good vittles and plenty of it. Real beds. Nice sea breeze. Hell, it'll be like a vacation.

YOUNG MAN: He sure took the cake.

CON MAN: And the plate too. But thirty years ago who knew any better? And wasn't that fellow our best buddy? And didn't we smile and laugh right into the boat? And didn't they slam the hold shut? And didn't they put that big lock on it? And there we were—in spaces dark and narrow as coffins. And buried in the vomit and the shit and the smell of our own bodies.

YOUNG MAN: Heard the trip used to be rough.

CON MAN: The sickness wormed right inside my brother. Nothing I could do. Might as well have tried holding onto smoke. So when that boat landed, I was the first one off; and I've always stayed one step ahead of everyone else after that. And I don't trust anyone just 'cause they say so.

YOUNG MAN: *You* set up the rules.

CON MAN: It's a great game. Up one moment. Down the next. Five dollars?

YOUNG MAN: Five dollars. My call. Twenty.

CON MAN *(Using a feint)*: Ten. *(He wins)*

YOUNG MAN: Whoa. That's new.

CON MAN: You catch on too quick. Got to use my bag of tricks. Twenty. *(He wins)* Ten. *(He wins again)* Twenty. *(He wins again)*

YOUNG MAN: This doesn't feel very friendly.

CON MAN: Keeps you alive. Don't want to snore through the rest of your life, do you?

YOUNG MAN: Let's keep it simple.

The con man gets into a rhythm where he anticipates the young man's hands.

CON MAN: Don't stop. Five! *(He wins)* Get it back. Five! *(He wins)* Double or nothing. Ten! *(He wins)* Say, that's sixty dollars you owe.

YOUNG MAN: I didn't mean to gamble that much.

CON MAN: I lost track too. Tell you what. Double or nothing again.

YOUNG MAN: Can't chance my cousin's money too.

CON MAN: I'm not going to play with someone who insults me.

YOUNG MAN: I was just talking about the risk.

CON MAN: It's what you suggested. I'm not asking you to run off with his money. It's an investment in a likely thing.

YOUNG MAN: I just lost seven times in a row.

CON MAN: Exactly. The odds are that you'll break even.

YOUNG MAN: My fiancée said to save up slow and steady. Should have listened to her.

CON MAN: Caution's going to lose her. She's not going to wait forever.

YOUNG MAN: She swore she would.

CON MAN: And what did her folks swear? They don't sound like the romantic type. Probably sell her to the first rich man.

YOUNG MAN: You hear stories.

CON MAN: Expect the worst from the folks back home. Expect the worst here too.

YOUNG MAN: Anyway, I didn't come over here to stay poor.

CON MAN: The sooner you go home, the better.

YOUNG MAN: Your call.

They put up sixty dollars apiece.

CON MAN: Ten.

YOUNG MAN: Five.

CON MAN: Twenty. *(He wins)* I feel like it's my fault. Let's do it again.

YOUNG MAN: That's plain reckless.

CON MAN: This place is all one big gamble. White demons all around us.

YOUNG MAN: Americans.

CON MAN: Always been white demons.

YOUNG MAN: Names are power. Call them demons and they are demons.

CON MAN: This is the third Chinatown. First one used to be over there in the demon town. But a mob of demons burnt it down. So the Chinese built a new one on this side of the river. And the mob torched that one down. So the Chinese put up a third. Stubborn.

YOUNG MAN: Maybe the Americans ran out of matches.

CON MAN: Listen to me. This could mean your life.

YOUNG MAN: Is that you or the whiskey talking?

CON MAN *(Annoyed)*: Most guests wouldn't give you the time of day. Just let you get yourself killed. But I try and help you. And all you do is bullyrag me.

YOUNG MAN: Don't fess yourself.

CON MAN *(Growing angry)*: Shouldn't make fun of someone older than you.

YOUNG MAN: Did I laugh?

CON MAN: Don't like feeling awkward.

YOUNG MAN: Don't like being bossed either.

CON MAN: Then maybe you'd just better pay up.

YOUNG MAN: Don't you tell me what to do.

CON MAN: Aren't you the little prince. Only you're not in China anymore. Cut a real swell there, didn't you? Silk on your back?

YOUNG MAN: In the summertime.

CON MAN: And slick little maids all around. One to carry a stool in case you get tired. One with a tray of snacks. One with a pipe.

YOUNG MAN: I had two servants. Men.

CON MAN: Hot? Let me fan you, dear sir. Thirsty? I'll fetch tea right away. Tired? I'll carry you up to the palace.

YOUNG MAN: Our house wasn't that big.

CON MAN: And now you know how the bills were paid.

YOUNG MAN: I'll pay my share. Out of your pockets. Double or nothing.

CON MAN: Whoa. You've got a temper just like my son.

YOUNG MAN: Where is he?

CON MAN: Where he ought to be.

YOUNG MAN: I guess I just lost my head. What am I going to say to Papa now?

CON MAN: Thought it was a cousin?

YOUNG MAN: Cousin was just smoke. Don't like to tell folks how my father got sharped.

CON MAN: Wish I had a dollar for every person that I saw get slicked.

YOUNG MAN: He left a friend in charge while he fetched me from China. Only when we landed in San Francisco, this "loyal friend" said that the store had gone bankrupt. But the friend had sold everything and pocketed most of the money. What I got is all he gave us. Even have to wear castoffs.

CON MAN: Nothing more wicked than cheating a friend.

YOUNG MAN: I'm no better. Thought I could take you. Wanted to surprise my father. He's too old to start over. Serves me right to lose.

CON MAN: Don't be so hard on yourself. All right. Let's set up the target and you can take another shot at it.

YOUNG MAN: How much?

CON MAN: A hundred.

YOUNG MAN: A hundred.

They both put a hundred dollars down.

CON MAN: Ten. *(He wins)* I'd better give you another try.

YOUNG MAN: Appreciate your offer. But you don't pour water into a jar after it cracks.

CON MAN: More than you reckon.

YOUNG MAN: How?

CON MAN: Maybe it's better if you don't know. You don't want my help.

YOUNG MAN: Speak plain.

CON MAN: Soon as the harvest is over, the demons will come.

YOUNG MAN *(Uneasily)*: I heard rumors, but my father said that was just talk.

CON MAN: Fifteen years ago, there used to be Chinatowns all over the state, but mobs came in and burnt them to the ground. Up in Chico the demons even chopped up the hoses.

YOUNG MAN: Why us? Why here? Take down the signs and the ducks; and it'd look like any American town.

CON MAN: Can't change your skin. Now it could be like Fresno or Tacoma or Seattle. Might be satisfied with just robbing you and kicking you out.

YOUNG MAN: Then we'll just go some other place.

CON MAN: You could lose everything.

YOUNG MAN: We'll start over.

CON MAN: I said everything.

YOUNG MAN: Our lives too?

CON MAN: Might be like Butte. Came at night and shot the men in their bunks. Polite names didn't stop them then. Burnt the bodies.

YOUNG MAN: There's police. There's sheriffs.

CON MAN: Ought to let you learn the hard way—just like that boy.

YOUNG MAN: What boy?

CON MAN: Young boy. 'Bout your age. Friendly as a pup. Stopped at this shack on a big farm. He talked the others into letting me stay for the night. Just had to do a little doctoring. And I hadn't had a roof over my head in a week so wasn't I glad?

YOUNG MAN: And the demons wrecked the shack?

CON MAN: Set fire to it. Foreman says not to panic. Just lie down in the dirt. Wait for the farmer and the sheriff. But the fire's going up the walls. So I go to the back and get on my hands and knees and I start digging. Digging. Digging. Like a dog. And the next moment, the pup's there too. And doesn't that dirt fly?

YOUNG MAN: What about the fire?

CON MAN: It's only a matter of time. But me and the pup, we don't stop. We just dig faster and harder. I go headfirst into the hole. I scoop. I claw. And then my hands break into the air. The blessed, cool air. And then I can see the night sky.

YOUNG MAN: And the boy?

CON MAN: He follows. He's got his head and shoulders out of the hole when he jerks to a stop. "Hey!" he says. And the next thing he's sliding right back through the hole like an oiled pig. They were yanking him back inside.

YOUNG MAN: No!

CON MAN: I try to grab his hands, but they slip right out of mine. And the next thing I know, we both hear a demon howl. I twist around and see him—head and hair red as blood. And I just spin right around and hightail it out of there. And behind me, I hear a bang. Bang. Bang. Bang. Like New Year's. But it's not firecrackers chasing the demons away. And they're laughing that mean, liquored laugh.

YOUNG MAN: All dead?

CON MAN: It's the land of opportunity. Only they don't say what kind.

YOUNG MAN: The money's supposed to set up the barber shop. Can't lose any more.

CON MAN: Didn't think you wanted charity either. The risk is part of it. Might lose your money. Or you might take mine. Want to be stuck on the Mountain for the rest of your life? And always wondering when the demons are going to come?

YOUNG MAN: You read omens? Wind and Water?

CON MAN: Read it on your face. I can go into any bar in any Chinatown and see the timid. They're the ones washing the spit off the floors.

YOUNG MAN: But if I lose . . .

CON MAN: If you win.

YOUNG MAN: I'm the one spitting on the floor.

CON MAN: We'll make a guest out of you yet.

YOUNG MAN (*Walking backwards around the con man*): That should turn my luck around.

CON MAN: Two hundred.

YOUNG MAN: Two hundred.

They both put up two hundred dollars.

Your call.

CON MAN: Ten!

YOUNG MAN: Ten!

CON MAN: Five!

YOUNG MAN: Twenty! *(He wins)* Glad you talked me into that. Mighty neighborly of you to let me slip off the hook.

CON MAN: Let's match the pot.

YOUNG MAN: Never heard of inviting the fish to tie himself to the line.

CON MAN: Don't tell me you can't use the money.

YOUNG MAN: We sure could. Our family ought to sell the estate and move into a smaller place. But my papa won't let them.

CON MAN: No face.

YOUNG MAN: The family sucks you dry and calls it face. They keep spending money like we still had the store.

CON MAN: It was okay as long as you were in China.

YOUNG MAN: Your son take it any better?

CON MAN: You hear me and hear me good: when you meet demons and they say things to you, be patient. Be silent. But above all be invisible.

YOUNG MAN: I've got more grit that that.

CON MAN: So you'd talk back to the demons and they'd knock you down.

YOUNG MAN: And I'd get right back up and teach them a lesson.

CON MAN: And when they got through pounding your head in, your own mother wouldn't be able to recognize you.

YOUNG MAN: Is that what happened to your son?

CON MAN: Talk just makes the time drag on. Let's play.

YOUNG MAN: Maybe one more game. *(Pause)* Four hundred.

CON MAN: Four hundred.

The stake is now eight hundred dollars.

YOUNG MAN: Fifteen.

CON MAN: Nothing.

YOUNG MAN: Five.

CON MAN: Twenty.

YOUNG MAN: Ten.

CON MAN: Fifteen.

YOUNG MAN: Five. *(He wins)* I don't believe it!

CON MAN *(Stunned)*: Only got the fare to go back home.

YOUNG MAN: I'll give you a break, old man. How much you got?

CON MAN: Two hundred.

YOUNG MAN: Two hundred it is.

CON MAN: Then let's switch games. *(He takes out his deck of cards)* High card then?

YOUNG MAN: Can I shuffle too?

CON MAN: Don't you trust me?

YOUNG MAN: That's to skin your luck off the deck. Scared?

CON MAN: Go ahead.

The young man sets the cards down and shuffles as clumsily as a small child.

A king.

YOUNG MAN: Not bad. *(He cuts the remainder of the deck)* Ace. *(His other hand scoops up the money)*

CON MAN: You cheated.

The young man now seems relaxed and confident—even exaggeratedly tough.

YOUNG MAN *(Runs a finger along the edge of the cards)*: I can read your markings as well as you can.

CON MAN: You're not fresh off the boat, are you?

YOUNG MAN *(Rolling up his sleeves)*: This rig gets you oldtimers everytime.

CON MAN: I have to get out.

YOUNG MAN: Game's over, old man.

CON MAN: You fix this in your heart. There really is a storm coming. But with fire and bullets instead of raindrops.

YOUNG MAN: You old fart. It was all right to strand me.

CON MAN: I thought you were stuck anyway.

YOUNG MAN: And instead, you are. I can live well in Frisco on what I've got now.

CON MAN: I've been trying to tell you how to survive. You've got to give me another chance.

YOUNG MAN: You had your boat fare, old man.

CON MAN: When a guest goes home, he's got to have a real blowout. Got to have presents. Got to have face.

YOUNG MAN: Didn't you already send home enough?

CON MAN: I sent the money to buy ten acres back home—all of it bottom land. And my family goes everywhere in chairs. Their feet never touch dirt.

YOUNG MAN: It's really something when a con man cons himself. Not a bad barber. *(Takes razor from his shirt pocket and flips it open)* Shaved you that close.

CON MAN: You should be down on your knees thanking guests like me. You know how many people used to starve before we came over?

YOUNG MAN: I know all about it, old man. The old farts used to hammer the stories into my head. Told me about this young farmer: he's so poor, he can't grow rocks in his field. And along comes a drought. And the fields turn hard as iron. And folks are eating the leaves off trees and the weeds from the hills. And when there's nothing left, this young farmer looks at his poor old mommy and daddy and sees that they're just like skeletons. *(Pretends to cut his own arm with the razor)* So he slices the flesh from his arms. Slices it away in strips thick as your finger, and he puts it into a pot with their water ration. And he gives the broth to his parents. The old farts said he was just so grateful. But I thought he was crazy then. And I think he's crazy now.

CON MAN: His flesh came from their flesh.

YOUNG MAN (*Puts the razor in his pocket*): They just said, "Here's money. Here's food. Here's clothes." No one said it was only for eighteen years.

CON MAN: It's a balance. Your parents sacrifice for you; you sacrifice for them. Your father knows.

YOUNG MAN: My father was the biggest fool on two continents.

CON MAN: Was?

YOUNG MAN: He's dead. After we lost the store, we were on this farm shoveling shit and his heart busts. Just like an old, worn-out sack.

CON MAN: Didn't you tell him to rest?

YOUNG MAN: I should have told him to shut up.

CON MAN: Don't mock the dead, boy.

YOUNG MAN: Be grateful, *boy*. Lie down, *boy*. Let me walk all over your back, *boy*. I'm the boss now.

CON MAN: But back then, you weren't. And I know guests. They always make sure of one thing before they give up the ghost: they always see that someone will keep sending money back home.

YOUNG MAN: You guests got real sand, all right.

CON MAN: You said no?

YOUNG MAN: I wasn't going to wind up like him.

CON MAN: But he was dying. He only wanted some comfort.

YOUNG MAN: I told him the family's on its own now. Just like me.

CON MAN: And your father knew before he died. All his work. All his plans. All ruined.

YOUNG MAN: You're no better. What really happened to your son?

CON MAN: Dollar for a trim and an answer. (*Covering his fist with a hand*) You can pretend you're a prince back in China.

YOUNG MAN: Don't you have any pride?

CON MAN: Maybe you don't trust me with a razor?

YOUNG MAN (*Contemptuously throws a coin on the ground*): You're not that kind of fool. (*Sitting down abruptly*) Did he get beaten up?

CON MAN (*Picking up the coin and then taking the razor*): I ordered him not to go to the beach; but the fool went anyway.

YOUNG MAN: Who listens to a con man?

CON MAN: I quit the road. I had an honest job.

YOUNG MAN (*Flings a second coin down*): Well, what's wrong with visiting the beach?

The con man begins the shave the young man.

CON MAN (*Shaving one cheek*): Jobless demons camp there. They'd like to get one of us alone where there's no police. No place to hide. Nothing but sand dunes. And the ocean. (*Shaving the other cheek*) And them. And their fists. And their feet.

Tilting the young man's head back, he brings the razor along the young man's throat as the young man's eyes widen in fear.

And you can scream and scream and nobody to hear.

The con man folds the razor as the young man recovers.

YOUNG MAN (*Scornfully tosses down a third coin*): How'd you know it was your son?
CON MAN (*Getting the coin*): By the fancy embroidery on his shirt.
YOUNG MAN: Or was it that carving?
CON MAN (*Tucking the razor into the young man's shirt pocket*): You listen to me and don't go near the beach.
YOUNG MAN: Maybe I like salt air.
CON MAN: You could die.
YOUNG MAN: Son go for a swim?
CON MAN: He went to get some driftwood. He was going to carve it for his mother. It was still clutched in his hand.
YOUNG MAN: So you kept it.
CON MAN: And worked it. (*Fingering the carving*) So a little of him would stay alive.
YOUNG MAN: What exactly did you tell him?
CON MAN: I told him not to go out.
YOUNG MAN: You didn't warn him about the beach?
CON MAN: He should have obeyed me.
YOUNG MAN: Had to play the emperor, didn't you? No explanations. No warnings. Just orders. You killed him, old man.
CON MAN: I was his father.
YOUNG MAN: More face. More lies.
CON MAN: There's a way to do things.
YOUNG MAN: You're nothing but a windbag—like my father and all his friends. Big talkers and big cheats.
CON MAN: You belong in this hellhole.
YOUNG MAN: Let's gamble for the carving.
CON MAN: No, not that. You've left me with just three dollars.
YOUNG MAN: We're still not even.
CON MAN: What did I do to you?
YOUNG MAN: This is for your boy. Should've left him back in China, old man. Shouldn't have been selfish. Shouldn't've dragged him over here to die.
CON MAN: I was lonely.
YOUNG MAN: You couldn't even talk to him. And now that he's dead, you carved the wood so you can fox everyone into feeling sorry for you.
CON MAN: I feel sorrow. Not like you.
YOUNG MAN (*Fingering the carving*): You hypocrite. You only care about what people think. This is a lie—just like all the other lies you old farts tell.
CON MAN: Sometimes it's genuine. Sometimes it's not fake.

YOUNG MAN: Feelings are sticks that move the other puppets. Only I'm not going to leave you any tricks, old man. Going to shave you down to the bone.

CON MAN: You can't even tell what's real anymore.

YOUNG MAN: I'm the one who gives the orders. I'm the one who does the conning. When I'm done with you, there won't even be a ghost left to wail in the wind.

CON MAN: What's money, boy?

YOUNG MAN: You wanted mine bad enough.

CON MAN: If you don't have your souls, you've lost it all.

YOUNG MAN: I'm a winner. And you're going to help me. How much? Ten bucks? Twenty? A hundred?

CON MAN: I can always get more money. But can you get back what you lost?

YOUNG MAN: Will the demons give you that long? And if they do, what if the tonic doesn't sell and the cards turn cold?

CON MAN: How touching. Worried about an old man's final years. If your father could only see you now.

YOUNG MAN: Or your son.

CON MAN: I gave my son what I could.

YOUNG MAN: Funny. I gave the same thing to my father.

The young man bets all his money. The con man takes the carving from around his neck.

Here. I'm emptying my pockets. I'll bet it all, *old man.*

CON MAN: What's the game, *boy?*

YOUNG MAN: I'm the impatient sort. High card again.

CON MAN *(Putting the carving down)*: We'd just match ace against ace.

YOUNG MAN: Someone's bound to make a mistake sometime.

CON MAN: I get to shuffle?

YOUNG MAN: But I draw first.

As the con man shuffles, there is almost the intensity of a duel.

(Drawing) A five. Wait.

CON MAN *(Drawing)*: Too late. An ace.

YOUNG MAN: You cheated.

CON MAN: So you hate to lose too.

YOUNG MAN: How?

CON MAN: I marked the five when I was picking up the cards.

YOUNG MAN: But you couldn't be sure.

CON MAN: Sometimes you really do have to go out on the tightrope. *(Picks up the money)* I knew I'd find a way to hook you.

YOUNG MAN: So don't ever let anyone know what you're thinking.

CON MAN: Or who you are. Or what you are. Give people a blank page and they draw their own picture.

YOUNG MAN: Do anything to hook the marks.

CON MAN: Even use your own pain.

YOUNG MAN: Maybe I'll just drink all the tonic and kill myself.

CON MAN: Won't do you any good. You'll just go blind for a few days. (*Shoves the basket over*) But you can have it.

YOUNG MAN: So you really are going home.

CON MAN: Every now and then I slip in the truth. Spices up things.

YOUNG MAN: And the storm?

CON MAN: It's still coming.

YOUNG MAN: Then why'd you try to con the town?

CON MAN (*Puts the money away*): Call it habit. Or vanity. A kind of farewell tour. Dumbest thing I've ever done.

YOUNG MAN: So I did have you for a while.

CON MAN: Don't brag till the fish is in the pan.

YOUNG MAN: I don't make the same mistake twice.

CON MAN: Neither do I. (*He picks up the carving*) You might need this too.

YOUNG MAN: You even lied about that.

CON MAN: Maybe I heard it from the man I took this from.

YOUNG MAN (*Admiringly*): You bastard.

CON MAN (*Tosses the carving to the young man*): Or maybe it's the truth.

YOUNG MAN: Why give it to me then?

CON MAN: Maybe it just makes for too many awkward questions. Maybe I like slicking through things now.

YOUNG MAN: Which is it?

CON MAN: It's a new age of wonders, friend. A new age.

The young man slips a folded wad of dollars from his stocking. He begins counting his hidden stake. Lights out.

END OF PLAY

Between Worlds is made possible, in part, with public funds from the New York State Council on the Arts.

TCG also gratefully acknowledges public funds from the National Endowment for the Arts, in addition to the generous support of the following foundations and corporations: Alcoa Foundation; Ameritech Foundation; ARCO Foundation; AT&T Foundation; Beatrice Foundation; Center for Arts Criticism; Citicorp/Citibank; Common Wealth Fund; Consolidated Edison Company of New York; Eleanor Naylor Dana Charitable Trust; Dayton Hudson Foundation; Exxon Corporation; Ford Foundation; Jerome Foundation; Andrew W. Mellon Foundation; Metropolitan Life Foundation; National Broadcasting Company; New York Community Trust; New York Times Company Foundation; Pew Charitable Trusts; Philip Morris Companies; Scherman Foundation; Shell Oil Company Foundation; Shubert Foundation; Lila Wallace-Reader's Digest Fund; Xerox Foundation.

TCG also wishes to thank Artists Space, and particularly Hendrika Ter elst, who is in charge of their Artists File, for their assistance in finding the cover painting by Ron Gee.